# A SHORT INTRODUCTION TO
# OLD TESTAMENT

By

## Robert Gnuse

**Linus**
Publications, Inc.

Published by Linus Publications, Inc.
Deer Park, NY 11729

ISBN: 1-60797-177-1

Printed in the United States of America.

Print Numbers 5    4    3    2    1

# Table of Contents

# Chapter 1

# Introduction

"Of making many books there is no end" (Koheleth 12:12), and perhaps the same might be said of introductions to the Bible. Why, might the reader ask, should another introduction of the Hebrew Bible or Old Testament be generated? I believe a place exists for a volume such as this in light of the current climate of critical biblical scholarship. The past generation has seen a shaking of the foundations and a shifting of the paradigms in Old Testament research. This introduction will endeavor to present the basic information necessary for an overview of the Old Testament in a way that reflects the new paradigms and insights of critical study.

What are the paradigms that make this textbook different from those of a former generation?

1. There is a tendency among most critical scholars to date the emergence of written literature later in the history of the Israelites and Jews. Increasingly we date the written literature to the time of the exile, especially Pentateuchal traditions, which formerly we suggested had arisen in the pre-exilic era. In particular, a paradigm called the "Solomonic Enlightenment" is gone. We used to suggest that the court of Solomon experienced a literary renaissance in the 10th century BCE, and literature was produced in the court by intelligentsia who had come in contact with the great cultures of their age. This literature supposedly included much of the narrative in Genesis, Exodus, and Numbers, as well as accounts about David in 1 and 2 Samuel (the "Yahwist," the "Rise of David," and the "Succession Narrative"), and in addition, the wisdom literature in Proverbs 10-31 and the wisdom novel of Joseph in Genesis 37, 39-50

(the "Joseph Novella") were projected into this era. Now all of that literature is dated to later eras, usually the Babylonian Exile of the 6th century BCE, and different intellectual contexts are suggested (for example, the "Joseph Novella" is no longer considered wisdom literature).

2. Since we now date much of this literature to the exile or the post-exilic period, after the 6th century BCE, we have a new perception of that era. In the past we often characterized the six centuries after the destruction of Jerusalem in 586 BCE down to the time of Jesus as an era that lacked religious creativity. At times we even spoke of it as an era of dead legalism and ritual. Now we sense that is was a creative and productive age in which much of the biblical literature was produced and meaningful new religious pieties arose. Now we appreciate how Christianity arose out of an intellectually vibrant and religiously active Jewish background.

3. There is an increased awareness, created both by our study of the text and by recent archaeological evidence, that the monotheistic faith of Israel arose at a much later date than heretofore we had assumed. At least, this is certainly the case for the common Israelites and Jews. Monotheism and its concomitant values did not successfully capture the minds of these people until the Babylonian Exile in the 6th century BCE. Prior to exile only an unreflective monotheism existed; it took the crisis of exile in a foreign land to make people self-consciously monotheistic. Monotheism was not an early radical breakthrough; the foundations for this belief system grew over the years. It leads us to appreciate that any great intellectual system of thought may take many years to win the minds of people, and that the implications of such a new worldview may take many years to unfold in terms of the religious and social implications.

4. Our appreciation for the diversity of the thought in the biblical literature has increased. After the Babylonian Exile people began to search for new ways to envision and experience God. Much of the literature reflects the different pieties of that age. Thus, we shall consider the post-exilic literature from the perspective of a religious quest for God which moves in different directions: the cultic piety of the priests, the hope for a golden age in history found among the later prophets and apocalyptic thinkers, and the search for God in the everyday life, the human mind, and created order undertaken by the wisdom thinkers. This latter category of literature and thought, the wisdom tradition, has received increased respect and attention by scholars as a serious mode of discourse about the divine among Jews in the post-exilic era.

5. Finally, a new way of understanding many biblical texts and customs is an approach called "social world" analysis, which seeks to appreciate the cultural dynamics of the East Mediterranean world. Though it is beyond the scope of this introductory textbook to engage in the presentation of "social world" theory and a thorough analysis of the Bible with that method; nonetheless, whenever possible this textbook will introduce observations about the life,

customs, and cultural assumptions of the ancient Israelites and Jews in order to understand crucial texts and concepts. Significant new understandings have arisen concerning the Israelite and Jewish cultural experience. For example, we no longer perceive them as people who emerged from the desert with a nomadic ethos. Rather, they historically were both pastoralists (animal herders) and farmers, moving back and forth between economic life-styles depending upon economic needs and environmental circumstances. Their relationships with each other were defined in terms of kinship, but we now sense that this was a form of "fictive kinship." People were adopted into clan and tribal relationships, which were actually artificial concepts. Related to this is our modern understanding of the Israelite conquest or settlement of the land around 1200 BCE. We now perceive that the majority of the Israelites were actually Canaanites who evolved into Israelites. The settlement process was an internal and peaceful process, not a military conquest, as it sometimes was portrayed in the past.

Beyond these particular perspectives, this introduction also will focus on only certain aspects of the Hebrew Bible. This is a short introduction, and so it will not attempt to be comprehensive. The focus will be on the thought or the theology of the Hebrew Bible, and its development as religious spokespersons responded to their experience of the divine and subsequently attempted to address the religious and existential questions of their audience through the vicissitudes of history. The text will not dwell extensively upon the actual political history of the Israelites as it is recorded in the Bible, nor will extensive attention be given to archaeological discoveries, unless they are germane to the discussion.

Throughout the text the terms Old Testament and Hebrew Bible will be used interchangeably. Old Testament is the term that Christians use for this corpus, and it obviously implies that there is a New Testament to be included with it. The Jewish term for this literature is TaNaK, an acronym for Torah (Pentateuch), Nebiim (Prophets), and Kethubim (Writings), the three parts of the Old Testament. Another term more neutral in usage is the term Hebrew Bible, for it respects the identity of this literature as a separate sacred canon used by both Christians and Jews. References to biblical books are not abbreviated for the sake of clarity for the students. This volume arose out of involvement in teaching in graduate level extension programs in the Loyola Institute of Ministry of Loyola University, New Orleans for the past twenty-five years. The generation of this text owes much to the efforts and editorial direction provided by Prof. Charles Winters and Prof. Bernard Lee, both of the Loyola Institute of Ministry.

# Value of the Old Testament

The Bible is the most significant source for Jewish and Christian piety and theology. As sacred literature, some people read it for devotional and inspirational values, others draw from it for liturgical and artistic inspiration, and on a more advanced level Christian theologians use it to articulate theology and ethics. Some theologians are asked to create official statements for their denominational churches using biblical passages as a foundation. For Jewish thinkers the Hebrew Bible is interpreted through the lens of the Talmud to provide guidelines for leading a moral and ritually pure life. For Christians the Bible, both Old and New Testaments, is interpreted through the primary event of Jesus' death and resurrection in order to proclaim a message of salvation and to provide guidelines for a Christian lifestyle. Biblical scholars and theologians generate studies of the Bible for advanced students, textbooks for college and high school students, and curricular material for Bible classes, Sunday schools, and confirmation training. Preachers study biblical texts to preach Sunday morning sermons, and many lay people study it in order to teach Sunday school. How you read the Bible is determined by your needs and what you wish to obtain.

Some Christians, who believe that use of the Bible is important, limit their attention solely to the New Testament. They ask why should Christians read and study the Old Testament? Does not the New Testament provide us with our beliefs and preachers with enough topics for sermons? Some think that the Old Testament portrays God as a deity of wrath and war who threatens to punish people for sinning against the hash demands of the Law. However, a closer reading of the text discloses God as a deity who loved and elected the Israelites to be the chosen people. This God gave the Law to provide a sense of identity to Israelites and Jews, who then obey the Law as a way of thanking God for choosing them. The Old Testament view of God does not differ from the New Testament view of God.

After some debate in the 2nd century CE, Christians decided to use the books of the Old Testament as scripture because these writings helped them to understand more clearly the teachings of Jesus, Paul, and other writers of the New Testament, most of whom were Jewish. New Testament authors were deeply indebted to the language and ideas of the Old Testament, and many early Christians understood this language well. Jesus was Jewish and Christianity arose out of Judaism. Christianity was Judaism's most successful heresy, according to one witty Jewish scholar. Another Jewish scholar, the Apostle Paul, described Christianity as a branch growing out of Judaism. If Christianity had evolved after the 1st century CE without retaining the roots provided by the Old Testament, it would have been a very different religion and it might have disappeared.

Christians and Jews study the Old Testament or the Hebrew Bible because it contains the accounts of their origins and the texts foundational to their identity. Many accounts describe human experience in a deep existential fashion common to people everywhere. Even those who have no strong religious identity resonate with the experiences of persons in the biblical narratives. The Old Testament testifies to the beginning of beliefs and values that ultimately shaped Judaism, Christianity, Islam, and western culture as a whole. It speaks of a grand drama wherein people of faith related to a God whom they believed cared for them and directed their lives.

# The Grand Story

The events of the Old Testament narrative may be divided artificially into six eras. To some extent we shall follow this narrative in our textbook. As the Jewish authors told their story in the written accounts of our Bible, these were the great events: 1) The Exodus out of Egypt, Lawgiving at Sinai, and Wandering in the Wildness (1200 BCE) were recalled in the books of Exodus and Numbers. 2) The Settlement in Canaan (also portrayed as a conquest) (1200-1050 BCE) was recalled in Joshua and Judges. 3) The United Monarchy (1050-922 BCE) of Saul, David, and Solomon was recounted in 1 Samuel, 2 Samuel, 1 Kings, 1 Chronicles, and 2 Chronicles. 4) The Divided Monarchies of Israel and Judah (922-586 BCE) were remembered in 1 Kings, 2 Kings, and 2 Chronicles. Indirect memories were located in the prophets Amos, Hosea, Micah, Isaiah 1-39, Zephaniah, Nahum, Habakkuk, and Jeremiah. 5) The Babylonian Exile (586-539 BCE) was alluded to in the oracles of the prophets Ezekiel and Isaiah 34-35, 40-55. 6) The Post-Exilic Era or Second Temple Period (539 BCE-70 CE) was partially recalled by Ezra, Nehemiah, 1 Maccabees, and 2 Maccabees. Indirect memories can be found in prophetic oracles in Haggai, Zechariah, Isaiah 56-66, Obadiah, Joel, and Malachi; Wisdom Literature such as Proverbs, Job, Koheleth, Sirach, and Wisdom of Solomon; hymnic materials in Psalms, Lamentations, and Song of Solomon; and Novels such as Ruth, Jonah, Esther, Daniel, Tobit, and Judith. The list does not refer to the Primeval History (Genesis 1-11) or the Patriarchal Narratives (Genesis 12-50), because these accounts are not the story of Israel, they are a pre-history of Israel. The book of Genesis functions as the Old Testament of the Old Testament. The biblical authors remembered their past as a drama of divine protection and salvation for faithful believers. They were not interested in historical details but they believed in God's presence among them in their corporate and personal experience of God.

**Exodus and Wilderness:** Jacob and his twelve sons, the symbolic ancestors of Israel, came to Egypt to seek haven in a time of famine, but were forced into slave labor. God sent Moses to liberate them, defeat pharaoh at the sea, and take them to Sinai where they received the Law. Though they sometimes murmured against God and Moses in the wilderness, they survived numerous threats and eventually entered the land as a unified people under Joshua's leadership. Perhaps the Ten Commandments in an early form served as civil law code to bring order to this community of escaped slaves.

**Settlement in Canaan:** Under Joshua's leadership Israelites seized Jericho and Ai and won battles north and south in the highlands, after which Joshua assigned portions of the land to the various tribes. The narrative appears to portray Joshua's campaign as a total conquest of the land, but a slower reading of the text reveals that Joshua's people only conquered the tribal area of Benjamin, and more land was absorbed by peaceful alliances made with the local inhabitants. Joshua's group was small, so over the years Israel grew by peaceful amalgamation with the local inhabitants. Traditions about the judges testified to the social disorder and lack of unity among the people, and the author of the book justified the emergence of kingship to bring order to society. In the narratives Israelites appeared to be like the Canaanites, because most of them really were Canaanites. The chaos recorded in the book of Judges reflected the early evolution of Israelites in the highlands of Palestine as a fairly disjointed group of diverse peoples.

**United Monarchy:** Israelites in the highlands of Palestine found themselves threatened from the southwest, as the Philistines, a people who immigrated into the land from the Aegean Islands and Turkey, attempted to unify all Palestine under their rule. Saul arose to oppose them and in the minds of the biblical authors he became Israel's first king. Whereas he failed and died in battle, David succeeded and created a unified country, ruled from the city of Jerusalem, which David conquered. This country was inherited by Solomon, a king made famous by his wealth and the construction of the Temple in Jerusalem. After Solomon's death the kingdom divided into two separate kingdoms. David was remembered as the paradigm for the ideal king, while Solomon was recalled in later years as the ultimate tyrant. We observe that the real force behind the emergence of the monarchy was probably economic: the highland population increased and developed economically and socially, and trade drew them together. The United Monarchy was simple and rustic, more of an advanced chieftaincy than a truly unified state.

**Divided Monarchy:** Solomon's oppression alienated people so that his son Rehoboam faced rebellion and the ultimate split of the kingdom. Rehoboam retained Jerusalem and the small southern state of Judah, while the northern kingdom, Israel or Ephraim, was ruled by Jeroboam. Wars occurred between the two kingdoms, and occasionally the northern state ruled the southern state, although the biblical authors tried to downplay that in the narratives. Both countries found themselves at the mercy of Egypt and various Mesopotamian empires. Prophets proclaimed that divine judgment would occur for social and religious evils, so when Assyria destroyed Israel in 722 BCE and Chaldean Babylon destroyed Judah in 586 BCE, the prophets were vindicated as spokespersons for God. The ten tribes of the north were exiled to northern Mesopotamia where they were settled, intermarried, and disappeared, while imported subjects of the Assyrian empire merged with surviving Israelites to create the later Samaritans.

**Babylonian Exile:** Biblical authors in the books of Kings condemned all the kings save only David, Hezekiah of Judah (725-710 BCE) and Josiah of Judah (636-609 BCE), for they alone were seen as truly faithful to Yahweh. Chaldean Babylonians under Nebuchadrezzar or Nebuchadnezzar conquered Judah and took exiles in Babylon in 597 and 586 BCE, destroying the city and the Temple. Jewish religious intellectuals declared this destruction was caused by the sins of the people. These intellectuals created literature that would evolve into the Hebrew Bible, and they preserved customs to be observed by Jews forever (especially Sabbath, kosher food, and circumcision). Prior to the exile we call the folk Israelites or Judahites, but after 586 BCE we call them Jews. The former terms were national-political, but the latter was a religious term of identity, for after 586 BCE what held Jews together was religion, not political allegiance.

**Post-Exilic or Second Temple Era:** Cyrus of Persia conquered Babylon in 539 BCE, and allowed prisoners of war, including Jews, to return home. Those few who returned to Jerusalem rebuilt their city and Temple, and organized their society according to the newly emerging written literature of the Pentateuch and the Prophets. Ezra and Nehemiah, both sanctioned by Persian authorities, reconstructed Judaism in the late 5th century BCE using the biblical text. Jews were ruled by Persians (539-330 BCE), Alexander and his generals (330-301 BCE), Egyptian Greeks, the Ptolemies (301-199 BCE), Syrian Greeks, the Seleucids (199-164 BCE, and Romans (63 BCE-70 CE), with only a brief period of independence under the Maccabees (164-63 BCE). During these years scribal intelligentsia generated more literature: hymns or psalms, wisdom literature, novels, historiography, and apocalyptic texts, much of which would become the Bible.

This textbook will pay attention to the grand drama in its discussion, but the actual sequence of chapters will follow more closely our understanding of how the literature arose. Many memories of the Israelites were recalled in oral tradition but not written into a form that we would recognize until late in their history. 1) We shall first consider the 8th century BCE prophets (Amos, Hosea, Isaiah, Micah), for their message had a tremendous theological impact upon how the later historical narratives developed. 2) The Deuteronomistic History, the books of Deuteronomy, Joshua, Judges, Samuel, and Kings, were written down in some initial form around 620 BCE to actually become the core of what would later be the Bible. 3) In the middle of the 6th century BCE perhaps the prophetic texts were committed to writing, and several contemporary prophets were included (Jeremiah, Ezekiel, Isaiah 34-35, 40-55). In later years additional prophets were added. 4) In the late 6th century the Yahwist Historian recalled the experience of the Exodus and the Wilderness in the books of Exodus and Numbers. 5) The Yahwist crafted a prehistory of the Israelites with narratives about the Patriarchs and a pre-history of all people in Genesis 2-11. 6) Priestly Editors made additions to the grand narrative and added priestly legislation (Leviticus) in the 5th century BCE. 7) Post-exilic intellectuals generated further historiography (Chronicles, Ezra, Nehemiah), hymnic literature (Psalms, Lamentation, Song of Solomon), wisdom literature (Proverbs, Job, Ecclesiastes, Sirach, Wisdom of Solomon), novels (Ruth, Esther, Jonah, Daniel 1-6, 13-14, Tobit, Judith), and apocalyptic (Daniel 7-12). We shall follow this format primarily because this textbook seeks to present the account of how scholars believe the intellectual tradition of the Hebrew Bible emerged.

# Bibliography

Gösta Ahlström. *The History of Ancient Palestine*. Minneapolis, MN: Fortress, 1992.

Rainer Albertz. *A History of Israelite Religion in the Old Testament Period*. Old Testament Library. Louisville, KY: Westminster John Knox, 1994.

Michael Coogan, ed. The Oxford History of the Biblical World. New York, NY: Oxford University Press, 1998.

William Dever. *What Did the Biblical Writers Know, and When Did They Know It?: What Archaeology Can Tell Us about the Reality of Ancient Israel*. Grand Rapids, MI: Eerdmans, 2001.

Israel Finkelstein and Neil Asher Silberman. *The Bible Unearthed: Archaeology's New Vision of Ancient Israel and the Origin of Its Sacred Texts*. New York, NY: Free Press, 2001.

Baruch Halpern. *The First Historians: The Hebrew Bible and History*. University Park, PA: Penn State University, 1996.

B. S. J. Isserlin. *The Israelites*. London: Thames and Hudson, 1998.

Donald Redford. *Egypt, Canaan, and Israel in Ancient Times*. Princeton, NJ: Princeton University, 1992.

Hershel Shanks, ed. *Ancient Israel: From Abraham to the Roman Destruction of the Temple*. Washington, DC: Biblical Archaeology Society, 1999.

Hershel Shanks, ed. *The Rise of Ancient Israel*. Washington, DC: Biblical Archaeology Society, 1992.

# Chapter 2

# Ancient World Before Israel

When Israel entered upon the scene of the ancient Near East, the world was already very old. Great civilizations had been in existence in the river valleys as well organized states for nearly two millennia, and farming in small villages had occurred for nearly eight millennia. As Israelites emerged in the highlands of Palestine around 1200 BCE, they were, in some ways, a rustic people, but in other ways they were heir to a great heritage of culture from both Mesopotamia and Egypt. The degree to which they adopted and modified political and religious concepts from their neighbors is debated by historians. The Israelites, like the Greeks, were an Iron Age culture (1200 BCE and thereafter) highly indebted to those beliefs and customs held by predecessor cultures, but they advanced understandings and attitudes about the divine realm and the human world in significant ways that would ultimately lay the foundation for western civilization. It is worth reviewing briefly the world out of which Israelites and Jews arose in order to understand their place in history. Though we cannot undertake a thorough review of the ancient Near East in a short introduction such as this, we at least should be familiar with the historical parameters of the age in which Israel was born and those significant pieces of literature with which Israelite authors might have been familiar.

## History of the Ancient Near East

The earliest settlements in the ancient Near East may be dated to the period after the last ice age, when hunters came down from the Eurasian plains and began to establish somewhat permanent camps in the highlands in the Middle East from which they would hunt and forage for food (11,000 BCE). By 9000 BCE these camps began to seem more like villages, and people began to plant the wild grains around their villages rather than foraging for them in the highlands. With agriculture, the Neolithic Era began (New Stone Age), whereas we classify all human accomplishment prior to this era as the Paleolithic Era (Old Stone Age). In the Neolithic Era (9000-4500 BCE) people domesticated animals for livestock, invented pottery for food storage, and began the division of labor that evolved into the three-class system--upper class priests and warriors, middle class craftsmen, and lower class farmers and herders. By 6000 BCE increased population led people to move into the river valleys of the Nile in Egypt, and the Tigris and Euphrates of Mesopotamia (and further east into the Indus valley of India). With the emergence of copper tools along with stone tools (usually obsidian was the hardest stone for such tools), the Chalcolithic Era began (4500-3100 BCE). During this period population grew in the river valleys and urban sites developed to become centers of power. Increased population demanded agricultural intensification, which led to organizational leadership, which, in turn, led to state formation.

Around 3100 BCE state formation occurred in Mesopotamia and Egypt. In Mesopotamia significant city-states emerged, including Eridu, Ur, Uruk, Nippur, and Kish as major centers, and at various times certain cities had hegemony over large areas. In Egypt unification of the entire Nile valley occurred under Pharaoh Menes who built his capital at Memphis. With state formation, the river valley cultures took the systems of notation used for keeping records of gifts to temples and taxes to rulers, and developed these systems into true writing (cuneiform in Mesopotamia and slightly later the hieroglyphs in Egypt). Also, monumental building projects emerged within the first few centuries as an expression of the power of the newly created states in both river valleys (temples, Egyptian pyramids, Mesopotamian ziggurats). From this point onward we know more about the political, cultural, and religious life of these peoples, as they recorded more and more information with their newly developed skills of writing.

Modern historians thus divide the history of the ancient Near East into certain eras. The Early Bronze Age lasted from 3100 to 2100 BCE, the Middle Bronze Age from 2100 to 1550 BCE, the Late Bronze Age from 1550 to 1200 BCE, the Iron Age from 1200 to 550 BCE, the Persian Period from 550 to 330 BCE, the Greek or Hellenistic Period from 330 to 30 BCE, and the Roman Period from 30 BCE to around 500 CE. These ages represent political eras with interregnums of social dislocation before a new political era began. Often cultural artifacts recovered by archaeologists reflect these political divisions. From 3000 BCE we may summarize the history of the ancient Near East most easily by speaking of people and events in Egypt and Mesopotamia respectively, with reference to other significant cultures on the periphery of those river valleys.

With Egyptian history we divide the ages up into periods that Egyptians also would have recognized as distinctive. The pre-dynastic years span the time from the earliest significant settlements in the Nile valley (5500 BCE), which were later than comparable settlements in the Mesopotamian valley, to the times of unification under Menes (3100 BCE). We speak of the Old Kingdom (3100-2200 BCE), the First Intermediate Period (2200-2050 BCE), the Middle Kingdom (2050-1800 BCE), the Second Intermediate Period (1800-1550 BCE), the Empire or New Kingdom (1550-1100 BCE), the Third Intermediate Period (1100-650 BCE), and the Saite Period (650-500 BCE). The Egyptian historian Manetho divided the history of his people into 31 dynasties or royal families that ruled from 3100 BCE to 500 BCE. It is easier for us is to speak simply of the three kingdoms, which somewhat correspond to the three divisions of the Bronze Age.

1.  The Old Kingdom in Egypt saw the emergence of a strong unified state. The period was characterized most by the building of pyramids during the Third and Fourth Dynasties (2800-2500 BCE), especially the three great pyramids of Giza built by Cheops, Chephren, and Mycerinus (their Greek names). (Pyramids were built not by slaves but by professionals and free Egyptian peasants.) Also, typical of this era was a blossoming of great intellectual and technological breakthroughs, accompanied with a fairly optimistic worldview on the part of the intelligentsia. The capital was at Memphis, in the northern part of the country. This era was followed by a period in which central government collapsed and regional rule arose. For some, the First Intermediate Period was one of chaos, but for others the relaxed rule may have stimulated new religious and ideological developments.

2.  The Middle Kingdom saw the country reunified by strong pharaohs from Thebes in the south. They undertook empire building in the south, in Nubia, and engaged in extensive trade. The spirit of this age was more subdued, and pharaohs were portrayed artistically in more relaxed fashion and called the "shepherds of the people." The Twelfth Dynasty was the strongest, and it produced a number of pharaohs named either Amenemhet or Sesostris. This era slowly edged into decline as Semitic foreigners from Palestine infiltrated the northern part of Egypt and established rule there. Later Egyptians viewed these foreign Hyksos as rulers who brought shame to Egypt by their presence. Later Egyptians engaged in military campaigns in Palestine, almost in paranoid fashion, in response to this perceived invasion and occupation by the Hyksos.

3.  A strong revival in Thebes during the Seventeenth and Eighteenth Dynasties created an empire in Palestine and Syria that would be maintained throughout the Nineteenth Dynasty. This Empire period would be an era of wealth and military might. Intellectually we sense that the Egyptian psyche was somewhat paranoid about the threat of the dreaded Asiatics and religious piety tended to be more pessimistic, personal, pious, and introspective. Great Eighteenth Dynasty pharaohs included the empire builder Thutmosis III (1490-1436 BCE) and the opulent Amenhotep III (1405-1367 BCE), ruler of Egypt at its zenith. Amenhotep IV renamed himself Akhenaton (1367-1350 BCE) when he began his religious reform at Amarna. Modern scholars debate as to whether or not Atonism, created by Akhenaton, was a form of monotheism. Most famous, of course, is the Nineteenth Dynasty Pharaoh Ramses II (1290-1224 BCE), who held together the Egyptian empire in the face of Hittite military strength and the pressure of foreign Sea Peoples. Romantically considered by some to be the pharaoh of the Exodus and called by others the greatest pharaoh, he receives far more credit than he deserves. The Egyptian empire was weakened after 1150 BCE and in the Third Intermediate period, contemporary with Israelites, the Egyptians were not really the powerful state they once had been. Occasion periods brought a brief flash of power and cultural accomplishment, such

as with some pharaohs in the Saite Period, like Psammetichus (663-610 BCE) and Necho (610-595 BCE), but those times were few. Eventually Egypt would become a Persian province after 525 BCE and subsequently be ruled by Greeks and then Romans.

Other related cultures with whom the Egyptians and the Mesopotamians had dealings also deserve mention at this point.

1.  Syria was a significant area in the trade route of the Fertile Crescent between Egypt and Mesopotamia. We cannot write a political history of these people, and our cultural knowledge is brought to us courtesy of the archaeologist's spade. In Syria or northern Mesopotamia there was a blossoming culture with many cities, one of which was Ebla. Ebla flourished from 2400 BCE and rivaled the Akkadian Empire until it was defeated. The Eblaites were the first significant West-Semitic culture we know about, and we believe insight into their religion and literature may help us learn more about the roots of Israelite religion and culture. The Amorites were culturally significant in north Mesopotamia in the first half of the second millennium BCE. (Years ago some scholars suggested that Abraham was an Amorite, but few suggest that today.) By the beginning of the first millennium BCE a new people called the Arameans settled in Syria, and they were occasional enemies and allies of the Israelites over the years. Ultimately, the language of the Arameans (Aramaic) became the common political language of the Assyrian and Persian empires, and the Hebrew Bible was written in this Aramaic script during and after the Babylonian Exile.

2.  Phoenicia was a term for a number of cities along the modern coast of Lebanon, who were also part of the West-Semitic culture, and closer to the Israelites in some ways than the Syrians. Their major cities were Tyre, Sidon, Arvad, Byblos, and Ugarit (moving from south to north away from Israel). These people were coastal Canaanites, thus inviting us to compare their culture to that of Israel. Texts from Ugarit dating to 1400 BCE in an alphabetic script using cuneiform sigla have been used precisely for such comparisons. Phoenicians colonized much of the Mediterranean, as far as Spain, and their most famous colony was Carthage (750-150 BCE).

3.  Canaan is a term used for Palestine by Egyptians and Mesopotamians, ironically, however, not by the people themselves. Israelites used the term to describe those people in Palestine who differed from themselves, and, in actuality, they were describing what they had been before they evolved into Israelites. The most cohesive group were the Philistines who lived in numerous cities on the coastal plain in southwestern Palestine (Ashkelon, Ashdod, Gath, Ekron, Gaza), but even they had no real sense of unified identity. They may have been part of the Sea-Peoples who were displaced from the Aegean and migrated by land and by sea down the east Mediterranean coastline for many years (1200-1100 BCE) destroying and seizing cities on the coastal plain. Stopped by the Egyptians around 1200 BCE and 1100 BCE, they may have settled on

the coast to become Philistines.  They became a nemesis to Israel and helped precipitate the emergence of kingship under Saul and David.

4.  Hittites were a confederation of peoples in Anatolia or central Turkey who exercised great power in the second millennium BCE (1750-1200 BCE). Around 1590 BCE Mursilis I destroyed the city of Babylon, in the 1300's Shuppiluliumas created a strong Hittite empire in Turkey and Syria, and in 1286 BCE Mutawallis II engaged Ramses II of Egypt in an indecisive battle at Kadesh in Syria, which nevertheless weakened Egyptian control over its northern Asiatic domains.  Hittites were a major military and cultural force in the Syro-Palestinian area, and perhaps in some ways their ideas and beliefs influenced later Israelite literature and thought.  Hittites may have mediated Mesopotamian thought to the later Greek world, and their historiography and political ideas foreshadowed the later sophisticated Greek concepts.

With Mesopotamian history we divide the political cultural eras according to significant ethic groups who moved into the river valley and exerted significant social and political domination.

1.  Though there appear to have been three cultural groups of people prior to 3100 BCE (Uruk, Ubaid, and Jemdat Nasr), we usually speak of the Sumerians as the first truly significant cultural entity in Mesopotamia (3100-2400, 2150-1950 BCE).  They were a non-Semitic people (perhaps kin to the contemporary folk in the Indus Valley at Harrapa and Mohen-jaro), who left us a number of clay tablets, written in a pre-cuneiform script, concerning economic dealings, political statements, and some literature (myths).  They predominated in southern Mesopotamia in a number of significant cities, including Ur, Uruk, Nippur, Kish, Lagash, Adab, Eridu, Mari, Shuruppak, and others.

2.  The first true empire was created by Sargon the Great, a Semite from the northern part of the valley, who unified rule over Semites and Sumerians.  He built the city of Akkad, and his people and empire are called Akkadian (2400-2150 BCE).  He and successors, such as Naram-Sin, campaigned widely from the Mediterranean Sea to the Iranian highlands.  They subdued great northern Mesopotamia cities, such as Ebla in Syria, which appear to have been more in the West-Semitic or Syro-Palestinian cultural sphere.  Akkadian was written in cuneiform script, and it became the language of law, literature, and international correspondence for a thousand years. Mesopotamia would be called Sumer and Akkad throughout the rest of ancient Near Eastern history.

3.  After a brief revival of Sumerian rule at Ur III under Ur-Nammu and Shulgi (2100-1950 BCE), the next people to assume significant power were the Amorites.  They were strong in a number of cities, such as Larsa and Isin, and it was the Amorite dynasty in Babylon under Hammurabi (c. 1750 BCE) that unified the entire land.  Texts from this era were written in the cuneiform dialect we call Middle Babylonian.  This period was famous for laws, economic edicts of reform, and some of the great epic cycles.  Babylon remained powerful until it was sacked by the Hittites in 1590 BCE.

4. The Kassites were the next powerful entity in Mesopotamia (1500-1100 BCE). Under their aegis building projects, epic literature, and divinatory skills, such as astrology, developed. They vied with the Assyrians over the years for political domination of the valley. Their most famous king was Nebuchadrezzar I around 1100 BCE (after whom the later king who caused the Babylonian Exile would be named), and his famous Assyrian nemesis was Tiglath-Pileser I.

5. From 1100 to 612 BCE the Assyrians from north Mesopotamia were the dominating power that sought to extend their rule from Elam to Egypt in the name of the god, Ashur, who called Assyrians to a manifest destiny of world dominion. Famous for their brutality, theirs was an empire that created homogeneity by massive deportations of people. They imported so many people into their own realm that they evolved from being Assyrian into becoming Aramean (Syrian), and Aramaic thus became the common language of the world (and continued to be under later Persian rule). Assyrians destroyed the northern state of Israel in 722 BCE and deported the urban population. Israelite prophets railed against "wolf" of Assyria that God used to punish sinful Israel.

6. The destruction of Nineveh in 612 BCE by king Nabopollasar began the ascendancy of the Chaldean Babylonians, who essentially inherited the Assyrian Empire and continued the same policies of rule, including the deportation of defeated peoples. Nebuchadrezzar (spelled Nebuchadnezzar in the book of Daniel) destroyed Jerusalem and exiled the urban population of Judah in 586 BCE. In turn, the Chaldean Empire collapsed during the reign of Nabonidus in 540 BCE when Cyrus the Persian conquered Babylon. With the fall of Babylon, rule over the Mesopotamian valley passed out of the hands of Mesopotamians and into the hands of outsiders for more than a thousand years (until the Abbasid Caliphate in 750 CE).

If we switch from the perspective of Mesopotamian history to a wider view of the ancient Near East history, especially in regard to the experience of the Jews, we should at least mention three other significant peoples and corresponding cultural eras they represent. Our review then takes through the entire history of Israelites and Jews.

1. The Jews found themselves ruled by Persians from 540 BCE to 332 BCE. Persian rule permitted Jews to return to Judah after 539 BCE as part of a policy to create loyal buffer states between themselves and Greek influence. Hence, Ezra and Nehemiah were sponsored by Persian rule. After Cyrus the Great other famous Persian rulers included Darius I (522-486 BCE) and Xerses I (486-465 BCE), both of whom unsuccessfully invaded Greece. Ultimately, Darius III was defeated by Alexander the Great, who campaigned in Asia from 333 BCE to 323 BCE.

2. Jews fell under Greek rule with Alexander's entry into Jerusalem in 332 BCE. After Alexander's death civil war between Alexander's generals ravaged the Middle East for over twenty years. After 301 BCE Jews found themselves ruled by Egyptian Greeks, called the Ptolemies, out of Alexandria in Egypt.

Eventually after a series of many battles, the Seleucid Greeks from Syria gained control of Palestine by 199 BCE. Seleucids sought to hellenize the Jews more aggressively than the Ptolemies had done, so the Jews rose up in rebellion under the leadership of the Maccabees from 167 BCE to 164 BCE. An independent Maccabean state existed from 164 BCE to 63 BCE.

3. Roman expansion brought Jews under their control with the entrance of general Pompey into Jerusalem in 63 BCE. Jews remained a Jewish province either under the rule of client kings, like Herod the Great (30-4 BCE), or Roman procurators until the destruction of Jerusalem by the Romans in 70 CE, which effectively ended the Second Temple Period of Judaism. A failed revolt against the Romans led by Bar Cochba in 132-135 CE sealed the fate of any possible Jewish state in Palestine for two thousand years.

Though this brief summary cannot begin to do justice to a fuller history of the ancient Near East, at least this review has mentioned significant nations and peoples that were part of the social-cultural experience of the Israelites. Throughout the textbook allusions will be made to Israelite and Jewish interactions with these peoples.

# Literature of the Ancient World

The efforts of archaeologists have provided us with many texts from the ancient Near East that shed light on much of the Hebrew Bible. The biblical authors were part of their cultural environment and were sometimes well educated (at least if they knew how to write, they had more education than most of their people). Thus, biblical authors may have been familiar with the literary accounts and the typical political language of the other societies around them. For example, we have found a fragment of the great literary work, the Gilgamesh Epic, at Megiddo, and we would assume that educated Israelites were at least familiar with the legal customs, international treaties, and the language of economic dealings in the first millennium BCE. Certainly during the Babylonian Exile many Jews would have come into contact with literary traditions and the visible religious and social customs of the Babylonians around them, and the exile was the time in which much of our present Hebrew Bible was written. Hence, a consideration of the texts of the ancient Near East often can be helpful in understanding the deeper meaning of many biblical texts. We cannot enumerate all the relevant literary texts in our introduction, but we can acknowledge the most important ones.

# Creation of the World, Flood, and Foundational Accounts

## Mesopotamian

The most fascinating texts for comparison are those accounts dealing with the creation of the world, and they are the ones that have captured popular imagination the most.

Mesopotamian texts, in particular, appear to demonstrate the greatest similarity with biblical accounts in Genesis 1-11.

*Enki and the World Manor Myth.* In this third millennium BCE Sumerian myth, Enki created order in the world with eight creative acts, which was similar to the eight creative acts of God in the six days of creation in Genesis 1.

*Enki and Ninmah Myth.* Enki and Ninmah fashioned people from clay to relieve the gods of labor in this third millennium BCE Sumerian myth. But while drinking at a banquet they both boasted about their importance and ability in the creative process. On a challenge Ninmah created a palsied man, a blind man, a lame man, a moron, a barren woman, and a sexless creature. Enki found social roles for each. Enki created an "umul," an immature fetus, and Ninmah could not find a place for it, so she lost the bet. Thus, deformities entered into our world due to a drunken contest among the gods. This origin of evil myth contrasted with the free will decision of the man and woman in Genesis 3.

*Dumuzi and Enkimdu Myth.* The farmer Dumuzi and the shepherd Enkimdu both wooed Inanna, but the farmer won her in this third millennium BCE Sumerian myth. When they reconciled, they determined that the shepherd should possess the highlands and the farmer would own the lowlands. This story favored the lifestyle of the farmer, which was the reverse of the Cain and Abel story.

*Ziusudra Myth or The Eridu Genesis Myth.* This late third or early second millennium BCE Sumerian myth told about the flood. Enki created people to build cities, but the gods (Enlil especially) decreed their destruction by a seven-day long flood. The priest of Enki, Ziusudra, survived in an ark, afterward offered sacrifice to Utu, and was granted immortality and lived at Dilmun, while Enki recreated people.

*Adapa Myth.* In this second millennium BCE Akkadian account, Adapa, the priest of the god Enki, was called to the heavens for breaking the wing of the west wind while he was fishing. Enki warned him not to eat or drink anything when appearing before Anu, lest he be poisoned. But due to the intercession of the divine gatekeepers, Tammuz and Gizzada, Adapa was offered the bread and water of immortality. Thinking it to be poison, Adapa turned down the food and thus lost immortality for humanity. This, also, contrasted with the loss of the tree of life in Genesis 3 by human free will.

*Atrahasis Myth.* This Akkadian account from the early second millennium BCE told the story of both creation and the flood. When the gods went on strike to protest their onerous work, seven pairs of humans were created from clay and the body and blood of the dead god We-ila to do the work of the gods. Ea (Enki) commissioned the goddess, Nintu-Mami to make people by pinching off pieces of clay. Hence, people were meant to be the slaves of the gods. The noise of humanity disturbed Enlil who thinned them out with plague, famine, and other disasters, which Enki softened by telling Atrahasis what sacrifices to offer. A flood was decreed, and Enki was prevented from talking to humanity, so he communicated to Atrahasis by addressing the wall of Atrahasis' reed hut and telling him to build an ark to save human and animal life. The ark had seven floors, with nine compartments on each. The flood lasted seven days, and then Atrahasis sent out a raven, swallow, and a dove. After the flood his family was divinized and taken to a distant land.  The gods created people again and used sterility and stillbirths to control human population.  The similarities with the details of the biblical flood are great, but there are significant religious and moral differences.

*Gilgamesh Epic.*  The Sumerian king Gilgamesh was a hero who overworked his people, so the gods sent a wild man to Uruk to distract Gilgamesh.  After Enkidu became civilized, he and Gilgamesh became friends and went to the Cedar Forest to bring back wood.  They killed the beast, Humbaba, and later the bull of heaven, thus offending Ishtar.  The gods decreed Enkidu's death, and grief over Enkidu's death sent Gilgamesh off on a quest to find immortality.  On his quest, on the island of Dilmun, he met Utnapishtim who told him the story of the flood.  In this version of the flood the gods decreed human destruction by flood, Enki warned Utnapishtim by talking to him through a reed hut and a brick wall, giving him the instructions for the ark.  The ark survived the flood, landed on Mt. Nisir in Urartu (which sounds like Ararat), and sent out the same three birds as Atrahasis did.  (Noah did not have a swallow.)  After Utnapishtim sacrificed and the gods swarmed like flies to the meal, the gods granted him immortality and put him on Dilmun.  Perhaps, this story was dependent upon Atrahasis, and it also merits comparison with the biblical flood account.  Also, in the Gilgamesh Epic the story of Enkidu's "fall" into becoming a civilized man occurred after he had sex with a temple harlot, who was the symbol of civilized urban society.  It was comparable to the man and the woman leaving the garden in Genesis 3 and assuming the responsibilities of adulthood.  Toward the end of the epic the snake ate the plant of youthful rejuvenation, which Gilgamesh got from the bottom of the ocean, and this was comparable to the loss of the tree of life in Genesis 3.

*Enuma Elish.*  This creation epic told of the genealogy of the gods and then of how Ea or Enki defeated his ancestor Apsu, who desired to kill the noisy younger deities.  But when Tiamat, spouse of Apsu, challenged the gods and gained allies, Ea would not fight, but Marduk was chosen instead.  Marduk killed Tiamat and cut her in half to create the waters above and below the firmament.  After this Marduk created in order: 1) the Esharra temple, 2) sun, moon, and stars, 3) clouds, 4) mountains, 5) firmament, and the 6) Milky Way.  People were created by Ea (Enki), who used the blood of one of the evil defeated gods, Kingu, the boyfriend of Tiamat.  Hence, people were meant to be the slaves of the gods and served the gods by working on the "Temple Manor" of the gods (their own land) and by paying tribute to the king and the priests.  This myth of "social legitimation" was countered by the monotheistic hymn in Genesis 1, which also affirmed the royal status and equality of all people in the creation of the man and the woman.

# Egyptian

*Hymn to Ptah.*  Ptah created the world and people like a potter, shaping their form with his hands in a manner similar to creation of people and animals by Yahweh in Genesis 2.

*Heliopolitan Cosmology.*  The primal hillock emerged and Atum sat upon it and created the world by self-masturbation.  The separation of land from the watery muck reminds us of the third day in the creation story in Genesis 1.

*Memphite Theology.* Though the text purported to come from the Old Kingdom, it may have originated in the first millennium BCE in the form we have it. Ptah created the world by the power of his siu, which may be translated as spit, semen, tongue, or word. So the image may be earthy or it may be sophisticated, depending on how the text is translated. Most believe the text is late and that Ptah created by the command of his tongue or word. We are reminded of Genesis 1.

## Syro-Phoenician

*Baal Myth.* This second millennium BCE myth told of how the storm god Baal defeated the god of the sea, Yam, in a manner similar to Marduk's defeat of Tiamat, but then Baal submitted to Mot, the god of the underworld and death, until Anat killed and winnowed Mot's body and presumably released Baal. The myth appears to be seasonal to some scholars: the defeat of Yam was the passage of the winter rains and the coming of the spring showers, while the success of Mot over Baal paralleled the hot summer's supremacy over vegetation until the fall harvest came. The myth contains creation imagery, but does not seem to be a well-developed creation myth.

*Aqhat Myth.* Dan'el, a venerable ancient figure, who was childless, prayed for a son and received the promise of Aqhat in a dream theophany from El. Aqhat was an archer, whose bow was coveted by Anat, but she failed to seduce him. Anat had Yatpan kill Aqhat, but the bow was lost to the underworld, and Aqhat's death brought loss of fertility (or perhaps the summer season, if this was a seasonal myth). Pisgah, sister of Aqhat, found Yatpan, killed and winnowed him like grain (also like Anat did to Mot). Aqhat was restored to become the hunter in the sky (Orion), comparable to the revival of Osiris by Isis in Egyptian myths.

*Keret Epic.* Keret, a king who was childless, prayed to El for a son and received a dream theophany (like Dan'el). He was told to lay siege to the city of Udum where he would obtain a wife. This plot reminds us of the Iliad. He finally married the girl, had children, ruled wisely, and though he became sick for a time, he returned to the throne to remove the incompetent son who tried to rule in his stead.

# Legal Materials

*Ur-Nammu's Law Code.* We are uncertain whether this fragmentary Sumerian law-code came from Ur-Nammu or his son Shulgi, both of the Sumerian Ur III dynasty. This short text of casuistic or conditionally stated laws dates to about 2000 BCE.

*Lipit-Ishtar's Law Code.* This fragmentary law-code came from the Amorite king of Isin, named Lipit-Ishtar, and dates to about 1850 BCE. Though Lipit-Ishtar was an Amorite ruler in south Mesopotamia, the code was written in Sumerian.

*Law Code from Eshnunna.* We used to attribute this fragmentary law-code from central Mesopotamia to king Bilalama, and some now attribute it to king Dadusha, both of whom were kings of Eshnunna. But given such uncertainty, it is best to simply characterize it as an Amorite law-code from between 1900 BCE and 1700 BCE. It has a variety of laws reflecting a money economy.

*Hammurabi's Law Code.* This was the longest version of Amorite Babylonian laws from 1750 BCE, created by Hammurabi to unify law in his newly created empire, but it was apparently advisory (perhaps like all law-codes), not truly binding upon judges. It reflected a money economy, and the laws were designed to protect the leaders, the rich, and the powerful in society (especially those people from Babylon, capital of the empire). Like the previous law-codes, it had many interesting similarities with Israelite laws, especially the Book of the Covenant in Exodus 21-23, but the differences also invite attentive analysis. Since it was longer than the previous codes, people often fail to acknowledge their existence, as this law-code receives the attention of textbooks.

*Hittite Laws.* A number of laws date to the Old Kingdom of the Hittite Empire (1600-1500 BCE) and are attributed by scholars to various kings: Telepinus, Mursilis I or Hattushilis II. These laws had a great concern with purity in addition to criminal law.

*Nuzi Archives.* Archives from this north Mesopotamian city, including courtroom decisions dating to the 14th century BCE, familial customs, including inheritance guidelines, adoption, surrogate wives, and deathbed blessings, recorded here, are highly reminiscent of practices mentioned in the patriarchal narratives of Genesis.

*Middle Assyrian Laws of Tiglath-Pileser I.* These laws are usually attributed to Tiglath-Pileser I of Assyria (1100 BCE), an empire builder like Hammurabi, and they are characterized by harsh retribution for many of the crimes.

*Neo-Babylonian or Chaldean Laws.* These laws date to the time of the Babylonian Exile of the Jews (550 BCE), and Jews may have been familiar with these laws. Family customs practiced by the patriarchs in Genesis conformed to these laws more closely than other laws or courtroom decisions (including those from Nuzi). The laws addressed economic and familial issues. Nabopolassar or Nebuchadrezzar might have commissioned these laws to emulate earlier empire builders, like Hammurabi.

# Political Documents

A significant number of political documents also deserve mention, though not all can be listed here. What they share in common with the biblical literature is the chronicle style to record events of the past, a style found in Samuel and Kings. But even more important is that these documents also testify to deities who act in the social or historical arena. The biblical materials developed this concept of a God who acts in history more than is observed in these documents. In addition, some of these documents display the same covenant language found throughout the Hebrew Bible.

*Ebla Archives.* A number of tablets at the north Mesopotamian city of Ebla reflected the political, economic, and religious agenda of the late third millennium BCE. Ebla for a time withstood the Akkadian Empire before it was absorbed.

*Mari Archives.* Mari was a major city in north central Mesopotamia during the Akkadian and Amorite eras. Over 20,000 Akkadian tablets discovered since 1936 contain numerous references to political, economic, and religious issues. In particular, about 50 texts have references to the activity of Mari prophets, which bear striking resemblance to the activity of prophets in Israel in terms of language and actions. The tablets come from the time of Hammurabi in the Amorite period (1800-1700 BCE)

*The Weidner Chronicle*. This second millennium BCE document overviewed the history of Mesopotamian dynasties and rulers from 3000 BCE to 2000 BCE. It was an early form of historiography coming from the city of Babylon, which viewed history from the perspective of Marduk's cult in Babylon. It came from either the Amorite or the Kassite era. It was like the Deuteronomistic History, which viewed events from the perspective of the Yahweh religion.

*Hittite Covenants*. From 1400 BCE to 1200 BCE more than 35 covenants or treaties were made between Hittite rulers and various small states in Anatolia and Syria. These covenants would list: 1) a historical prologue, 2) stipulations of the covenant, especially the obligations of the vassal nation toward the suzerain nation, 3) oath of allegiance before the gods by both parties, sometimes involving the cutting of animals, 5) blessings and curses for keeping or breaking the covenant respectively, 5) stipulations for the deposit of copies of the covenant, and 6) provisions for public reading. All of this language is highly reminiscent of covenant language in the entire book of Deuteronomy, Joshua 24, the Decalogues in Exodus 20 and Deuteronomy 5, as well as scattered allusions in the prophets.

*Amarna Correspondence*. These were tablets written in Akkadian from Palestinian rulers in cities such as Ashkelon, Shechem, Gezer, and especially from Abdiheba of Jerusalem, to Akhenaton of Egypt (1367-1350 BCE), which reflected the political situation in Palestine prior to the emergence of Israelites. The texts made references to the Habiru or Hapiru, lawless and landless people in the land, who might have been some of the people who evolved into Israel.

*Deeds of Shuppiluliumas*. These annals of the great warrior Hittite king (1350 BCE), who extended the Hittite empire, remind us of the memory of David's conquests in 1 Samuel.

*Ten Year Annals of Mursilis II and Annals of Mursilis II*. These Hittite royal annals (1325 BCE) demonstrated a historiographical style that foreshadowed later Greek historiography. They spoke of how gods acted in the social arena for people and individuals in a manner which reminds us of biblical literature.

*Apology of Hattushilis III*. This Hittite apology (1250 BCE) explained why Hattushilis revolted against and killed his predecessor in order to become king. The similarity with David's rise to power (1 Samuel 15-31, 2 Samuel 1-8) is haunting, especially since there are other court apologies by usurpers with the same plot.

*Merneptah Stela*. The oldest historical reference to "Israel" was recorded by Pharaoh Merneptah (1209 BCE), who claimed to have defeated them. This "Israel" may have been folk who joined the Joshua people, or it may refer to the Joshua people.

*Nebuchadrezzar's Chronicles*. These annals reported how the Kassite king Nebuchadrezzar I (1100 BCE) brought back images of Marduk from Elam to Babylon.

Nebuchadrezzar reported that Marduk left Babylon in anger during war but eventually returned, and this reminds us of the account of the loss of the Ark of Covenant in 1 Samuel 4-6, 2 Samuel 8.

*Sheshonq Inscription.* Pharaoh Sheshonq of Egypt devasted Palestine in a raid around 920 BCE after the death of Solomon. 1 Kings 14:25-26 described this invasion, and archaeologists have found evidence of its magnitude.

*Tell Dan Inscription.* This late 9th century BCE inscription by a Syrian or Aramean king provides the oldest historical reference to the "House of David" (which may or may not prove the historicity of David). The inscription claimed that the Syrian king killed both kings of Judah and Israel, which contradicts the biblical account that attributed this to king Jehu of Israel. The text may also mention king Ahaziah of Judah.

*Moabite Stone.* In this inscription from the Transjordan, king Mesha of Moab declared that the god Chemosh allowed Israel to conquer Moab as a form of punishment, but Chemosh allowed him to liberate Moab. The similarity with language in the book of Judges is striking. In general, the inscription described Chemosh as a God who acted in history, like Yahweh.

*Black Obelisk.* This 9th century BCE inscription by king Shalmaneser III of Assyria recorded how king Jehu of Israel paid tribute to him (842 BCE), but the Bible did not mention this event.

*Synchronistic Chronicles of Assyria.* These historical annals from 800 BCE recorded the political rule of kings in Babylon and Assyria from 1500 BCE to 800 BCE in a synchronistic manner reminiscent of how the book of Kings reported affairs in Israel and Judah. The reports justified Assyrian military actions.

*Sennacherib's Prism.* This monument described how king Hezekiah of Judah paid tribute to the Assyrian king Sennacherib after his attack and siege of Jerusalem in 701 BCE. Sennacherib did not say he took the city of Jerusalem. The Bible spoke of an Assyrian retreat after plague, which Sennacherib did not mention, but the Bible did not acknowledge that tribute was given by Hezekiah.

*Assyrian and Sefire Treaties.* There are a number of treaties (800-600 BCE) that the Assyrians made with many of the vassal states they conquered or ruled. Their format came from earlier Hittite treaties (mentioned above), and the biblical materials are now seen to be more dependent upon these Assyrian treaties rather than the older Hittite treaties. The Deuteronomistic Historians and prophets may have used the Assyrian diplomatic language most directly.

*Deir Alla Inscription.* This inscription from the Transjordan (800-700 BCE) spoke of a seer named Balaam, who averted some great disaster. The text may be Ammonite or maybe Israelite, and it testified to the same shadowy figure described in the book of Numbers.

*Babylonian Chronicles.* These Chaldean annals recorded the actions of Babylonian kings from 750 BCE to 550 BCE and viewed actions of people from the perspective of Marduk. We are reminded of the religious perspective of the Deuteronomistic History.

# Poetry and Novels

*Sumerian Lamentations.* About five second millennium BCE Sumerian and Akkadian laments mourned the destruction of great cities. Usually the destruction came as punishment from the gods because of some cultic offense against the patron deity of the city. Famous cities lamented included Akkad, Eridu, Nippur, Ur, as well as the land of Sumer in general. One of the best known of these was "Lamentation Over the City of Ur," which recalled the destruction of Ur III when the god Enlil deserted the city. In the "Curse of Akkad," the destruction of the city by the Gutians was attributed to the sin of the ruler, Naram-Sin, who dishonored the shrine of the goddess Inanna. The book of Lamentations in the Bible was a comparable lament over the fall of Jerusalem. One is reminded of how the Deuteronomistic History explained the destruction of Jerusalem, in part, because kings did not worship Yahweh exclusively at the Temple, though the biblical account additionally stressed human sin and worship of other gods as causes for the destruction. The language of lament is also found in the lament hymns of the Psalter.

*Egyptian Love Songs.* Over 50 examples of love songs from various periods in Egyptian history may be likened to the Song of Songs, or Song of Solomon. Nothing comparable came from Mesopotamia. In Papyrus Chester Beatty I a number of Egyptian songs contained comparable imagery to Song of Songs: lush nature imagery, erotic body imagery, lovers described as brothers and sisters, and references to love-sickness and pinning by the lovers.

*Akkadian Laments.* A number of lament hymns addressed to Marduk or Ishtar from the second millennium BCE were written in Akkadian. The language bore a fair resemblance to the language of the lament hymns in the Psalter as well as the book of Job.

*Hymn to Aten.* This lengthy and beautiful hymn was supposedly Akhenaton's hymn of praise to the sun disk, Aten, in language that sounded very monotheistic. This 14th century BCE hymn could have inspired Psalm 104, either directly or through Phoenicia intermediary hymns we do not possess.

*Testimony of an Eloquent Peasant.* This delightful Egyptian tale described how a peasant appealed to officials in the bureaucracy of Egypt to get justice for his mistreatment by a lower official (2150 BCE). It may reflect times during the First Intermediate Period in displaying a mistrust of the bureaucracy and its possible corruption, or it may be an optimistic portrayal of government because the peasant finally got justice in the end due to his speaking ability.

*Tale of Sinuhe.* Sinuhe fled Egypt after a Middle Kingdom pharaoh was assassinated, and he lived among the Bedouin in Palestine experiencing many romantic adventures before he returned home to a warm reception in his beloved Egypt. Years ago scholars used this tale to describe the life in Palestine at the time when the patriarchs supposedly lived (Middle Bronze Age).

*Tale of Two Brothers.*  This New Kingdom tale reminds us of the temptation of Joseph by Potiphar's wife.  The wife of one brother falsely accused the other brother of adultery after attempting to seduce him.  Though enraged at first, the enraged brother was finally convinced of the honesty of his younger brother, who actually cut off his penis.

*Tale of Wen-Amon.*  This romantic tale of a merchant tells us much about the time when Egypt's power was declining (1100 BCE).  Wen-Amon went to Phoenicia, lost his money, tried to get wood for pharaoh, encountered dangers and exciting adventures, including a large magical snake.  Notably, there was mention of an ecstatic prophetess, and we use this reference to reconstruct the pre-history of West-Semitic prophecy.

# Wisdom Literature

## Egyptian

*Wisdom of Ptah-hotep.*  This was a collection of wisdom sayings from the Old Kingdom period (2450 BCE), which stressed self-control, hard work, learning, and good speech.  It had an optimistic view of how intelligence and hard work brings success.

*Dispute Over Suicide or A Debate between a Man and his Ba.*  This was a piece of literature reminiscent of the negative observations about life in Koheleth or Ecclesiastes.  In this work (2050-1750 BCE) the author considered suicide.

*Wisdom of Merikare.*  This was a collection of sayings from the Middle Kingdom (2050 BCE) concerned with affirming the need for establishing order in society to avoid chaos.  It also had a high sense of social justice.

*Satire on the Trades.*  This was a humorous spoof on various jobs in Egypt, which concluded that the life of a scribe is the best life to have (2150 BCE or later).

*Song of the Harper.*  This pessimistic work (2150 BCE or later) considered the possibility that there was no afterlife, and it reminds us very much of the pessimism of Koheleth or Ecclesiastes.

*Wisdom of Amenemhet.*  This collection of Middle Kingdom sayings (1960 BCE) supposedly came from beyond the grave, from a Pharaoh Amenemhet I, who was assassinated and then sought to give advice to his successor and son, Sesostris I.  It obviously lacked the optimism of comparable Old Kingdom documents, and pharaoh was clearly not the divine personage portrayed in religious-political propaganda.

*Wisdom of Amenemope.*  This New Kingdom collection of sayings (1100 BCE) may have been partially paraphrased in Proverbs 22:17-24:22.  Though the material in Proverbs appears to us as optimistic and secular, the fuller collection in Egyptian was more religious and pessimistic about the world, stressed individual piety, trusted in the gods, and slightly doubted the idea of corporate retribution (fairness) in the world.

*Ani.* This was the advice given by a father to his son, after the son argued with him. The father counseled quietism and piety, and he negated the simple optimistic dogmatism of the past found in early wisdom.

*Onchsheshonqy.* This work purported to be written by a man unjustly imprisoned, and as it offered advice on how to survive in the world, it sounds both cynical and humorous (450-250 BCE).

# Mesopotamian

*Instructions of Shuruppak.* The supposed father of Ziusudra gave him advice on how to survive in life (third millennium BCE) in this Sumerian text.

*A Man and his God.* Like the book of Job, this was the complaint of a man with his deity as to why so much evil had befallen him (third to second millennium BCE) in this Sumerian text.

*Counsels of Wisdom or The Babylonian Counsels.* This was a collection of Akkadian proverbs (late second millennium BCE), often sarcastic and humorous (actually entertaining to our modern sensitivities), which reflected clearly that the Mesopotamian view of life was rather pessimistic compared to the more optimistic Egyptian worldview.

*Tamarisk and the Date Palm.* These two trees debated each other as to which of them provided more benefits to people (second millennium BCE). This Akkadian text was part of a genre in which several third millennium BCE Sumerian texts also existed ("Hoe and Plow," "Mighty Copper and Silver," "Summer and Winter," and "Cattle and Grain"). These were teaching tools for youth to list things in their world. The debate format reminds us of the debate between Job and his friends.

*Ludlul Bel Nemeqi or "I Will Praise the Lord of Wisdom."* This Akkadian hymn (second millennium BCE) recounted a sufferer speaking of how he struggled with Marduk over why he suffered, but the sufferer confessed that ultimately Marduk delivered him in the end. It reminds us greatly of the book of Job.

*Pessimistic Dialogue between a Man and His Slave.* This humorous spoof in Akkadian had a man consider the good and the bad things about jobs and activities in life, and he finally concluded that suicide is the best action. His servant humored him by agreeing with every suggestion until the master proposed a suicide pact for both of them (second millennium BCE).

*Dialogue of Human Misery or Babylonian Theodicy.* This Akkadian disputation between two individuals over the question of why one them suffered (late second millennium BCE), written in acrostic form, seems the closest in format to the book of Job. It lacks Job's dramatic divine theophany or any real resolution.

*Ahiqar.* This is a 5th century BCE wisdom tale told in Aramaic which told of how Ahikar, unfairly sentenced to die by Assyrian king Sennacherib, was saved and finally restored to his position, while his deceitful nephew, Nadin, died. It is reminiscent of the Joseph tale in Genesis. The advice given by the hero in proverbial form may have influenced the sayings in the book of Proverbs.

This review of ancient Near Eastern literature cannot be thorough in this short review. But this particular list provides us with the key resources, many of which may have been known to biblical authors. If some of these were not known by the biblical authors, perhaps there were other works that we do not have, with which the biblical authors were familiar. When we read such texts, we are often able to discern the deeper meanings found within our biblical texts, because we enter more deeply into the world in which ancient Israelites and Jews lived.

# Conclusion

Study of ancient Near Eastern culture and society is an interesting topic by itself. The historical eras, the significant personages, and most importantly, the key pieces of literature are a valuable preliminary study in our consideration of the Old Testament/Hebrew Bible and its intellectual message. Throughout the following chapters we shall refer back to some of these literary works, and we shall elaborate further upon their significance for the biblical text. We shall focus upon how certain ancient texts inspired their biblical counterparts, and at other times how the biblical authors may have reacted against certain ideas and values articulated by these texts. On many issues Israelites and Jews thought about things no differently than their contemporaries, but on certain religious and intellectual issues, they diverged significantly. In these areas of divergence, they not only moved forward intellectually, they contributed to the assumptions of our modern intellectual worldview.

# Bibliography

Bernard Batto. *Slaying the Dragon: Mythmaking in the Biblical Tradition.* Louisville, KY: Westminster John Knox, 1992.

Richard Clifford. *Creation Accounts in the Ancient Near and the Bible.* Catholic Biblical Monograph Series 26. Washington, DC: Catholic Biblical Association, 1994.

Michael Coogan, ed. *Stories from Ancient Canaan.* Philadelphia, PA: Westminster, 1978.

Henri Frankfort, ed. *The Intellectual Adventure of Ancient Man.* Chicago, IL: University of Chicago, 1946.

William Hallo, and Lawson Younger, eds. *The Context of Scripture.* 3 vols. Leiden: Brill, 2003.

Victor Matthews and Don Benjamin, eds. *Old Testament Parallels: Laws and Stories from the Ancient Near East.* New York, NY: Paulist, 1991.

James Pritchard, ed. *Ancient Near Eastern Texts Relating to the Old Testament.* 3rd Ed. Princeton, NJ: Princeton University, 1969.

H. W. F. Saggs. *Civilization Before Greece and Rome.* New Haven, CT: Yale University, 1989.

Jack Sasson, ed. *Civilizations of the Ancient Near East.* 4 vols. New York: Scribner, 1995.

# Chapter 3

# The Classical Prophets

Reading: 1 Kings 1-19,2 Kings 1-2,Isaiah 36-39

mos, Hosea, Isaiah, and Micah were great 8th century BCE prophets, who shaped biblical religious beliefs tremendously. Although there were some Yahwistic traditions in oral form prior to these prophets, Yahwism was a minority movement. Even though some worshipped Yahweh exclusively, they did not know that they ought not worship other gods. Classical prophets developed the values of Yahwism greatly and were responsible for the eventual emergence of monotheism and concepts of justice in society in the late 7th and 6h centuries BCE.

## Characteristics of a Prophet

Around 200 BCE Jewish scholars in Alexandria, Egypt, began translating the Hebrew Bible into Greek for Jews who were no longer fluent in Hebrew. It was called the Septuagint because of the pious story that 70 scholars translated independent, but identical translations of the entire biblical text. Modern critical scholars assume the Septuagint arose piecemeal over many years. Septuagintal translators chose the Greek word prophetes to translate the Hebrew word for prophet, nabi. The old Hebrew word meant either "one who is called" or "one who calls or speaks." The Greek word referred to the latter meaning, so prophetes came to mean preacher or proclaimer. That was the most appropriate meaning for the function of a prophet; he or she proclaimed an oral message to communicate the will of God to people.

**Divination**?: When people today hear the word "prophet," they think of someone who predicts the future, or gazes into a crystal ball. The Israelite prophets would have rejected this definition, for predicting the future was "divination," activity often done elsewhere in the ancient world.  Divination assumed that the universe was a closed, fixed, determined environment in which both people and the gods were fated to perform certain actions according to some great cosmic plan.  If the future were fixed, you could predict it in ironclad fashion.  Israelite prophets rejected such a worldview. Actually, some ancient Near Eastern texts indicate to us that other intelligentsia in Mesopotamia and Egypt also qualified this deterministic understanding by the first millennium BCE, but the practices of divination still occurred, often under the aegis of kings and rulers anxious to know their fate.  (Well, we still read horoscopes today, don't we!)  Israelite prophets spoke of the future and of events that would transpire, but they spoke conditionally of the future, that is, the future was to be determined by actions freely chosen by people in the present.

Prophets saw the universe as open-ended; people were free and responsible for their own actions.  Yahweh was free, Yahweh's mind could change, and an oracle that spoke of future events, especially judgment, could be reversed by the gracious will of Yahweh. Sometimes prophets even gave oracles that overturned their own previous oracles.  Scribes who wrote our prophetic books included oracles that were later overturned, and thus communicated to their audience that the future was not fixed.  The best example was Ezekiel 26:1-21 wherein the city of Tyre was told that Nebuchadnezzar would conquer it.  However, according to Ezekiel 29:17-20 Yahweh will give the country of Egypt to Nebuchadnezzar instead of the city of Tyre (because Nebuchadnezzar's siege of the city failed).  That did not occur either.  The scribal editor put two failed oracles into the book of Ezekiel.  Though Ezekiel might look like a poor prophet; nonetheless, there was a good reason for recalling these "failed" oracles. Oracles had to be conditional when the future was described, for oracles were designed to elicit a human response in the time when the prophet spoke.  If the oracle came true absolutely, then there was no need for any human response, like repentance.  God could be gracious and forgive the people who were threatened with punishment or destruction.  The prophets did not want their oracles to be seen as immutable; their oracles warned of an anticipated future that would occur unless human beings made appropriate decisions to affect the future.  We should use terms like anticipation, warning, or expectation, rather than prediction, to describe prophetic oracles that spoke of future events.

Prophets uttered a conditional proclamation.  "If you do not stop sinning, you will be punished," or "If you repent, Yahweh will turn away this evil against you." Threats and blessing were not predictions!  Prophets spoke such words to get a response in their own age.  They did not speak of some distant future age; they addressed concerns of their own generation.  Eventually, many oracles were reinterpreted to have new meanings for later ages, but it should not be forgotten that the prophets had specific references in their own age.  Thus, the Immanuel oracle spoke about affairs in the time of kings Ahaz and Hezekiah, and only later did the symbols come to represent the coming messiah, and eventually, Jesus Christ for Christians.  Most prophetic oracles did not even speak of the future; they addressed issues in the prophet's contemporary society.  Most of our texts recall how the prophets criticized religious, political, and economic abuses.  Prophets sought to change the hearts of people, so when they proclaimed words of future judgment, they sought to persuade Israelites to do something.  This was preaching, not prediction; prophets were primarily forth-tellers, not foretellers.

**Oracles**: Spoken messages are the mode of communication for modern preachers as well as ancient Israelite prophets. Like most people in ancient Israel, classical prophets were not literate (except for Isaiah) and did not write their oracles, they lived in a pre-literate society. Later students of the prophets and scribes wrote down their oracles over a number of years to produce the books we have in the Hebrew Bible. Writing was a specialized profession for trained scribes, much like the practice of law today is only for lawyers. People who did not read or write were not uneducated, they had tremendous skills of memorization to recall their own traditions and sacred stories. The average person then could memorize texts the length of our New Testament; the bard could memorize material equivalent to our entire Bible. Prophets spoke orally and publicly, and many in the audience could remember what the prophet said. People truly interested in the prophet's message could recall his or her oracles for years, so that the oracles could be written down in later generations.

Speakers in a pre-literate society often articulate their messages in poetic form to facilitate memorization. Utterances with poetic rhythm and word plays help listeners to recall the message. (Even we remember little obnoxious ditties and songs from the radio.) A message in the form of a good poem would be remembered for a long time. Hence, prophets were not only good preachers, but also good poets. Our prophetic corpus contains good theology and excellent poetry. Perhaps 99% of all prophetic oracles spoken in ancient Israel were lost for us; so what was preserved were the oracles with an enduring message and a high literary quality. Because oracles were poems, modern English translations set the prophetic text in poetic stanza.

Prophetic oracles often were of two types: oracles of judgment and oracles of hope. Oracles of judgment proclaimed that Yahweh was angry at the sins of the people: either they were worshipping other gods or oppressing the poor. Some judgment oracles were "punishment oracles" in which the prophets declared that Yahweh would punish the people. Other oracles were "doom oracles" that declared Yahweh's wrath to be so great that Israel would be destroyed. Many of these latter oracles were rhetorical, designed to elicit human response rather than to proclaim an unavoidable future. Oracles of hope proclaimed that a gracious Yahweh would forgive people. Some of these oracles promised forgiveness to those who had repented or who were oppressed, others provided hope of restoration to those who had experienced extreme punishment or were in exile. There may not be a difference in the two types of hope oracles; rather, they may reflect different settings in which hope oracles were spoken. Oracles of forgiveness came from prophets prior to the exile, and oracles of restoration were exilic or post-exilic.

**Prophetic Immunity**: Prophets spoke to crowds of people, often at festivals or in cities, such as Jerusalem. Festivals could be emotionally charged times, and the crowd might react violently to judgment oracles spoken against them. Since prophets spoke with divine authority, they impressed that upon the audience for their own self-protection. Thus, they began oracles with the formula, "Thus says Yahweh," and they occasionally ended oracles with "It is said of Yahweh." These formulas were used in the realm of political diplomacy. If a ruler sent a message to another ruler, the messenger carried the message orally and announced the message with these formulas. The foreign king would know exactly what was said by the first king and that the words were not the words of the messenger. Careful use of these formulas by messengers kept them from offending the king with a harsh message and being killed. After 750 BCE Assyrians commissioned their diplomatic envoys to speak publicly to people in those cities they wished to control rather than speaking directly those in the royal court. This was done for public intimidation; threats of war with Assyria were designed to prod locals into pressuring their own kings. Thus, Israelites became familiar with this courtly language. Classical prophets after 750 BCE used this language to address the masses, since they would recognize the format. Prophets used diplomatic formulas also to indicate that the oracles came from God, not their own personal feelings, just as diplomatic messengers spoke the words of kings verbatim. Thus, the prophet wished to be seen as a messenger from Yahweh and his or her attitude was often, "Don't blame me. I'm only the messenger! This is Yahweh's message to you."

This formula was used also because prophets believed that when they were called, they were set apart. This is the other meaning of nabi, "one who is called." They felt compelled to speak, for even though the words they spoke were their own, their personal experience of Yahweh could not be put into human words, and that inspired them to speak the messages. (Jeremiah, for example, queried God as to whether he represented the divine will properly through his oracles. Clearly the words were his own, not words spoken into his ears by God.) The prophet had a divine experience and put the message into his or her own words, but no prophet would dare admit that. So the messenger formula, "Thus says the Lord," was an attempt to say to the people, "This is really what God wishes me to say to you!"

# Development in Prophecy

**Early Prophets:** Ecstatic behavior occurs in many religions. In Greek the word ecstasy means "standing beside oneself," which refers to a state in which a person no longer controls his or her thoughts and actions. Loud rhythmic music, excited dancing, fasting, self-inflicted pain, alcohol, herbal drugs, and other means are used by religious intermediaries in many cultures, past and present, to obtain an ecstatic state in which a message from the divine might be heard.

Early in Israel's history such behavior was connected with prophets because it was common among prophets and mantic diviners throughout the ancient world. When Moses called his seventy assistants, some prophesied (Numbers 11). Perhaps classical prophets disavowed this activity after 750 BCE, for they appear more calm and rational to us in the biblical text. Early prophets, including the students of Samuel and Elisha, apparently used ecstasy. At the same time, however, other early prophets like Nathan (1 Samuel 12), Gad (1 Samuel 22), and Ahijah (1 Kings 11, who told Jeroboam he would rule ten tribes), exhibited no ecstasy in the reception or delivery of oracles.

Divination was condemned by classical prophets, but early prophets apparently did some forms of divination. Samuel was called a "seer" and he divined the location of Saul's lost asses (1 Samuel 9:6-9). This text also stated that the term "seer" was no longer used at the time when this story was written down, which indicated some evolution had occurred in the prophetic movement. Elisha was a grand wonder-worker (2 Kings 2-6), and both Elijah and Elisha raised someone from the dead (1 Kings 17:17-24, 2 Kings 4:18-37), stories that contrasted their roles as Yahweh prophets against the claims of Baal, who supposedly had the power over life and death. By comparison, later classical prophets were portrayed as finite human beings. Stories about the earlier prophets were colored by the desire to make serious theological statements in addition to recalling the words and deeds of the prophets.

**Classical Prophets:** Some prophets from the time of Amos onward (750 BCE) functioned quite differently. Prophets of the old way continued, but the individuals whose oracles appear in our Bible seemed to diverge from the old patterns. They functioned as individuals, rather than in groups. They neither learned to be prophets by serving as prophet apprentices ("schools" of the prophets connected with Samuel and Elisha), nor did they train students. Amos might have stressed this difference when he said, "I am not a prophet, nor am I the son of a prophet" (Amos 7:14). (The exact meaning of that statement is debated among scholars, however.) Classical prophets had followers who later wrote down their oracles, but these "students" were not prophets themselves. For example, Baruch the scribe may have written the early version of Jeremiah's oracles. Thus, these later prophets appear to have viewed prophecy as a vocation, a "calling," rather than a learned profession.

Classical prophets do not appear to us to have had ecstatic experiences; at least, they did not speak of them. They rejected methods of inducing a revelation from Yahweh, such as ecstasy. Yahweh was free and would send a "word" at the proper time; human beings should never manipulate a revelation from Yahweh. Isaiah was silent for a long time during his ministry when no "Word of the Lord" came to him. Amos might receive dreams (Amos 7:1, 8:3), but they were not sought by him, and later Jeremiah condemned dreams as a form of false prophecy (Jeremiah 23:25-32, 27:9-10, 29:8-9). Dreams may have been regarded as way of manipulating God to receive a revelation, because often in the ancient world dreams were incubated by ritual activities in cultic shrines. The classical prophets were critical of any attempt to induce revelation.

Revelation was a "word" or a message that could be received, perhaps as an "inner voice." Scholars have debated what this meant, but the form of revelation received by the classical prophets was portrayed as different than that of the earlier prophets. Classical prophets may have appealed to Elijah's experience with the "still, small voice" on Horeb, which marked a turning point for them in the history of prophecy. The "still, small voice" may have referred to a quiet, internal awareness of God's will instead of a dramatic external experience.

The differences we see in the biblical text between the early and the later prophets may be created by our sources. Early prophets were remembered in folk tales and prophetic legends recorded in the books of Samuel and Kings. These narratives were recalled orally for generations before they were woven into the Deuteronomistic History, hence spectacular aspects were emphasized over the years for the audience. The prophets were portrayed in powerful and romantic fashion, especially Samuel, Elijah, and Elisha. For the classical prophets we have their oracles, which were generally committed to some fixed or written form within one or two generations after they spoke. The concern was with their message, not their deeds; thus, they appeared more calm and rational. If they received messages from God in dramatic or ecstatic fashion, the later biblical writers chose not to tell us this.

Ultimately, with the classical prophets it was the quality of the message, the style of the oracles, and their disdain for the professional prophets that indicated some evolution must have occurred beginning in the 8th century BCE. When Judah and Israel came into political contact with great imperial powers, especially Assyria, the economic and social changes required a new type of religious spokesperson to arise for the challenge. Forms of international diplomatic discourse were adopted from Assyrian culture, including public address formulas (which the Assyrians proclaimed to the crowds and not just the king), messenger formulas ("thus says the Lord"), the notion of covenant and public covenant making ceremonies (which the Assyrians used in treaty making ceremonies with their vassal states), and some stereotypic curses found in the prophets and Deuteronomy (which were used by Assyrians to intimidate smaller nations into obedience). The prophets modified this formal political language to talk about Yahweh's relationship to Israel and Judah to put real sting into their message. The adaptation of this language was used to declare that Yahweh was the true suzerain or lord over the people, and that an earthly power, like Assyria, was not. Thus, the 8th century BCE was a time when a significant evolutionary leap occurred in the prophetic movement.

# Theology of the Prophets

The prophets spoke to the needs of the people in their own age, not in general or universal terms. Hence, we can observe differences between various prophets, or even within the message of a prophet who functioned for a number of years, but we will still make general observations about the overall theological message of the classical prophets.

This brings us to a great question often debated by scholars. When we read the prophetic literature recorded for us in the biblical text, how much of that material actually reflected the words spoken by those historical prophets and how much was creatively generated by the authors who wrote down those oracles years or centuries later? Most of the prophetic corpus appears to have been written in the 6th century BCE by theological authors during the Babylonian Exile. Were they remembering the faithfully memorized oracles of those great prophets accurately with only a few of their own critical observations? Or were they capturing the essential spirit of a bygone prophet's message, but really generating new oracles meaningful to their own generation? All scholars agree that the later exilic editors added some materials to the prophetic books. For example, the prophet Amos was an 8th century BCE prophet who spoke a word of judgment to the northern state of Israel, but the very last oracle in his book was a hope oracle addressed to the southern state of Judah promising a return from the 6th century BCE exile. Clearly the scribe who wrote down Amos' oracles added this final word to make the book relevant for his own age. But were the additions so extensive, that it would be better to say that the prophetic books were created in the exilic setting? In favor of the view which attributes most of the oracles to the original prophets, one could point out that the older the prophet, the shorter the book (Amos, Hosea), the more proximate in time that the prophet was to the exile, the longer the book (Jeremiah, Ezekiel). In this textbook we will speak of the setting of each historical prophet as the point of origin for most oracles, but we shall acknowledge that to some degree all the oracles have been revised by the final editors. Having said that, let us now discuss the theological themes of the prophetic tradition, regardless of whether they came from the prophets or later editors.

**Yahweh:** Prophets believed that they existed in a personal relationship with God, a revolutionary concept in the ancient world. They believed they sat in the "council of Yahweh" and were privy to the divine will. In this prophetic encounter with Yahweh, they perceived certain characteristics of the divine nature: 1) Holiness (kadosh) pointed to the majestic power of Yahweh and the inability of evil to stand before the divine. Holiness was associated with fire, a purifying force, which would destroy not only sin, but the sinner also. People must be shielded from Yahweh's holiness, and even the prophet must be cautious in his or her treatment of the divine message that came from a holy god. Holiness as an attribute described God in transcendent fashion. 2) Yahweh was righteous (sedek) and that demanded the response of righteousness (sedekah) from human beings. Whereas holiness described Yahweh in an absolute way, righteous described the relationship of the deity to people. Yahweh was righteous and that placed a serious demand upon people to be obedient and just. Righteous accentuated the immanence of God among people. 3) The Hebrew word hesed can be variously rendered as "faithfulness," "loving kindness," "mercy," "forgiveness," "covenantal faithfulness," and "steadfast love." In prophetic oracles "faithfulness" might provide the best meaning, but in the later post-exilic Psalms the word assumed the meaning of "grace" and "holy one" at times. It referred to Yahweh's undeserved acts of love, but it could also mean that Yahweh drew near to punish sin. To say that Yahweh drew near is good or bad depending upon one's actions.

The prophetic understanding of history was not like ours, it was like a proto-historical view of reality. Their understanding of history stressed the inter-relationship of the divine and the human in determining the course of events. They viewed Yahweh as one who primarily guided people in social and political affairs. Yahweh still brought fertility for fields and animals by their understanding, so Yahweh was active in nature, but prophets stressed Yahweh's actions in the social arena primarily. Yahweh acted mightily in the Exodus to save and create the nation, and this was the model for past and future actions. Yahweh was lord over the destinies of other peoples and nations, for Assyrians and Babylonians could be brought to punish the chosen people. Israelites were not unique in speaking this way, for Assyrians spoke similarly of Ashur, their god, and Babylonians spoke of Marduk leading their nation to a great national destiny. We suspect that Israelites stressed this dimension of the divine presence in the political arena more than their contemporaries did, and herein we observe one of the intellectual foundations for the emergence of a sense of history in western culture. For those foreign peoples the description of their deities in natural terms remained a significant aspect of their discourse about the divine; Ashur and Marduk remained storm gods in the minds of most Mesopotamians. But in Israel the language of social relationship and action in the human social arena began to predominate, especially in the language of the prophets.

The prophetic belief that Yahweh controlled the destiny of other nations became a seedbed for monotheism. If Yahweh controlled other nations, then foreign gods must either be subordinate to Yahweh or not exist. Eventually, the latter idea would prevail.

The 8th century BCE prophets were "incipient monotheists" or "monolatrists," for they did not deny the existence of other gods, but declared that the people should ignore them and worship only Yahweh. Such "practical monotheism" could lead to real monotheism, which denied all other deities, but only when the Jewish people were thrown into exile and had to live directly among people whose gods they ignored. In Babylonian Exile everyone had to decide whether to worship the gods of the land where he or she resided or deny their existence. People who chose the latter stayed Jews; those who did not, lost their Jewish identity. Hence, Jeremiah and Ezekiel were close to absolute monotheism, but Second Isaiah clearly advocated it in the late exilic period.

People who worship only one deity must attribute all things to that deity, while polytheists attribute various natural and social functions to diverse deities. Monotheists must view their God as the source of both good and evil, a distant deity (transcendent) and a personal deity (immanent), a high creator deity (who crafts the cosmos) and an immanent redeemer (as in the Exodus), a god of love and a god of wrath, and so forth. For us, positing such tensions in one divine being comes naturally, but we must appreciate that this was a great monotheistic intellectual breakthrough provided to us by the classical prophets. Polytheists had a wide and varied range of deities and lesser divine beings from which to choose when they attributed the various specialized functions of the divine realm. For them, that was the natural way of thinking, for they could see diverse forces in nature, each of which reflected a separate divinity. For the monotheist it was an intellectual challenge and a leap of faith to posit that all things came from one god.

Polytheists usually relied upon nature metaphors to speak of the divine realm, for within nature there were different forces operative: sun, wind, sky, moon, stars, water, earth, etc. Polytheistic belief systems used nature metaphors extensively. Those who moved toward monotheism gradually dropped such categories. A single deity in the divine realm must be lord over all things in nature, and eventually, the more important arena for divine activity became the social or historical realm. Whether perceiving the existence of one god arose first, or whether stressing the social dimension over nature came first, we do not know. Some cultures in the Near East were moving in a monotheistic direction long before Israel, but none came to a complete monotheism because of the social and economic chaos that would result. Envision unemployed priests and artists as well as political groups representing those people whose gods were lost. This was most likely what happened for a time in Egypt in the 14th century BCE when Akhenaton so radically enforced the closure of temples for the other gods, especially Amun-Re, and elevated the worship of Aten, the sun disk. His movement probably failed because he alienated so many people, including priests, builders, artists, and those who provided supplies to the various temples. Emergent monotheism in a complex society causes chaos. Generally monotheism most readily can emerge in a simple society ready to disavow complex societal structures with their concomitant religious and economic values. This is what the Israelites and post-exilic Jews were able to accomplish, especially when they were socially dislocated in exile.

The prophets represented the first serious intellectual movement to advance toward consistent monotheism and the conversion of the masses. The process took over two centuries after the classical prophets first emerged, but seeds of emerging monotheism appeared already with Amos who spoke of Yahweh's control over foreign nations. Hosea attributed both anger and love to Yahweh in ways that the audience could comprehend, and thus he portrayed Yahweh as encompassing diverse divine attributes. Gradually the prophets moved the people toward a monotheistic religion that would emerge in the crucible of the exile.

To speak of freedom of action for the god(s) was a radical concept for an ancient Near Easterner. Traditional views in the ancient world emphasized a fixed and static universe, willed by the gods, with an emphasis upon nature imagery where seasonal cycles impressed the mind with unchanging repetitive patterns of life. To some extent, however, that worldview was changing throughout the ancient Near East after 1000 BCE. Israelite conceptualizations may have been in the forefront of this transformative process. Israel's worldview focused on divine actions in the social and historical arena, and this posited a more open-ended view of reality and greater freedom in the human and the divine realm. Unlike cyclic nature that repeats the seasons, history can be viewed as moving through singular and distinctly new events.

Yahweh was lord of human events and free to change the divine will, which was why prophetic oracles were not immutable predictions. People were free, and with freedom came responsibility for personal actions. Connecting human freedom to divine freedom stressed moral behavior over cult, and actions in the social arena or everyday life became the more pleasing activity for Yahweh. Morality replaced ritual as the most important human response to the divine. Sacrifice was a way of praising or thanking Yahweh; it was no longer the way of bending the predestined cosmic cycles to protect life and humanity. Cultic behavior became less significant than ethical behavior, and the norms for ethics came from the laws. Israelites and Jews slowly became a people of the book.

These ideas were manifest elsewhere in the ancient world also. Greeks began to belittle their gods and speak of human freedom and the value of the individual. Great historians, philosophers, artists, dramatists, and scientists emerged in the Greek age of inquiry and reflection. In India the Upanishads spoke of the divine as a transcendent force and of the value of human meditation, rather than Brahmanic ritual. Buddhism arose and turned its back on priests, cult, and ritual in favor of the meditating monk seeking bodhi, wisdom and enlightenment. In China this was be the age of Lao-Tzu and Confucius, as well as the subsequent Confucian rationalists. Thus, Israel was part of a worldwide intellectual advance, which we sometimes call the "Axial Age" (800-400 BCE), in which new great religions replaced the old, archaic religions. The value of the individual was elevated, while the ritual and cult of great sacrificial systems faded.

**Human Finitude:** As we read the prophetic oracles we discern that the prophets condemned two forms of sin: the worship of other gods and economic oppression of the poor. These two sins, however, were related in the minds of the prophets, which strikes us as unusual, for we have grown up with the assumption of a division between affairs of church and state, so that the prophets appear to us as attacking separate religious and social sins. For the prophets, however, Yahweh was lord of all things; matters of politics, economics, society, and religion all were circumscribed by the will of Yahweh.

There was a connection between these two types of sin. If people worshiped a nature deity, or regarded Yahweh primarily as a nature deity, then the most important religious act was sacrifice. Laws and ethics were less important. If people worshiped one God and stressed ethics, morality, and law, then concern with justice took precedence over sacrifice and ritual. To worship other gods, or to treat Yahweh like Baal, muted the social concerns, the demand to obey the laws, and the concern for justice. Kings sponsored devotion to the golden bull/calf at Dan and Bethel, and for most people it made Yahweh into a fertility god, so traditional Yahwistic values were ignored. This enabled kings, their family, and their friends to manipulate the economy to their own financial benefit and to the disadvantage of the poor highlanders. Religion in Israel then legitimated social injustice. For the prophets, the worship of other gods and the oppression of the poor were the same sin, for the former permitted the latter.

The prophetic imperative to the people was that they must repent and change their ways. When prophets spoke of repentance, they meant that a change of attitude leading to a different set of actions should result. Israelites and Jews did not envision ideas occurring separately from concrete human actions. The Hebrew word shub meant, "to turn around and walk in the opposite direction." It meant far more than our modern concept of "to feel sorry." True repentance meant to be sorry and change one's behavior.

Yahweh was a merciful deity, for if the people repented, they would be restored. When the prophetic corpus was committed to written form, words of hope and forgiveness were the ultimate message over against the words of judgment, even though the judgment language predominated in the prophetic corpus. Jews saw that the words of judgment were fulfilled with the exile, but the words of hope would refer to a greater future yet to come.

**Covenant**: Prophets used the term covenant infrequently; the later Deuteronomic theologians used the concept much more to envision the relationship of people and God. But the prophets had a concept of election, which evolved into the language of covenant, and after the 8th century BCE prophets used the word covenant increasingly due to its political use by the Assyrians. Election or covenant could be envisioned two ways. Prophets declared that Israel should obey the laws of Yahweh, lest they forfeit their election. Prophets also stressed the enduring permanence of the election or covenant due to Yahweh's mercy. The first model has been called the Mosaic or Sinaitic covenant, a conditional covenant, for it used imagery associated with the giving of the Law at Sinai. It may have evolved in the northern prophetic movement. The second model has been called the Davidic, Abrahamic, or Zion covenant, an unconditional covenant, associated with Abraham in Genesis 15 and David's dynastic oracle in 2 Samuel 7, as well other literature connected to kingship in Jerusalem.

Mosaic covenant imagery was used rhetorically when a prophet stressed the judgment of Yahweh and the need for repentance, lest the covenant be broken and the land be lost. This imagery under-girded oracles by Amos, Hosea, early oracles by Isaiah, early oracles by Jeremiah, early oracles by Ezekiel, and the Deuteronomic theologians. Davidic covenant imagery was used when the prophet proclaimed hope, forgiveness, and restoration, reassuring the people of Yahweh's perpetual faithfulness, lest they despair of Yahweh's presence. This model under-girded the later oracles of Isaiah, Jeremiah, Ezekiel, all post-exilic prophets, and the Yahwistic and Priestly Editors in the Pentateuch. That particular prophets used both covenant models tells us that there were not two covenants; rather, there were two ways of speaking about the same covenant, even if the images and vocabulary arose in different areas of Israel and out of different social settings. The message of the prophet was determined by the religious needs of the audience.

When the prophets addressed the people they addressed them corporately, for in kinship systems, like that of Israel, people had a strong sense of group or family solidarity. Our modern individualism would have been strange to them, for they were more prone to say "we" than "I." Every Israelite was "kin" or "neighbor" to other Israelites, and the welfare of the poor and weaker members of society was the responsibility of everyone in the community. This mentality had begun to deteriorate in the 8th century BCE, and the prophets appealed to this old value system. The covenant relationship established at Sinai especially reflected this sense of solidarity. They knew that attending to the welfare of individuals really supported the welfare of the whole group, especially in the marginal economy of Palestine.

**The Future:** Among the pre-exilic prophets we sense no attention to the hope of a personal afterlife. With their strong sense of group identity, their vision of the future was a vision of national existence. The may have had a sense of a personal afterlife, they were attentive to burial customs and had great respect for the departed elders. Some poetic texts hint at the possibility of a life beyond the grace, but it was not mentioned in prophetic oracles. Only with Jeremiah and Ezekiel during the exile was there an emphasis upon any given individual's relationship with Yahweh, and only after the exile did developing references to the hope of an afterlife appear.

When prophets spoke of a future for Israel and Judah, they often used the concept of the "Day of the Lord." Originally this meant a day on which Yahweh would fight Israel's enemies to save or deliver the people, as happened during the Exodus, the conquest under Joshua, and Gideon's defeat of the Midianites. Tracing the development of this motif in the prophetic tradition can be a good summary of the entire prophetic movement. Amos changed the "Day of the Lord" image to make it a day of total destruction because of Israel's sin (Amos 2:4-16, 3:14-15, 5:18-20, 8:9-14). In the next generation Isaiah and Micah in Judah used the same notion (Isaiah 5:30, 7:10-25, Micah 5:10-15). Isaiah added the motif that a remnant would survive (Isaiah 10:20-27), which was what happened in the Assyrian wars: a lucky remnant in Jerusalem survived the Assyrian onslaught. With the 7th century BCE prophets, Zephaniah, Jeremiah (Jeremiah 46-52), and Ezekiel (Ezekiel 25-30), the day was portrayed as one of punishment for Judah. But the day was envisioned as international in scope; other nations who were Judah's enemies would be punished. The remnant was now a "righteous remnant"; survivors would be those who were faithful to Yahweh. The day was portrayed in much more dramatic fashion, but history would continue after its occurrence. With post-exilic prophets the day became grander and more final (Zechariah 9-14, Isaiah 56-66). It was a day of hope for Jews once more, for the enemies of Judah would be defeated and the righteous Jews would be elevated to a position of power and respect in Jerusalem (Isaiah 60:15-16, 62:1-3, 66:18-20, Joel 3:1-21). In some texts, it sounded like a military empire would be created (Isaiah 61:5-7, 63:1-6, 66:12-24, Obadiah 15-21, Zechariah 9:1-17, 10:3-12, 12:1-9, 14:1-21); in others, it sounded like Jerusalem would become a respected religious center (Isaiah 56:3-8, 60:1-16, Zechariah 2:10-12, 8:13, 20-23). It seems as though there would be one dramatic day according to the authors, but history would continue. Finally, after 200 BCE the "Day of the Lord" became a cosmic day in the texts (Isaiah 24-27, Daniel, and other Jewish Apocalyptic Literature) in which good and evil warred against each other, and Yahweh ended world history. The Golden Age became a messianic kingdom in another dimension or in the afterlife. The "Day of the Lord" evolved into judgment day, and this was the image used by Jesus and the New Testament authors to characterize the Kingdom of God.

The "Day of the Lord" motif evolved throughout the prophetic movement. It was a day of judgment with the pre-exilic prophets and then a day of restoration in the hope oracles of the post-exilic prophets. It developed from being a regional event in Palestine to an international war and ultimately to a cosmic event. The motif became grander in the vision of the messianic age offered by post-exilic prophets. Finally, the prophetic movement gave rise to Jewish apocalyptic literature, and the motif became a key apocalyptic image.

# Conclusion

The message of the prophets was seen by 19th Christian commentators as the heart of the Old Testament, because of its understanding of monotheism and its high moral vision, which especially included a call for justice in society. Their focus on the message of the prophets was well deserved. The prophets, or at least the exilic authors who wrote down and collected their oracles, may have been most responsible for the creation of the core messages in the biblical tradition. Were it not for the message of the prophets, perhaps monotheism would not have arisen among the Jews, for there would have been no memory of a religious and social critique for them to reflect upon.

In prophetic oracles we see a message that resurfaced in the teachings of Jesus, thus becoming the heart of Christian ethical teaching. In their vision of hope we see images that Christians applied to the teachings and actions of Jesus. In their oracles we see the rhetoric that under-girded the emergence of democratic values in our modern age. Churches have drawn upon the message and the rhetoric of the prophets to speak to the modern age a message of reform and justice. In the 19th century abolitionists and other reformers were inspired by the message of the prophets. Today Christians quote the words of the prophets in social statements, especially language in Roman Catholic social encyclicals. Their vision of an age in which peace will prevail and people will be treated justly is a vision of hope for all of us. Prophets inspired the later Jewish tradition; they were people who spoke the truth and represented God to the people. A prophet was seen as one willing to suffer for the sake of his or her message and ultimately suffer for the sake of the people to whom he or she spoke. The prophet is one who has a valuable message to speak, one who has the courage to speak it despite criticism, and one who is willingly to suffer for the message. Clergy in seminaries are often inspired by the image of the prophet and seek to imitate it.

We can speak of the overall message of the prophets, but that requires us to make some broad generalizations. Ultimately, each prophet spoke to a particular time and place, and the message of each prophet was distinct, with its own themes and its own special message. Hence, a truly fair treatment of the prophetic corpus requires us to give a closer consideration to each of the significant prophets within the prophetic corpus.

# Bibliography

Joseph Blenkinsopp. *A History of Prophecy in Israel*. Rev. ed. Louisville, KY: Westminster John Knox, 1996.

Robert Gnuse. *No Other Gods: Emergent Monotheism in Ancient Israel*. Journal for the Study of the Old Testament 236. Sheffield, Eng.: Sheffield University Press, 1997.

Abraham Heschel. *The Prophets*. 2 vols. New York, NY: Harper and Row, 1962.

Johannes Lindblom. *Prophecy in Ancient Israel*. Philadelphia, PA: Fortress, 1973

Victor Matthews. *Social World of the Hebrew Prophets*. Peabody, MA: Henrickson, 2001.

Marti Nissinen et al. *Prophets and Prophecy in the Ancient Near East*. Atlanta, GA: Society of Biblical Literature, 2003.

David Petersen. *The Prophetic Literature*. Louisville, KY: Westminster John Knox, 2002.

Gerhard von Rad. *The Message of the Prophets*. Trans. D. M. G. Stalker. New York, NY: Harper and Row, 1967.

Robert Scott. *The Relevance of the Prophets*. New York, NY: Macmillan, 1968.

Marvin Sweeney. *The Prophetic Literature*. Interpreting Biblical Texts. Nashville, TN: Abingdon, 2005.

# Eighth Century Prophets and the Elohist

Reading:  Amos 1-9,Hosea 1-14,Isaiah 1-11,Genesis 15,20,22

Prophets of the 8th century BCE are characterized as the great classical prophets, spokespersons for God who addressed serious social and religious issues. Theirs was an age in which both Israel and Judah had become truly organized states and experienced the problems that such socio-political development brought. Archaeological finds testify to the presence of record keeping, taxation, building projects, and a well-developed economy. With this came economic wealth for a select group of people, mostly city dwellers in Samaria and Jerusalem, and a great degree of poverty and displacement for poor, marginal highlanders. On the international scene Assyria was ascendant and made an impact on the political and social life of both monarchies. To this tumultuous age came these prophets. Perhaps the age made them great, or perhaps they were great prophets, because such an age needed men of this caliber. Regardless, they spoke a message of judgment against religious and economic practices of their age that would never be forgotten. The style and the depth of their message was a quantum leap beyond that of prophets in the past. For this reason their oracles would be written down, mostly during the Babylonian Exile, and they would be seen as the first in the line of the great prophets.

## Prophets in the North (Israel)

In the late 8th century BCE Israel and Judah were overwhelmed by the Assyrian colossus. Amos and Hosea in Israel, Isaiah and Micah in Judah, all proclaimed their vibrant message. They condemned sin and announced the threat of divine punishment by the Assyrians. Though their message was not well received, later generations recalled how the dire course of events vindicated their warnings. By the 7th century BCE there may have been a small written collection of their oracles, which in turn continued to grow until it may have taken final written form during the Babylonian Exile.

**Amos**: Jeroboam II (786-746 BCE) brought prosperity to the northern state of Israel while Assyria waged war in Syria to the north. Trade brought wealth to those in the cities, especially for those who were already rich, but the poor farmers in the highlands lost their land to the rich. In this atmosphere Amos arose, coming from Judah in the south to proclaim his message of judgment at the royal shrine of Bethel in the north.

By proclaiming his message at the royal shrine of Bethel, he appealed to a popular understanding that God or the gods of a nation made covenants with the royal house at the shrine on a periodic (perhaps annual) basis. Political covenants also were made between states at such shrines. Perhaps Amos was portraying himself as lodging a formal complaint, or lawsuit formula, at the shrine. Festivals at royal shrines were a time of nationalistic fervor among the people, and to speak judgment against the king and nation flew in the face of such fervor. In Amos 1:1-2:11, a very long oracle, the prophet declared that on the "Day of the Lord" Israel would be punished for sin. We suspect that the "Day of the Lord" was a motif used by nationalistic prophets to stir up the feelings of the people in patriotic settings, such as festivals at royal shrines. The "Day of the Lord" occurred when Yahweh defeated Israel's enemies in battle. Thus, Amos turned nationalistic imagery upside down and made it into a judgment oracle, so as to bluntly communicate his message about social justice. The "Day" became one in which Yahweh would use foreign enemies to punish Israel. We believe Amos was the first to add this twist to a well-known nationalistic motif and bequeath its new meaning to later prophets.

Elsewhere in his oracles, Amos declared after the Assyrian attack all that would be left of Israel would be like the tip of a sheep's ear after the wolf's attack (Amos 3:12). Samaria would be destroyed, its inhabitants killed, their bodies dismembered (typical Assyrian war practices) and carried off in baskets, and the people exiled. Rich women were compared to the fattened cows of the Bashan readied for slaughter (Amos 4:1-3). Israel was condemned for social injustice--the poor were bankrupted by dishonest economic dealings and forced into slavery (Amos 2:6-8, 8:4-6). Highland farmers were driven into debt by unfair market practices such as high interest rates and dishonest scales. They sold their family members as debt-slaves, lost their land, and either became sharecroppers on their land or poverty-ridden servants in the urban centers.

The rich and powerful worshipped Yahweh at shrines, such as Bethel and Gilgal, where sacrifices were offered to Yahweh as though everything was morally acceptable. To Amos such religion was mockery, for if you offered sacrifice to Yahweh while you oppressed the poor, greater judgment will follow, not blessing or forgiveness (Amos 4:4). Yahweh desired that "justice roll down like waters, and righteousness like an ever-flowing stream" (Amos 5:24). Ethical demands of Yahwism were less important than the cultic regulations for most people; Yahwism was more like the cult of Baal for them.

Israelites assumed their status as Yahweh's chosen people meant that Yahweh would never let them fall and would intervene for them. Amos turned this image around and offended many by saying that Yahweh was angry and would come to punish them by using the foreigners they thought Yahweh would defeat. Amos was a stern social critic, and he implied that there was little hope for the people. His language describing the impending doom in war was very graphic and violent. Language from his oracles has often been quoted by religious leaders seeking social reform in modern society.

When criticized by the high priest Amaziah at Bethel for being a professional prophet from Judah, he declared, "I am not a prophet, nor am I the son of a prophet" (Amos 7:14). He may have meant I am not now a prophet, he may have meant I was not a prophet but I am now, or he may have meant I am a prophet, but not a professional court prophet. Though scholars have disputed what he meant, most believe he sought to distance himself from some professional class of prophets. Though he felt that he was not a "prophet," ironically, he became the first in a line of classical prophets, the standard by which we measure all who would call themselves prophets.

**Hosea**: Hosea criticized Israel for religious apostasy as well as social injustice. He declared that Israel deserted Yahweh who led them through Exodus, Sinai, and the wilderness, and now they worshipped the gods of Canaan (Hosea 4:11-19, 5:4-7, 8:5-12, 11:2). Hosea meant that most Israelites worshipped Yahweh as though Yahweh were another Baal; Yahweh was perceived primarily as a fertility god rather than a deity of ethical demand. For most people in Israel, especially for lowlanders in the valleys and the plains, this actually was the type of piety that they had always practiced; it was not very different from the religious piety of the second millennium BCE. Yahwistic religiosity was practiced only by a few folk in the highlands. Hosea's rhetoric was more innovative than traditional.

Practices at Bethel, Gilgal, and Dan, all national Yahweh shrines, were indistinguishable from the general religious practices found elsewhere in Syria and Palestine. Yahwistic highlanders, like Amos and Hosea, found this unacceptable. Since most Israelites did not perceive their religious piety to be inappropriate, the king promoted this form of Yahwism to lessen attention to the ethical demands for a just society. This thereby allowed the leaders to manipulate the economy and to abuse the poor for economic gain. How often has religion been used by the powerful to overlook or even justify oppression of the poor? How often have Christian leaders been silent, while only a few prophets dared to speak, like Archbishop Romero or Dietrich Bonhoeffer?

Hosea's criticism of the leaders of his society was bold. He attacked priests (Hosea 4:4-19, 5:1-2), other prophets (Hosea 4:5, 6:5), the king and his advisors (Hosea 5:1, 7:3-7, 13:10-11), and leaders in general (Hosea 5:10, 7:16, 9:15). The oppression of the poor weakened the nation, and ultimately the people would not fight to defend their country in the case of foreign invasion. This explains why the country fell so quickly before the military onslaught of Tiglath-Pileser III in 734-733 BCE. In a sense, Hosea was not an idealist in his political accusation; he was a realist. Social injustice weakened the national fabric by eroding the middle-class.

Sacred prostitutes, sexual practices, and ritual defloweration occurred at Yahweh shrines in Israel. The extent to which these activities were practiced has been debated by scholars, but such activities did occur and offended the prophets greatly. Hosea believed that sexual activity should not be used in religious worship, especially in the Yahweh religion. Hosea declared that Yahweh was not a fertility god, like Baal. Granted, it was by Yahweh's blessing that the land experienced agricultural blessing, but Yahweh could not be manipulated by worshippers using the sympathetic magic of cultic activity. Much of what Hosea said was new for most in his audience who worshipped Yahweh as their ancestors had worshipped El and Baal in the second millennium BCE. For the vast majority of Israelites, the prophets were proclaiming a new religion.

Hosea used powerful metaphors to communicate his ideas; he appropriated Baal imagery to describe Yahweh's relationship to Israel. Yahweh was the husband of Israel: Yahweh wooed Israel in the Exodus, married her at Sinai, honeymooned in the wilderness, and homesteaded with her as newlyweds in the settlement, but once in the land Israel chased after other lovers--the Baals, and committed adultery. Yahweh wished that Israel would return, but if Israel continued to be unfaithful, destruction would result. Perhaps, mused Hosea, Yahweh will take Israel into the wilderness (a metaphor for exile), and new faithfulness will result. The last image of the marriage relationship, renewed faithfulness in the wilderness, never came to pass; Israel was destroyed in the war with Assyria and subsequent deportation. (Judah would return from exile two centuries later, and the oracles of Hosea would be included in the Bible for the reason that Judah fulfilled Hosea's vision of hope.) Hosea's use of marriage metaphors recast the symbolic relationship between Israel and Yahweh from one of sex and fertility (as with Baalism) to a familial setting (with the overtones of covenant). By transforming these Baal myths and metaphors into Yahwistic categories, Hosea did something that we observe throughout the Hebrew Bible, he appropriated pagan images to oppose pagan thought. This is a good lesson for Christian leaders, who too often in the past have feared and rejected new systems of thought.

Paralleling the relationship of Yahweh and Israel was Hosea's marriage to his wife Gomer. Hosea used the symbol of his wife's unfaithfulness to describe Israel's unfaithfulness to Yahweh. Though Hosea was angry with his wife, he still loved her, so also Yahweh loved Israel while threatening judgment. This metaphor explained how Yahweh could both hate and love Israel, thus attributing diverse attributes to the divine being. When compared to a common human experience, the audience could understand attributing tensions to the divine nature.

Scholars have debated the nature of Gomer's unfaithfulness. Authors usually suggest that she married Hosea and then became unfaithful (Hosea 1) but he brought her back, perhaps out of debt slavery (Hosea 3). Others have suggested that perhaps she was a sacred prostitute or an immoral woman before their marriage, and she returned to her old ways, and then the prophet had to go bring her back. The best theory seems to be that as a young girl she underwent ritual defloweration in the puberty rites at a Yahweh shrine; something we would expect at a Baal shrine. If so, her "unfaithfulness" to both Yahweh and Hosea was unfaithfulness common for many women in Israel because of the cult at the shrines of Dan and Bethel. The two chapters (Hosea 1, 3) that referred to her infidelity do not describe two separate instances of how prophet married and redeemed her from slavery; they described the experience from two perspectives. Thus, the third option makes sense, for it requires only one marriage.

Hosea described the tension of anger and love in the divine nature, a theme that later Jeremiah inherited from Hosea. Hosea paralleled his own life with Gomer to Yahweh and Israel, and he dramatically portrayed Yahweh as husband to Israel. Hosea also attributed feminine imagery to Yahweh, especially with the metaphor of the mother who taught the child to walk (Hosea 11:1-4); here Israel was a son rather than a wife, and God was a mother. Hosea's deep familial imagery contrasted with the divine sex without family imagery in the Baal cult, and he raised the sensitivity of prophetic thought to new heights.

There were thematic connections between Hosea and later traditions. Hosea and the book of Deuteronomy both spoke of the divine love of Yahweh for Israel, the need for the exclusive worship of Yahweh, opposition to the golden calf, and the necessity for social and especially religious reform. The concept of covenant also appeared to be important for both. Perhaps the themes of covenant obedience began with Hosea and came to fruition in the Deuteronomic theological tradition.

# Prophets in the South (Judah)

**Micah**: Micah (710-700 BCE) spoke a word of judgment to Judah and Jerusalem in a mode reminiscent of Amos. Coming from Moresheth-gath, a rural town in Judah, he represented the country people who were being economically crushed by the rich classes of Jerusalem. His descriptions of oppression (Micah 2:1-10, 3:1-12, 6:1-16, 7:1-4) and his anticipation of Jerusalem's destruction (Micah 1:2-16) hint that he might have been a country judge. Legal formulas were cast as divine lawsuits by Yahweh against Judah in various oracles (Micah 1:2-9, 6:1-8).

Though Micah was a prophet of judgment, as later folk recalled (Jeremiah 26:16-19), there were passages of hope in the book of Micah. Scholars believe later editors placed hope oracles in Micah's collection because the words of hope were to be understood as the final word of Yahweh to the people. Micah 4:1-13, for example, also appeared in Isaiah 2:2-4, so some hope oracles of Isaiah or other later prophets were placed into the Micah collection by exilic editors. Micah's summary of his message is a deep expression of prophetic faith and a well-known quote today, "What does Yahweh require of you but to do justice, to love kindness, and to walk humbly with your God?" (Micah 6:8).

**Isaiah**: Isaiah was the greatest of the 8th century BCE prophets, and his oracles had significant impact on the later prophetic tradition. Oracles of later prophets influenced by his images would be included in the book of Isaiah. Thus, oracles in Isaiah 34-35 and 40-55 appear to be exilic, those in Isaiah 56-66 appear to be post-exilic, and Isaiah 24-27 is a very late apocalypse (250 BCE) and may be one of the last segments placed in the prophetic corpus. Isaiah 36-39 was a paraphrase of the same accounts found in 2 Kings 18:13-20:19, and may have been a conclusion to the book of Isaiah at an early stage. When we review the theology of the 8th century BCE Isaiah, we read oracles in Isaiah 1-11 and parts of 12-23 and 28-33. Isaiah 1-11 contained the classic motifs of this prophet. Scholars suspect that Isaiah 1-11 was written down and circulated under King Josiah's reign (636-609 BCE), because Josiah may have been seen as the messiah.

Isaiah functioned in the court of kings Ahaz and Hezekiah of Judah (740-700 BCE) as either a scribe (because of wisdom language in his oracles) or a priest (because he had access to the Temple). In his call experience (Isaiah 6) he received a vision in the Temple wherein he was taken up into the great heavenly Temple of Yahweh where he observed the seraphim, perhaps winged fiery snakes, and the glory of Yahweh. Because the pure holiness of Yahweh could have destroyed him, he declined to be a messenger until his tongue was touched by a burning coal, an appropriate symbol for a prophet who spoke the word of Yahweh.

King Ahaz was portrayed as a cynical ruler to whom Isaiah spoke primarily words of judgment. When Israel and Syria united militarily against Judah, Ahaz declined to trust in Yahweh as the prophet encouraged, but called to mighty Assyria for aid. Isaiah sought political alignment with neither side. Isaiah viewed the actions of Ahaz as a lack of faith and so he spoke the first Immanuel oracle as judgment oracle (Isaiah 7). The decision of Ahaz brought down Tiglath-Pileser III of Assyria in the brutal campaign of 734-733 BCE that destroyed Israel and Syria. Judah, the supposed ally of Assyria, discovered itself to really be Assyria's vassal. Isaiah became silent for years, maintaining Yahweh no longer gave him a "word" to speak.

Isaiah began to speak for Yahweh once again under Hezekiah, the son of Ahaz. Isaiah became a prophet of hope, for Hezekiah was dedicated to a more exclusive worship of Yahweh than his father had been. Hezekiah engaged in religious reform and perhaps some political change that led him to revolt against Assyria. In 705-701 BCE Judah was in revolt, and in 701 BCE, Sennacherib of Assyria destroyed 46 of 47 cities in Judah, fulfilling the judgment oracles of Micah according to some Judahites. Jerusalem survived, but for a time it appeared that Jerusalem would fall, and Judah would go into exile as Israel did 20 years prior. It was then that Isaiah uttered his message of hope: the king, the city, and the Temple would not fall to Assyria (Isaiah 37:1-7, 2 Kings 19:20-34). Few believed Isaiah during the siege, but when plague ("the angel of the Lord" is usually an expression for disease) drove away the Assyrian army, Isaiah was vindicated. Few knew that Hezekiah paid a heavy tribute to Assyria; we know it only from Assyrian records. The Assyrians gladly settled with a people whose god could so strike over a 1,000 men dead. (Our translation of 185,000 Assyrian dead is probably a mistranslation of 1,085, since Assyrian armies never exceeded 10,000.) The withdrawal of the Assyrian army in 701 BCE was seen as an act of divine deliverance comparable to the Exodus.

Isaiah 1-11 contain other authentic Isaianic oracles with both judgment and hope oracles, the judgment coming from Isaiah's early period under Ahaz and the hope imagery from late in his life with Hezekiah. This tells us that a prophet need not be consistently a prophet of judgment or hope. Prophets proclaimed the message of God, and that message was shaped by what the audience needed to hear, not what they wished to hear or what the prophet wanted to say. The same message may be expressed in different words and modes of thought depending on the human circumstances; the good prophet, preacher, or theologian knows how to apply the traditional message for each new age.

In Isaiah's oracles three significant motifs exemplified his theology: 1) the Davidic Covenant, 2) the Day of Yahweh and the Age of Peace, and 3) the Immanuel.

*Davidic Covenant*: Isaiah's message of hope was built on a "Royal Theology" of kingship going back to the united monarchy, which proclaimed that Yahweh's election of the David's family was everlasting. Not only the king, but also the city of Jerusalem (Zion), and the Temple were inviolable. The promise of Nathan to David (2 Samuel 7) must have been part of Jerusalem's courtly language and thus part of Isaiah's imagery. Thus, Isaiah declared that Jerusalem would withstand the Assyrian siege.

In later years, Judahites quoted Isaiah's oracles with self-confidence as they opposed the message of Jeremiah. (The orthodoxy of one age can become the heresy of the next, if it is not properly understood and reinterpreted.) When Jerusalem fell in 586 BCE, a crisis of faith occurred, for the covenant with David was broken. In exile, Second Isaiah (Isaiah 40-55) revived the image with the promise of restoration. When the exiles returned to Jerusalem after 539 BCE, this vindicated Second Isaiah and the imagery of the Davidic Covenant, for the city and the Temple were then rebuilt.

However, kingship did not return, and the construction of the Second Temple and the city were shoddy. Jews then envisioned a future age when a great messiah would bring a new Temple and a New Jerusalem. Imagery in the post-exilic prophets was grand in this regard. Ultimately, Christians saw the fulfillment of all these images in the Jesus movement. The fulfillment was quite different from what was popularly expected, for Jesus was the new king or messiah, and the Temple and the New Jerusalem became symbols for people, Christians in this life and the life to come.

*Day of Yahweh and the Age of Peace:* Isaiah's early oracles proclaimed the judgment of Yahweh for the sins of oppressing the poor (Isaiah 1:2-31, 2:6-5:30, 9:18-10:19), and some of these words of judgment may have come from the late period prior to the wars of 705-701 BCE. Isaiah viewed the day of the Lord as one of doom, but unlike Amos, he anticipated an age of peace following the destruction in which justice would prevail (Isaiah 10:20-11:16). In a small way, an age of peace occurred for Judahites after the siege of 701 BCE, since the vassalage of Assyria became lighter in the final years of Hezekiah's reign, and the wars had ceased. As with other hope oracles, people believed that even though they were fulfilled once, they would be fulfilled in grander fashion in the future. Students of Isaiah's message anticipated a great age that would come someday, and further oracles were generated that elaborated on this vision of hope (Isaiah 12-23, 28-33 contain oracles from this later generation after Isaiah's death).

*Immanuel:* When Isaiah first proclaimed the Immanuel motif, it was an oracle of judgment against Ahaz (Isaiah 7), for his lack of trust in Yahweh. Assyria would be the presence of Yahweh among the people to punish Judah. As a sign of that divine presence Isaiah spoke of a boy soon to be born in the court of Ahaz whose name would be "Immanuel," or "God" (*El*) "with us" (*immanu*). When the boy would be old enough to tell good from evil, the invasion would occur (under Tiglath-Pileser III in 734-733 BCE), and the boy would be forced to eat "curds and honey" in the desolate country. Perhaps, Isaiah spoke of his own son, or a son of King Ahaz, maybe even Hezekiah himself, who might have been born at this time. However, if Hezekiah began to rule by 727 BCE (2 Kings 18:1) or 715 BCE (2 Kings 18:13), one might suspect that he had to be born earlier than when the Immanuel baby was born. Thus, we are not sure of the Immanuel baby's identity. But the oracle came true. As the boy grew older, the Assyrian armies attacked.

Later in his prophetic ministry Isaiah modified the imagery of the Immanuel to be more hopeful and clearly focus on a royal figure (Isaiah 9). Isaiah might have referred to Hezekiah, whom Isaiah saw as an ideal king, and the oracle might have been given at Hezekiah's coronation. Isaiah 7 might have been revised at that point with the addition of the hope images that occur in the latter part of the chapter. After the rule of Hezekiah, Isaiah projected the image of the ideal king into the future to refer to some good Judean king who would conduct himself as David and Hezekiah. This king would come with a great age of peace (Isaiah 11). Perhaps Isaiah 1-11 written and circulated during Josiah's reign (636-609 BCE) because he was envisioned as this future ideal messianic king. Post-exilic prophets, Isaiah 56-66, Zechariah 9-14, Haggai 1-2, and Malachi 1-3, spoke of an ideal king who would rule with the Spirit of Yahweh and justice in a golden age for Jews. This person would be sent by Yahweh from the divine realm. Christians saw the image fulfilled by Jesus, but in ironic fashion, for his kingdom was not a military empire, but a kingdom of the heart that encompassed all peoples.

With all these symbols, there was evolution over the years. The images referred to phenomena in Isaiah's own lifetime; some referred to subsequent historical events after reinterpretation by later generations, all became part of a great vision of hope for post-exilic Jews, and finally all the symbols came together in a radically new way to be applied by Christians to Jesus. It is important for Christians to recognize that these symbols meant something concretely to Israelites and Jews long before Christians inherited them. These were symbols of hope for people in many different ages. Symbols capable of reinterpretation with deeper levels of meaning can be said to be "polyvalent." A powerful symbol can legitimately say different things to different people at any age in history or in changed social and historical circumstances. If we wish to speak meaningfully of divine inspiration, we could do well to speak of how God provided polyvalent symbols to sustain believers through the many centuries.

# Elohist Tradition

There is a northern prophetic tradition of narratives that scholars have sought to isolate. It is called the Elohist, due to its use of the word Elohim for the name of God. It has been dated anywhere from the 10th to the 6th century BCE by scholars, and often its very existence is denied. Locating its relationship to other biblical traditions is determined by what is included in the so-called Elohist tradition. Some believe this oral tradition is found only in the Tetrateuch of Genesis through Numbers, though others, including this author, believe that the prophetic accounts in Samuel and Kings should be connected with it. This author suggests that after the fall of the northern state of Israel in 722 BCE faithful Israelites who remained in the land crafted memories of the prophets, such as Elijah and Elisha, as well as traditions of the great foundational events of Israel. These accounts were recalled at the shrine in Bethel sometime around 700-550 BCE, but they never were organized into a unified epic, rather they remained "pools of oral tradition" until they were drawn into the exilic Yahwist history in the late 6th century BCE, who combined them with his own distinct and different theological themes.

Elohist accounts in Genesis, Exodus, and Numbers appear as though they might have provided an alternative memory those other stories primarily used by the Yahwist. They reflect different theological perspectives, which merit our attention and justify the discussion of the Elohist as a distinct theological tradition. These Pentateuchal stories bear a resemblance to prophetic narratives in the book of Kings, especially accounts about Elijah and Elisha. The stories we isolate cannot be put together to obtain a coherent narrative, for most of the oral traditions have been forever lost. If the emergence of the Pentateuchal Elohist accounts are dated after 700 BCE, that justifies combining them with the prophetic narratives for an overall theological evaluation. If these fragments were ultimately drawn together in the 6th century BCE Yahwist, that historian may have filtered out many of the northern Elohist narratives in favor of southern traditions from Judah, for they outnumber the Elohist portions at least three to one. Yahwist and Elohist materials were further edited to be a preface to the Deuteronomistic History.

We sense a strong continuity between Elohist themes and Deuteronomic theological themes. Both reflected the values of the prophets and both were critical of kings. Themes such as repentance, obedience to God, respect for the law, "fear of God," moral behavior, and the courage to stand up for religious beliefs were found in both traditions. Hence, we evaluate the Elohist before the consideration of Deuteronomic theology.

The Elohist narrative sequence appears to begin with Abraham's covenant (Genesis 15, the Yahwist covenant is in Genesis 12). It included the Abimelech affair (Genesis 20), the sacrifice of Isaac (Genesis 22), Jacob's dream of the ladder (Genesis 28), the Bethel pilgrimage to bury idols (Genesis 35), the resistance of the midwives (Exodus 1), Moses' call (Exodus 3), the account of the golden calf (Exodus 32), and various fragments throughout the patriarchal, Exodus, and wilderness wandering traditions. Some believe our present version of the Ten Commandments in Exodus 20 and the Book of the Covenant in Exodus 21-23 originated with the Elohist. Prophetic accounts include the nameless man of God (1 Kings 13) and the traditions of Elijah and Elisha (1 Kings 17-22, 2 Kings 1-8). Even though Elohist stories are few and fragmented, a careful reader can sense particular themes that permeate the texts.

Elohist accounts used "Elohim" for the divine name rather than "Yahweh." Perhaps reverence for the sacred name caused the Elohist to use "Yahweh" less; perhaps there was a tendency to prefer Elohim in the north because it was somehow connected to the divine name, El. At any rate, "Elohim" was the proper name for God until the revelation to Moses. This contrasted with the Yahwist who used the sacred name from the days of Cain. This difference in the northern and the southern traditions has led to interesting speculation about the evolution of Yahweh worship. It has been suggested that the name Yahweh might have been known by the people in the south much earlier than in the north, because the sacred name came into Palestine from Midian, Edom, or somewhere in the wilderness (presumably with the Joshua people).

**Elohist Theology**: Elohist stories stressed faithfulness and obedience. God fulfilled the promises to the patriarchs by giving Israel the land under Joshua (who is more important than David of the Yahwist tradition). Israel had to be faithful to keep the land. Abraham epitomized faithfulness in his willingness to sacrifice Isaac. "Fear of God" or deep awe prompted obedience. The midwives in Exodus 1 who courageously defied mighty pharaoh by not killing the babies had this "fear of God." Their act was an example of civil disobedience, for they chose obey God rather than a king, even though pharaoh called himself a "god." The Elohist spoke of obedience to God rather than to kings of Israel like Omri and Ahab, or the later kings who caused the destruction of the state in 722 BCE.

Israel and various heroes of the faith were tested by God many times. Abraham was tested to sacrifice Isaac; Israel was tested by God at Horeb (the Elohist name for Sinai). Injunctions not to worship other gods were the greatest test for the Israelites throughout history (Genesis 35:2-4, Jacob; Exodus 19:5, Israel). How Israel responded to tests and temptations was of grave importance in the Elohist view of history.

The Elohist traditions addressed a people in time of great crisis, either during an age of conflict between prophets and kings or more likely after the fall of the northern kingdom. A morality of high caliber pervaded the literature, and this moral sensitivity caused the Elohist stories to differ from Yahwist counterparts. While the Yahwist delighted in showing the human side of the patriarchs and their need for divine grace, the Elohist portrayed them as moral paradigms to emulate. Abraham's lie about Sarah (Genesis 20:12) was lessened by making her a half-sister, Abraham's fear was turned into concern about the lack of the "fear of God" in Gerar (Genesis 20:11), Abimelech clearly did not touch Sarah (Genesis 20:4, 6, 9) we are told repeatedly, Sarah sent Hagar away to protect her son, Isaac, but not out of jealousy (Genesis 21:11-14), Abraham agreed to Hagar's expulsion because it was God's will (Genesis 21:11-14), and Jacob obtained Laban's flock by divine direction, not magical manipulation (Genesis 32:6-13).

With this high moral vision, the Elohist avoided the bawdy humor and trickery found in usual folk tales, as in the Yahwist tradition. Years ago scholars assumed that general moral development among Israelites occurred between the time of the Yahwist and the later Elohist (for they dated the Yahwist tradition earlier than we do now). Now we think that the respective traditions reflect the style of the people who recounted the tales and the audience they addressed, not some major intellectual advance. The Elohist took sin and judgment seriously, and this concern went beyond the behavior of individuals to address the corporate actions of all Israel. If the nation forgets God, there will be great judgment (Exodus 32:4, "I will visit their sin upon them").

The prophet, or *nabi*, was very important for the Elohist. Abraham, Moses, and Miriam were called prophets (Genesis 20:7, Exodus 15:20-21), and Moses declared that all God's people should be prophets (Numbers 11:26-30). This suggests that these narratives circulated orally in northern prophetic circles. Furthermore, the stories that had the greatest affinity with Elohist materials in Genesis, Exodus, and Numbers were the prophetic tales found in the books of Kings. Moses had a very developed character in the Elohist texts; he was the agent by which God led the people in the exodus, a wonder worker who brought plagues and divided the Sea of Reeds with his rod or staff (Exodus 10:12-14, 14:16). The rod or staff of Moses reminds us of the prophetic mantle associated with Elijah and Elisha, and appears to be a later development of that theme.

Aaron contrasted with Moses, for he represented priests, while Moses represented prophets. Aaron led the people astray by making the golden calf, just as the later priests serviced golden calves for Jeroboam I at Bethel and Dan. Aaron excused himself by saying the calf "came out" of the oven, as if God had made it (Exodus 32-33). In contrast to Aaron, Moses received a clear call from Yahweh and spoke the divine message "clearly, and not in dark speech" (Numbers 12:7-8). He was willing even to die for the people to avert divine wrath, thus becoming an innocent sacrifice for the people (Exodus 32:32).

The story of the golden calves in Exodus 32 may have been veiled commentary on the abuse of kings, and the actions of Jeroboam in erecting the calves (1 Kings 12). According to the Elohist, kings like Jeroboam I led people into idolatry and brought punishment upon the entire nation. People ought to obey God and the prophets (successors to Moses) rather than kings and the Aaronide priests at the shrines. The Elohist would affirm the Samuel traditions wherein Samuel appointed both Saul and David to be kings and tore the kingship from Saul for his disobedience. Perhaps, some of the "Anti-Monarchy Source" may have originated Elohist circles before the Deuteronomistic Historians developed them. Kingship was acceptable only if it acknowledged the authority of the prophets. Such an idea was revolutionary in the ancient world where kings claimed to be divine or semi-divine. We who live with a democratic and constitutional government cannot appreciate how revolutionary these texts were in the first millennium BCE. Nor do we recognize how much these biblical texts influenced the emergence of democratic thought in western society. Once the Bible was placed into the hands of people in the English-speaking world (after the invention of the printing press and the translation of the text into the vernacular), the criticism of absolute kings and rise of democratic thought was accelerated.

**Elohist View of God:** The Elohist envisioned Elohim/Yahweh as a distant and awe-inspiring deity. Moses was appropriately fearful at the burning bush (Genesis 3:6), and at Mt. Horeb (Sinai) the people were forbidden to approach the mountain (Exodus 20:18-21). Whereas Yahweh stood beside Jacob at Bethel (Genesis 28:13) in the Yahwist version, in the Elohist version God did not come down from the exalted ladder or throne atop the ladder (Genesis 28:10-12). God was not portrayed in anthropomorphic or personal images as in Yahwist accounts.

Because God was distant, revelation occurred in different modes. Indirect revelation occurred in Elohist texts, unlike in the Yahwist where God spoke directly to people. Theophanies were fearful, dramatic, and distant. God was revealed through dreams, fire, a voice from heaven, in the thick cloud and thunder at Horeb, through the angel of the Lord/God (which was a pious and respectful way of saying God), and, above all, through human mediators such as Moses and the prophets. Fire occurred in Elohist theophanies, for fire was a symbol of holiness, power, and mystery. There was the burning bush, the pillar of fire that led Israel at night, and fire on Mount Horeb, and fire often destroyed the enemies of God and Israel. This emphasis upon a distant deity who communicated through indirect revelation called correspondingly for human respect and obedience as a proper response. The "fear of God" was the response from those who truly understood God. People led by the fear of God obeyed to the highest degree, even to sacrificing their only child (Abraham) or defying pharaoh (midwives).

Perhaps the account of Elijah's experience upon Mount Horeb (1 Kings 19) originated in Elohist circles. By this account, God was no longer found in the powerful theophanies of the past–fire, wind, storm, and earthquake, but in the still, small voice. This might have implied the emergence of the "prophetic word" as the new mode of revelation to replace the ancient theophanies. If so, the prophets claimed for themselves the awe, fear, and obedience earlier demanded by these terrific phenomena.

In conclusion, the Elohist offered a dramatic and moral theological message, envisioning God as transcendent, worthy of fear and respect, and one who must be obeyed over kings. The Elohist provided courageous theology in time of great social and religious crisis, perhaps after the destruction of the northern state of Israel. These texts still provide us with powerful inspiration today. Elohist traditions were probably preserved by the Yahwist Historian who blended them together with his own distinctive themes. We should not view the traditions as contradicting each other; rather, they complement each other. The Yahwist spoke of divine grace and a personal deity to one age; the Elohist spoke of a distant God and human fear and obedience to a different age. When human religious needs change, a different message must be spoken, but it remains the same religion. Jews and Christians have inherited both messages, and they hold these views in tension: modern believers speak of God as both transcendent and immanent, as both loving and demanding. Like instruments in a symphony, producing different sounds that arise and blend into a harmony, these biblical texts speak their individual message and finally produce a unified message in the entire biblical canon.

# Conclusion

The 8th century prophets BCE carried the vision of Yahweh as the Lord of all aspects of life to conclusions unprecedented in Israelite religion. That their values seem commonplace to us today reflects their impact upon the development of thought in the Judeo-Christian tradition and Western culture. They are used by Jews and Christians as a resource for proclaiming justice in society. What is significant is that their message was most important for the religious evolution of Israelite and Jewish belief, particularly the emergence of monotheism among the Jews during and after the Babylonian Exile.

Though scholars are puzzled about the exact history and development of the Elohist traditions, there was clearly the message that we ought to fear God rather than other people, and obedience to God leads to a high moral life-style. Some of these Elohist stories are among the most powerful memories in the Hebrew Bible, and they can inspire audiences even today.

## Bibliography

John Barton. Isaiah 1-39. Old Testament Guides. Sheffield, Eng.: Sheffield Academic Press, 1995.

Joseph Blenkinsopp. *A History of Prophecy in Israel.* Rev. Ed. Louisville, KY: Westminster John Knox, 1996.

Brevard Childs. Isaiah. Old Testament Library. Louisville, KY: Westminster John Knox, 2000.

Richard Clifford. Fair Spoken and Persuading: An Interpretation of Second Isaiah. New York, NY: Paulist, 1984.

Robert Gnuse. "Redefining the Elohist." *Journal of Biblical Literature* 119 (2000): 201-220.

James Mayes. Amos. Old Testament Library. Philadelphia, PA: Westminster, 1969.

James Mayes. Hosea. Old Testament Library. Philadelphia, PA: Westminster, 1974.

James Mayes. Micah. Old Testament Library. Philadelphia, PA: Westminster, 1976.

David Petersen. *The Prophetic Literature.* Louisville, KY: Westminster John Knox, 2002.

Gerhard von Rad. *The Message of the Prophets.* Trans. D. M. G. Stalker. New York, NY: Harper and Row, 1967.

Hans Walter Wolff. *Amos the Prophet: The Man and His Background.* Trans. Foster McCurley. Philadelphia, PA: Fortress, 1973.

# Chapter 5

# Deuteronomy and Jeremiah

Readings:  Deuteronomy 1-11,Jeremiah 1-7,12-20,31-38

## 7th Century Judah

2 Kings 21-23, Deuteronomy 4:44-11:32, and Jeremiah 1:1-4:4, 7, 26-45 contain historical background to this era.  Scholars suggest that when the northern kingdom of Israel fell to Assyria in 722 BCE, many fled to the southern kingdom of Judah, including the circle of faithful who viewed the destruction of their nation as divine punishment.  They preserved the oracles of Amos and Hosea as well as many legal and epic traditions.  We think that legal traditions emerged in the northern state, which had been proposed by prophets and other intelligentsia as a way of reforming religious and social abuses.  These were written in Deuteronomy 12-26, although our present text was expanded.  Some of the narrative traditions in Joshua, Judges, Samuel, and Kings may have come with these refugees, especially those associated with Joshua and the early prophets. Thus, the Deuteronomistic History shows signs of northern origin, even though the production of the literary corpus took place in Judah from 620 to 550 BCE.  Northern origins may be reflected in the theological continuity shared by Deuteronomy with the Hosea on themes such as the love of Yahweh for Israel, need for religious reform, stress on the exclusive worship of Yahweh, disdain for the golden calf, and the theme of covenant.  Another good example is how the "Blessing of Moses" in Deuteronomy 33 showered more attention on the northern tribes of Manasseh and Ephraim, as represented by "Joseph" (Deuteronomy 33:13-17) than on the southern tribe of Judah (Deuteronomy 33:7).

ezekiah was succeeded by Manasseh (685-642 BCE), who bought peace for Judah and preserved the state from Assyrian onslaught by being a faithful vassal to Assyria.  To Yahwists he was a traitor when he paid tribute and recognized the gods of the Assyrians. The Deuteronomistic account in 2 Kings 21:1-18 portrayed him as the ultimately evil king. Scholars suspect he went beyond the basic demands for recognizing Assyrian and other foreign deities necessitated by political allegiance by introducing religious customs from the greater Syro-Palestinian world. He sacrificed his own son as a burnt offering, a practice undertaken by religious devotees in Syria and Palestine, although we do not know to what extent it was done elsewhere. Manasseh sponsored fortunetellers and divinators, and he put the image of Asherah--the consort of Yahweh in popular Yahwism--back into the Temple (2 Kings 21:6-9). Furthermore, he tried to crush the Yahweh party by killing prophets (2 Kings 21:16), including Isaiah who was sawn in half according to later pious Jewish tradition. Yahwists resisted the king and preserved the legal, narrative, and prophetic traditions secretly. References to the "people of the land" (perhaps rural landowners) may describe the supporters of these Yahwist dissidents, and sometimes we think that the Levites were intellectual leaders in this movement. The earliest written versions of some biblical traditions may have emerged in this era, and the Yahwists waited for the time when they might surface with their message.

After Manasseh died, his son and successor Amon was assassinated, subsequently Manasseh's grandson, eight-year old Josiah, ascended the throne (640-609 BCE). The Assyrians, under king Ashurbanipal (668-627 BCE), had subdued all their potential enemies, and Assyrian armies no longer went forth on campaigns. Ashurbanipal attended to the creation of his famous library in Nineveh and the empire slowly began to weaken. Nationalistic fervor arose throughout the empire, territories began withholding tribute, but no retribution came from the Assyrian heartland. Josiah, too, began to move Judah toward de facto independence. Josiah initially began some political reforms, and when no response came from Assyria, he engaged in more extensive changes. When Josiah refurbished the Temple, a "book of the Law" was discovered (1 Kings 22). Upon hearing the contents of this document, the king was distraught and declared that the contents of these "lost laws" must be obeyed. These laws were said to come from Moses, and his public reading of them was the "second giving of the Law": the deuteros ("second") nomos ("law"). Josiah proclaimed that obedience was necessary, if Judah was to escape the wrath of Yahweh. Scholars have suspected since 1800 that the "book of the Law" was Deuteronomy 12-26, due to the similarity of the reforms undertaken by Josiah (1 Kings 23) and particular laws in Deuteronomy. We suppose the document was "planted" in the Temple by the Yahwists who saw an opportunity to implement their reforms under the aegis of national independence. Josiah may have been aware of this Yahwist conspiracy, for their program dovetailed nicely with his political agenda. Thus Deuteronomic Reform became the law of the land in Judah from 622 to 609 BCE.

# Deuteronomic Theology

Deuteronomy may have been produced in 622 BCE and later expanded around 550 BCE, for Deuteronomy 1-11, 27-34 appear to be additions to the core of legal material in chapters 12-26. The reformers also may have circulated the first edition of the Deuteronomistic History: Joshua, Judges, Samuel, and Kings. Work on these historical books probably continued in the exile, until a second edition may have arisen in either Babylon or Palestine around 550 BCE.

The Deuteronomists were prophetically motivated scribes who wished to inspire the people of Judah, the southern kingdom after the division of Solomon's empire, not to make the same tragic mistake as the northern state of Israel had done. They called upon people to heed the warnings of the 8th century BCE prophets and turn their devotion solely to Yahweh and become a just society. Though they appealed to past values, in actuality, they called people to monotheism for the first time in their history. The Deuteronomistic History was formulated to arouse this awareness. The laws in Deuteronomy 12-26 were a revision of Exodus 21-23, the Covenant Code, and the first short draft may have been generated in the north around 750-700 BCE. Heavily indebted to prophetic theology, these laws sought to create a society governed by Yahweh's will. The longer Deuteronomistic History emerged in final form during the Babylonian Exile around 550 BCE, and herein we observe the Israelite worldview that had been slowly emerging for years. The message of this theologically interpreted history was simple: faithfulness to Yahweh and the Law was the foundation for a successful and healthy society; disobedience brought destruction and the loss of land. The Babylonian Exile vindicated this dire warning and insured that this literature would be regarded as sacred.

**Covenant**: Israelites were the only people in the ancient world who used the political concept of covenant to describe their relationship to their deity. Deuteronomic thought appealed to Sinaitic or Mosaic traditions, reflecting the northern prophetic perceptions of the election of Israel. This model differed from the Zion or Davidic-Abrahamic courtly traditions of Judah. According to the Sinaitic traditions, the covenant relationship between Yahweh and the people was conditional and dependent upon Israel's obedience to the Yahweh and the Law. If Israel broke the Law, the people would be punished by foreign conquest or loss of the land; if they kept the Law, they would be blessed, especially through land productivity. Exilic redaction of these biblical texts emphasized even more how disobedience would lead to the complete loss of the land, which is what happened with the exile. The final exilic version of the Deuteronomistic History explained why the destruction of Jerusalem occurred in 586 BCE.

Deuteronomic Reformers stressed the conditional nature of the covenant to elicit not only repentance from the people of Judah, but also to encourage their participation in the social and religious reform of Josiah. This conditional covenant contrasted with the permanent promises made to David (2 Samuel 7:4-17) and the royal understanding of Yahweh's election of the King, the Temple, and Jerusalem. A Yahwist rendition of the covenant with Abraham in Genesis 12 also appears unconditional. Biblical theologians today see these not as two distinct covenants, but as two aspects of the same covenant that can be conditional or unconditional depending upon the social context. In the New Testament unconditional covenant language was used to speak about divine grace.

This conditional covenant rhetoric was inspired by political treaties in the ancient Near East, especially contemporary Assyrian treaties in the 8th and 7th century BCE, including those of king Esarhaddon (681-669 BCE). Curses in Esarhaddon's treaties were remarkably similar to those listed in Deuteronomy 28. Scholars have seen great parallels in both the Hittite covenants from the late second millennium BCE and Assyrian covenants from the first half of the first millennium BCE, and over the years there has been debate as to which set of covenants was more important for the biblical text. If the

Hittite treaties were more important, the implication is that covenant language existed in Israel from an early date and the beginning of the legal tradition (maybe Moses himself). If the Assyrian treaties were the source of influence, it implies that covenant language was introduced into the texts by Deuteronomists. Most scholars favor the latter option.

Covenant language occurred in connection with the Decalogue in Exodus 20, in the prophets, and in the book of Deuteronomy and the Deuteronomistic History. Recorded Hittite and Assyrian treaties used a recurring format: 1) historical review of good things done by the superior political entity for the lesser political entity, 2) stipulations of what the lesser political entity owed the superior entity, 3) blessings and curses that came with either obedience or disobedience to the treaty, 4) a list of gods who witnessed the treaty and should enforce it, 5) mechanical references to where the copies of the treaty should be deposited in the respective nations and how often they should be read in a public assembly. One may observe striking similarities with Exodus 20 and the whole book of Deuteronomy. In Exodus 20 Yahweh referred to Israel's deliverance from Egypt (#1) and the Ten Commandments were issued (#2), subsequently Exodus 20:5-6 and 34:7 contained references to blessings and curses (#3), the Israelites heard the commands read to them and affirmed them in Exodus 24:3 (#5), and the tablets were deposited in the Ark of the Covenant (#5). The whole book of Deuteronomy conformed to the pattern: Deuteronomy 1-11 reviewed Israel's journey in the exodus and wilderness (#1), Deuteronomy 12-26 contained laws (#2), Deuteronomy 27-28 had blessings and curses for obedience and disobedience (#3), Deuteronomy 31:9-13 stipulated that these laws be read every seven years (#5), and Deuteronomy 31:26 stipulated that the Deuteronomic Laws be placed in the Ark of the Covenant (#5). This patterning was a deliberate attempt by the biblical authors to impart a sense of seriousness to the law by implying that Israel made a significant legal treaty with Yahweh in the distant past, swearing to observe the Ten Commandments and Deuteronomic Law.

**Call to Repent**: Deuteronomic Reformers stressed contingent election; they called for public repentance after years of public apostasy. The rhetoric of Deuteronomy reminds us of the style of a revivalist preacher. The preface to the laws, Deuteronomy 1-11, was an oratorical sermon, which we suspect was created for public reading in the age of Josiah. The word for "repent" was shub, a term which meant to turn around and walk the other way. The imperative to repent combined with publicly proclaimed blessings and curses for obedience or disobedience led to a strong belief in retribution, for Deuteronomic reformers wished to bring religious and social change. They understood retribution for sin to apply to the people as whole, in a corporate sense. However, in later years Jews popularly made this notion strict in its application to everyday life and to individuals, so that suffering was seen as divine punishment. Post-exilic authors had to counter these misinterpretations of divine retribution in their writings.

Wisdom Literature in the Old Testament (Proverbs) made a strong causal connection between folly and sin, wisdom and righteousness, and one's lot in life. As a corrective, the book of Job and post-exilic Lament Hymns in the Psalter disassociated individual suffering and divine punishment. Though Deuteronomy helped give rise to strict popular notions of retribution in Jewish piety, it did not teach strict individual retribution in this life. Deuteronomy's rhetoric spoke to the nation as a whole: "If you (plural) sin, you (plural) will be punished." To assume that the same terms held for an individual in this life was truly a misinterpretation.

The later Jewish tradition spoke of how one righteous person or a few righteous people might save the larger group from destruction. In the exilic edition of the Yahwist tradition, the story of Abraham debating with Yahweh over the fate of Sodom (Genesis 18) demonstrated that a few righteous people might save an evil city. The suffering servant in Isaiah 40-55 and the innocent lamb sacrificed on the Day of Atonement (Leviticus 18) were exilic and post-exilic texts that testified to the sacrifice of an innocent person or animal for sins of many. This Jewish understanding lies behind the Christian view of Jesus Christ's death. The post-exilic stress upon vicarious suffering was a way of reacting against misunderstandings of Deuteronomic retribution. Popular piety in any age can cruelly attribute retribution for sin to a person's life and create further suffering.

**Social Justice**: Deuteronomic Reformers inherited the legacy of the classical prophets. Like the prophets, they condemned the people for worshipping other gods and economically oppressing poor Israelites. But Deuteronomists were different from the prophets in that they advocated particular reforms for society with new laws. Deuteronomy 12-26 revised legislation from the Book of the Covenant in Exodus 21-23 to safeguard more directly the rights of slaves, widows, orphans, and foreign residents. Deuteronomy 12-26 reflected a society with more complex economic and political structures, which permitted a greater gap between rich and poor. Laws in Deuteronomy eliminated loopholes in older laws that allowed powerful people to victimize the poor. Whereas Exodus simply forbade interest on loans extended to Israelites, Deuteronomy prohibited some variations of interest that side-stepped the old laws, like taking a "bite" out of the loan before extending it. According to laws in Exodus, if a debt slave married and had children while in debt slavery, he could not take his family with him into freedom. But in the laws of Deuteronomy, the family may leave with the debt slave and the master must provide provisions to prevent their return to debt slavery. Furthermore, debt release was to occur throughout the land every seven years so that the master could not dishonestly count the six years of debt servitude owed by the debt slave (Deuteronomy 15).

If we read both the Book of the Covenant and the Deuteronomic Law Code closely, we may notice the following parallels: 1) Sabbath observance (Deuteronomy 5:13-14, Exodus 23:12), 2) exclusive worship of God (Deuteronomy 6:13, Exodus 23:13), 3) altars and other gods (Deuteronomy 12:1-28, Exodus 20:19-23), 4) worship of other gods (Deuteronomy 12:29-13:18, Exodus 22:19), 5) no boiling a goat in its mother's milk (Deuteronomy 14:21, Exodus 23:19), 6) Sabbath Year release or land rest (Deuteronomy 15:1-11, Exodus 23:10-11), 7) humanitarian slave laws (Deuteronomy 15:12-18, Exodus 21:2-11), 8) consecrating first born children and animals (Deuteronomy 15:19-23, Exodus 22:29-30), 9) festivals (Deuteronomy 16:1-17, Exodus 23:14-19), 10) fair judges (Deuteronomy 16:18-20, Exodus 23:2-3, 6-8), 11) worship of other gods (Deuteronomy 17:2-7, Exodus 22:20), 12) witchcraft (Deuteronomy 18:10-11, Exodus 22:18), 13) unintentional homicide (Deuteronomy 19:1-13, Exodus 21:12-14), 13) perjury (Deuteronomy 19:15-21, Exodus 23:1-2), 14) rebellious sons (Deuteronomy 21:18-21, Exodus 21:15, 17), 15) lost animals (Deuteronomy 22:1-4, Exodus 23:4-5), 16) seduction (Deuteronomy 22:2-29, Exodus 22:16-17), 17) interest on a loan (Deuteronomy

3:19-20), Exodus 24:25), 18) kidnapping (Deuteronomy 24:7, Exodus 21:16), 19) loan collateral (Deuteronomy 24:10-13, Exodus 22:26-27), 20) widows, orphans, sojourners (Deuteronomy 24:17-18, Exodus 22:22-24, 23:9), 21) 21) crop gleaning (Deuteronomy 24:19-21, Exodus 23:11), and 22) first fruits (Deuteronomy 26:1-11, Exodus 22:29, 23:19). The Deuteronomic Law Code was an expansion of the earlier laws in the Book of the Covenant with special attention to the needs and rights of women, slaves, and the poor. Deuteronomic laws were reform-oriented laws meeting the social and economic needs of a developed economy for a later generation, while the Book of the Covenant was for a simple village agrarian society.

The sequence of laws in Deuteronomy 12-26 seems to follow the order of the Ten Commandments. We can observe this, if we view Deuteronomic laws as loosely fitting under the category of each of the Ten Commandments: 1) no other gods nor idols (Deuteronomy 12:1-32), 2) misuse of the divine name (Deuteronomy 13:1-18, false prophetic words), 3) Sabbath (Deuteronomy 15:1-16:17, Sabbath Release and festivals), 4) honoring parents (Deuteronomy 21:18-21), 5) killing (Deuteronomy 19:1-21:14, cities of refuge, holy war, and bloodguilt), 6) adultery (Deuteronomy 21:10-14, 22:13-30, 23:17-18, 24:1-4, women, wives, and daughters), 7) theft (Deuteronomy 23:19-20, 24-25, 24:6-21, 25:13-16, interest, collateral, gleaning, wages, weights), 8) perjury and lying (Deuteronomy 19:15-21, 23:21-23), 9) coveting (Deuteronomy 25:13-16). With the exception of the perjury command and some other laws that overlap, there was quite a coincidence in the sequence of laws in Deuteronomy and the Decalogue. This again implies that Deuteronomy built upon previous laws.

Reforms advocated in Deuteronomy 12-26 appear so idealistic that we debate whether they could have been implemented effectively in Josiah's age. Perhaps this radical change caused some backlash, so that after Josiah's death reform legislation was ignored. Nevertheless, after the Babylonian Exile, Jews took these laws very seriously. Perhaps, the laws were expanded then into their present written form. Their vision inspires social reformers in any age, and their rhetoric reminds us of the teachings of Jesus and remains a cornerstone in the values of contemporary Judaism.

**Deuteronomistic View of History:** The Deuteronomists viewed obedience to the Law as bringing reward and disobedience as bringing punishment in the course of history. Hence, the narrative was highly selective in the stories it recalled. Sin and obedience, reward and punishment, were operative principles throughout Israel's history. The laws in Deuteronomy 12-26 were a prologue to this history, for they contained the laws by which the course of history unfolded: disobedience brought national decline, obedience brought national success. This pattern can be observed in the book of Judges, for here the biblical authors had loose, oral traditions around which they could place editorial comments. Comments connected with these stories created the following pattern: 1) people lived in a state of blessing, 2) people sinned, 3) enemies conquered Israel as a punishment, 4) people repented, and 5) Yahweh sent a deliverer to save them. This was similar to the Yahwist format of blessing, sin, punishment, and forgiveness, which we shall consider later, but in this format the addition repentance added an important aspect that the Deuteronomists stressed. These five stages were recorded in Judges 2:11-23 and then repeated as a refrain throughout the book connected with the story of each major judge. Emphasis upon repentance may sound legalistic to us, but it was necessary in the late 7th century BCE for monotheism to emerge and for social justice to be practiced. For the Deuteronomists it was a message of grace, for such obedience insured blessing.

Deuteronomistic Historians reinterpreted history by projecting into the past their monotheistic faith (or at least they were close to monotheism). Early Israelites were criticized for their failure to worship Yahweh exclusively, when historically the earliest Israelites did not know to surrender belief in other gods. The conquest under Joshua appeared as a major conquest, rather than the limited experience it was. For the concept of total "Holy War" was a symbol for spiritual war that should occur in the hearts of people. The interpretation of history with "holy war" categories was rhetoric not actual history. The "remnant" of Canaanites in the land, who were the cause of later apostasy, should have been destroyed according to the historians. In actuality, had all Canaanites been destroyed, most Israelites would not have existed, since Israelites evolved out of Canaanites. The so-called Canaanite "remnant," which deserved destruction according to the Deuteronomists, existed in contemporary religious and social values that needed change. (This is why it is wrong for Christians to use the book of Joshua to justify war, or unfair to view the Old Testament as primitive because it justified bloodshed.)

Deuteronomic authors envisioned the Temple as the only place where sacrifice should have been offered. The Temple was the place where Yahweh "caused His name to dwell" (the "name of Yahweh" was a reverent circumlocution for Yahweh, just as the "angel of God/Lord" was for the Elohist). The testimony of archaeology to other existing Israelite shrines and clear hints in the biblical text, such as editorial comments, imply that the early Israelites had no awareness that the Temple was the only place for sacrifice; the Deuteronomists projected this belief into the past. Deuteronomists stressed the historic centrality of worship in the Temple, because Josiah centralized all worship in the Temple in his age. In order to bring cultic practices under uniform control and to eliminate devotion to other deities in many local shrines, or "high places," Deuteronomic reform argued for centralized worship in the Temple. This enabled the reformers to impose their values of monotheism and social justice upon the masses. Shrines like Dan and Bethel in the northern state of Israel received severe criticism, and Josiah destroyed the shrine at Bethel during a military foray into the north. Josiah's efforts to close all shrines other than the Temple in Jerusalem were paralleled by similar efforts of Hezekiah in the previous century. Josiah's efforts were far more oriented at religious reform than those of Hezekiah, for Hezekiah may have closed shrines simply to protect sacred objects from Assyrian invasion. Deuteronomistic Historians interpreted history to justify social and religious reform in their own age.

**Critique of Kings**: The Deuteronomists conveyed two different perspectives toward the monarchy. They were critical of kings, for when evaluated by their stern standards, only David, Hezekiah, and Josiah were adjudged to be good. They alone worshipped Yahweh exclusively and undertook some religious and social reform. (But maybe only the historical Josiah really worshipped Yahweh exclusively.) Other kings, especially kings in Israel, were responsible for religious and social abuses according to the historians. Though we might disdain this biased presentation of history, we must remember that the Deuteronomists were primarily theologians and preachers, only secondarily were they historians. Their subjective interpretation of history was necessary, for ultimately it give rise to the religion and value system that underlies western culture.

Kings in the ancient world were not only above the law; they made the laws, or attempted to change them. They portrayed themselves as receiving law directly from the gods to mediate to the people. (Notice That Moses usurped this royal function in the wilderness.) Kings claimed divine (Egypt) or semi-divine (Mesopotamia) status to rule in authoritarian fashion. Laws in Deuteronomy reversed these age-old patterns, for Deuteronomy 17:14-20 was the first legislation in human history, to our knowledge, which sought to limit royal powers. To observe such a law in the first millennium BCE is amazing, since European culture did not think to do this until a few centuries ago.

Kings were seen as the cause of Israel's and Judah's downfall in the Deuteronomistic History, but the ideal king, one like David, was a source of inspiration. The first edition of the Deuteronomistic History around 620 BCE may have portrayed Josiah as a new David, a messiah who would bring an age of obedience to God's will. This image helped sow the seeds for post-exilic hopes for the coming Messiah of the golden age.

**Deuteronomistic Historical Books**: The Deuteronomists described events from the conquest of Palestine under Joshua (1220 BCE) to the Babylonian Exile, and the last event mentioned was the release from prison of king Jehoiachin in 561 BCE. Scholars suspect that there were two conclusions in 2 Kings (2 Kings 23:25, 25:30), implying that the Deuteronomistic History may have arisen in at least two editions. The first edition arose in the days of Josiah after the discovery of the law in 622 BCE to give concrete expression to the rhetoric of the book of Deuteronomy. It stressed that obedience would bring blessing and fertility to the land and military victory under leaders like Joshua. Yahweh's word was communicated through prophets, and the historians often indicated when early prophetic oracles were fulfilled by later historical events. Ahijah of Shiloh predicted the division of Solomon's kingdom (1 Kings 11:29-40), which transpired shortly thereafter (1 Kings 12:15). The "man of God" predicted the defilement of the Bethel altar by Josiah (1 Kings 13:2), and that occurred centuries later (2 Kings 23:15-20). Ahijah envisioned the end of Jeroboam's dynasty (1 Kings 14:7-14) and it was fulfilled a few years later (1 Kings 15:29-30). The prophet Jehu predicted the end of Baasha's dynasty (1 Kings 16:1-4) and its fall was recorded (1 Kings 16:7-12). Elijah envisioned the deaths of Ahab and Jezebel (1 Kings 21:17-29), which the historian recalled several times ((2 Kings 9:36, 10:10, 17). King Ahaziah would die according to Elijah (2 Kings 1:4, 16), and he did (2 Kings 1:17). Elisha predicted the defeat of Israel by Hazael of Damascus (2 Kings 18:12), and it occurred (2 Kings 13:3). Elisha also stated that Jehu would destroy the family of Ahab and his wife, Jezebel (2 Kings 9:7-10), and Jehu obliged the prophet (2 Kings 9:36). By these many references the Deuteronomists presented a unified vision of history bounded by the prediction and fulfillment of prophetic oracles. More importantly, the significant authority of the prophets and the need for kings to heed the words of the prophets was clearly stressed. Yet, on the other hand, the Deuteronomists portrayed prophets almost as divinators and placed this image of the prophet in tension with the prophetic corpus, which viewed prophets as anticipators of a potential future that could be created or avoided by freely made human decisions. Many of the prophetic predictions offered hope of an ideal king who would someday emerge and heed the words of the prophets. The 622

BCE edition of the Deuteronmistic History probably saw Josiah as that great king, who served Yahweh exclusively and heeded the word of the Lord and the Torah. The record of Josiah's reforms culminated the first edition.

The exilic edition was written after the death of Josiah (609 BCE) and the destruction of Jerusalem and the Temple (586 BCE), so more pessimistic imagery was added throughout the history. Negative attitudes toward kingship and dire predictions for the loss of the land were inserted. The final edition of the Deuteronomistic History explained that Jerusalem fell in 586 BCE because of sin, not because Yahweh was too weak to defend them. The history also implied in subtle fashion that there was hope of restoration, for repentance brought divine deliverance throughout the history, and this message may have given hope for an ultimate return to the land. All this was added by subtle comments inserted into the text, often in speeches made by leaders.

The Deuteronomists wove together numerous pre-existing sources although scholars debate how well organized those sources were before the Deuteronomists received them. Some scholars view these sources as fairly intact when they were adopted; others see the historians engaging in a freer rewriting of very fragmentary sources. Their work was comparable to contemporary historiography in Mesopotamia and Greece where sources were woven together into a continuous narrative and unified by ideological themes. Mesopotamian sources, including the Babylonian Chronicle, and biblical authors interpreted the past from the perspective of divine-human relationships. However, unlike their Mesopotamian counterparts, who stressed cult and temple restoration, biblical authors included ethical and social-religious concerns in addition to the Temple ideology.

**Sources for the Deuteronomistic History**: Scholars have hypothesized a number of oral cycles or perhaps even written sources that were woven into the Deuteronomistic History.

1. The Wars of Joshua, Joshua 1-12, perhaps were a cycle of tales associated with the Elohist traditions, later expanded by the Deuteronomists.

2. Joshua's land distribution, Joshua 13-22, was a census list either from the time of David or much later from Josiah's age.

3. The Savior cycle of the Judges, Judges 2-12, contained old tales of heroes who fought Israel's enemies, and some Deuteronomistic passages were inserted.

4. Samson Idyll, Judges 13-17 was a romantic and bawdy tale about a hero.

5. Samuel Idyll, 1 Samuel 1-3, was a romantic tale with maybe an Elohist connection, which contained several separate components woven together.

6. Ark Narrative, 1 Samuel 4-6, 2 Samuel 6, was an old tale which paralleled ancient Near Eastern stories about how an angry deity allowed his/her people to be punished by foreigners who took the sacred objects of those people into exile.

7. The Pro-Monarchical source, 1 Samuel 9-10:16, 11, 13-14, were early monarchical traditions, which portrayed Saul as a charismatic leader.

8. The Anti-Monarchical source, 1 Samuel 7-8, 10:17-27, 12, 15, was a rather late tradition, perhaps Deuteronomistic in origin, which viewed Saul and kingship rather negatively.

9. The Rise of David, 1 Samuel 16-31, 2 Samuel 1-8, was a combination of old, loosely connected folktales and selections from Davidic court annals used to justify the rise of David.

10. The Succession Narrative, 2 Samuel 9-20, 1 Kings 1-2, was a unified story with a plot, emphasizing human emotions rather than divine actions as the cause of history and explaining the rise of Solomon.

11. The Court History of Solomon, 1 Kings 3-11, was a court annal paralleling Egyptian court documents that praised pharaoh and his wars, building projects, trade, and wisdom, but Deuteronomistic insertions viewed Solomon negatively.

12. Prophetic Traditions, 1 Kings 13-14, 20, 22, were stories about diverse prophets who critiqued the kings; the material is reminiscent of Elohist traditions and may have been part of a loose Elohist cycle.

13. Elijah cycle, 1 Kings 17-19, 21, 2 Kings 1-2, were accounts of Elijah's opposition to the Omride dynasty that were part of the general prophetic traditions.

14. Elisha Cycle, 2 Kings 3-9, was material similar to Elijah narratives in content, with a more fanciful style, and it was part of the general prophetic traditions.

15. Annals of the Kings, 1 Kings 12, 15-16, 2 Kings 10-25, were narratives spun off of the chronicles of Israelite and Judean kings, with special attention paid to Hezekiah and Josiah. Some of the data may have been taken from royal monuments in Jerusalem.

Much of this literature already contained ideas that resonated with Deuteronomistic thought, but Deuteronomists expanded these sources with nuanced language and sharpened some of the assumptions in the pre-existing narratives. Throughout the sources were well-crafted speeches by major characters that conveyed the ideology of the Deuteronomists more directly than other texts. These included the speeches by Joshua (Joshua 22, 23), Samuel (1 Samuel 8, 12), Solomon (1 Kings 8), and a number of short editorial statements. The speeches were editorial comments from the Deuteronomists. One might say that the entire Deuteronomistic History was a sermon.

Some contemporary scholars believe that the Deuteronomists at some point edited the books of Genesis, Exodus, and Numbers before they were re-worked again by Priestly Editors. There appears to be Deuteronomistic language in a number of Pentateuchal texts, especially in the book of Numbers. One may sense Deuternomistic editing of the Ten Commandments in Exodus 20 and the surrounding narratives. (Sometimes scholars will argue over whether passages in the book of Numbers were Elohistic or Deuteronomistic.) If this is correct, then it means the Yahwist tradition in Genesis, Exodus, and Numbers was edited first by the Deuteronomistic Historians, who may have connected those books to the larger Deuteronomistic History, and then the entire corpus was edited by the Priestly Editors, which explains why we observe priestly texts in a book like Joshua.

Deuteronomistic texts are easily identified by particular vocabulary. A few examples of classic words include: "repent," "obey," "serve," "the ways of the Lord," "listen to the words/commands," "follow other gods," "oath He swore to our fathers," "the place I will cause my name to dwell," "fear," "name of God/the Lord," "cause to sin," "walk in the ways," "statutes, commandments, and laws," "covenant," and many others. (There is similarity between this language and the language of Jeremiah, for he was contemporary with the movement.)

**History of the Reform Movement:** Reform swept the land from 622 to 609 BCE. Josiah destroyed shrines in Judah and Israel (2 Kings 23:15-20), commanded that Passover become a pilgrimage festival to Jerusalem rather than a familial or local celebration, and enforced other laws in Deuteronomy 12-26. Most significant was his centralization of Passover in Jerusalem, where it remained a pilgrim festival until after the days of Jesus. Scholars date particular texts in the legal corpora on the basis of references to the Passover as a pilgrimage festival. It had not been such before Josiah's time, for 2 Kings 23:21-23 stated, "no such Passover had been kept since the day of the judges who judged Israel, or during all the days of the kings of Judah."

Tragically, Josiah died at Megiddo in 609 BCE. He moved his army northward into Israel to claim this land in defiance of Egyptian Pharaoh Necho who also wished to rule this territory. Egypt, which had been part of the Assyrian empire, claimed part of the empire as Assyria collapsed. Josiah opposed Necho's army as it moved northward to become an Assyrian ally and claim the northern land of Israel. Josiah died, either in battle or by treachery, at the hands of Necho (2 Kings 23:28-30), for the biblical text merely said that Necho killed Josiah at Megiddo. Perhaps Josiah thought he could oppose the mighty Egyptians because he was the righteous king, and the Deuteronomistic History declared that Israelites would not be defeated in battle, if they were faithful to Yahweh. Joshua's victory over Sisera and Jabin was at Megiddo, maybe Josiah thought he could win there also! His death discredited Deuteronomic Reform in the minds of many.

Judahites may have seen the defeat of Josiah as a sign that the other gods were angry, since the people had been worshipping Yahweh exclusively. They turned to a host of deities once more for protection during the next generation. People diversified their divine stock-portfolio of viable gods. Jeremiah, for example, recalled how people adamantly defended their veneration of the goddess Asherah. Deuteronomic Reformers continued to argue for reform, and Jeremiah was their best advocate, but they no longer had a royal patron or much of an audience. Only in exile would the Jews turn again to their ideas, for only the Deuteronomist History could explain why Judah was exiled from the land.

# Jeremiah

Jeremiah was called to be a prophet against his will and sent to a people who did not wish to hear his words. He proclaimed Deuteronomic values to people who blamed those policies for national defeat, and he was rejected as a false prophet. He was called to live a celibate lifestyle (extremely unusual for Jews) and told to neither rejoice at weddings nor to weep at funerals, for how could he engage in such activities while the fate of the nation hung in the balance? He spent his life trying to save Judah, but was ignored; he was accepted as a true prophet and vindicated only when Jerusalem was destroyed, but then his prophetic mission had failed. We speak of the tragic figure of Jeremiah, the weeping prophet, and we call a tragic lament a "Jeremiad."

We know about Jeremiah's life because of biographical details in the book, presumably provided by Baruch, scribe and friend of Jeremiah. Jeremiah 1-33 contained oracles in narrative context, chapters 34-45 were biographical accounts, and chapters 46-52 were oracles against the nations, appended in the last stages of the book's growth. Jeremiah commissioned Baruch to write a copy of his oracles (Jeremiah 36:1-4) for king Jehoiakim. Though destroyed by the king, Baruch rewrote them, and this might have become the first of several editions of the book of Jeremiah. We suspect this first edition might have been our present Jeremiah 1-25, especially with the reference in Jeremiah 25:13 to "everything written in this book," implying that chapter 25 was near the end of "this book." We suspect that later Deuteronomistic editors produced the final work.

In Jeremiah 1:5 Yahweh declared that Jeremiah was called to be a prophet in the womb, and in Jeremiah 1:1 we are told that Jeremiah's call was the thirteenth year of king Josiah (626 BCE). Either 626 BCE was the year of Jeremiah's birth or the year when he first gave oracles. Most textbooks say he first gave oracles then and was relatively quiet during the era of the Deuteronomic Reform. I believe he was born in 626 BCE and really did not function until the reign of Jehoiakim around 609 BCE, at which time he became an advocate of the discredited Deuteronomic Reform movement. Jehoiakim (609-597 BCE) was a poor king, a puppet ruler, installed by Necho, deserving of the judgment oracles Jeremiah directed at him (2 Kings 23:30-36).

An early oracle of Jeremiah proclaimed that the Temple would be destroyed unless people repented. This attacked the concept of the unconditional covenant, proclaimed by Isaiah in the past, and Jeremiah was subsequently arrested and almost executed (Jeremiah 26:8-24). It would not be the last time he would be beaten and imprisoned (Jeremiah 19:1-20:2). Good theology in one era can become bad, if it is used inappropriately in another era. Jeremiah found himself reacting against the message of Isaiah, which was being misused in his day.

Jehoiakim switched to the Babylonian side in 605 BCE after Nebuchadrezzer defeated Necho at Carchemish. (The real spelling of his name is Nebuchadrezzar, not Nebuchadnezzar, as the book of Daniel has it. Daniel reflects the later Aramaic vocalization of the 2nd century BCE.) Later Jehoiakim revolted against Babylonian vassalage, but he died before Babylonians seized the city, and his son Jehoiachin had the misfortune of being dragged into exile in the first deportation to Babylon in 597 BCE. Jehoiachin languished in prison until 561 BCE, and Jews perceived him as a suffering servant figure for the entire nation. Zedekiah became king in his stead (597-586 BCE). He, too, revolted in later years, and in 587-586 BCE the Babylonian siege ended with the destruction of Jerusalem and further deportation of exiles to Babylon.

Because Jeremiah advocated submission to Babylon during this era, he was regarded as a traitor by his people (Jeremiah 21:1-14). He believed Babylon to be Yahweh's tool to punish Judah for sin, and for this at various times he was almost killed, imprisoned, and placed under house arrest. Jeremiah criticized Judahite kings because of their poor leadership and their oppression of the poor. He attacked Jehoahaz (Jeremiah 22:10-12), Jehoiakim (Jeremiah 22:13-19), Jehoiachin (Jeremiah 22:20-30), and Zedekiah (Jeremiah 21:1-22:10). (He was fair, he criticized everyone!) In the eyes of many he was a traitor to the nation, and his call for submission to Babylon only further antagonized people. After the fall of Jerusalem, Babylonians allowed him to stay in Jerusalem (Jeremiah 39:1-43:7), but after the assassination of the Babylonian appointed governor, Gedeliah, Baruch and Jeremiah both were taken to Egypt for their safety.

**Message of Jeremiah**: Jeremiah assaulted the worship of foreign gods, social injustice, and the personal immorality of his age, an era when the social institutions of Judah were crumbling. The age after Josiah saw a wholesale return to polytheistic ways. People were confident that Yahweh would never forsake them, and Jeremiah attacked this false security, especially in the Temple Oracle (Jeremiah 7, 26). He declared that because they came to the Temple after oppressing the poor, they had "become a den of robbers" (Jeremiah 7:11), words quoted by Jesus when chasing moneychangers out of the Temple.

Jeremiah spoke to a stubborn generation, so to get their attention he sometimes acted out his oracles. He bought a linen waistcloth, wore it, hid it in a local stream (not the Euphrates, as some think), several days later displayed the rotten cloth, and declared this was how the people of Judah looked to Yahweh (Jeremiah 13:1-11). He paraded in Jerusalem wearing a yoke for oxen to symbolize that they would be taken captive to Babylon. When a false prophet of hope, Hananiah, broke his yoke as a counter-sign that Yahweh would return the exiles deported in 597 BCE, Jeremiah paraded the next day with a metal yoke to counter Hananiah's symbolic gesture (Jeremiah 27:1-21, 28:1-17). He sent oracles written on a scroll to king Zedekiah (Jeremiah 36:1-32), for presumably the written word gave more power to the oracles. He smashed a clay pot, in the same way a potter eliminated a defective pot, to symbolize how Yahweh would destroy Jerusalem (Jeremiah 19:1-5). Symbolic oracles were designed to grab the attention of the people, for the people believed an oracle would have double power if it were acted out. They viewed these oracles as divinatory curses. Jeremiah did not see his oracles this way, and stated clearly that he was a messenger, not a creator of magical oracle-curses, but he did not shrink from using theatrics to get his message across.

The book of Jeremiah contained the prayers, or laments, or confessions of Jeremiah, his personal prayers to Yahweh (Jeremiah 11:18-12:6, 15:10-21, 17:14-18, 18:18-23, 20:7-12, 20:14-18). Readers herein observe the inner struggle between the prophet and his God. Jeremiah spoke in bold and scandalous terms: "Cursed be the day on which I was born! . . . Cursed be the man who brought the news to my father, saying, 'A child is born to you, a son, . . .' Why did I come forth from the womb to see toil and sorrow, and spend my days in shame?" (Jeremiah 20:14-15, 18). "O Lord, you have enticed me, and I was enticed; you have overpowered me, and you have prevailed" (Jeremiah 20:7). The word for "prevail" can also mean "rape." Why did Baruch, or a later editor of the book, allow us to hear and read these violent words of Jeremiah? Yahweh accepted Jeremiah's rage, for it was part of the divine-human relationship. Anger comes from suffering, and the suffering of humanity is something with which Yahweh identifies (as we shall see in Job). The confessions told the audience that Jeremiah ought not to be put on a pedestal because he was a prophet. (Religious people of any age should not put their religious leaders on pedestals, or place themselves on pedestals before people if they are religious leaders.) Even though he was a prophet, he was still human. Furthermore, his earthy way of speaking to Yahweh can be viewed as a model of prayer life for Jews. When they hurt, the people of God can call upon God and express their pain and anguish. We find the same message in the Lament Psalms, the book of Job, the prayer of Jesus in the garden, and the cry upon the cross, "My God, My God, why have you forsaken me?" (Mark 15:34). Commentators have noted the similarities between the language of Jeremiah and the words of the Lament Hymns, and they have debated as to which corpus of literature might have influenced the other.

Jeremiah became a prophet of hope after the fall of Jerusalem in 586 BCE, when all had despaired and finally accepted the truth of his judgment oracles. The hope oracles of Jeremiah were found scattered in Jeremiah 30-34, a small section of the book, called "the Little Book of Consolation." Famous images appeared in this part of the book. First, after the time of judgment, God will break the yoke on Judah's neck (Jeremiah 30:5-9). Second, there will be a restoration (Jeremiah 30:12-22, 31:1-14, 16-20). Third, a new age will come in which "virgin Israel" will experience a "new thing on earth: a woman protects a man" (Jeremiah 31:21-22). Fourth, the covenant will be transformed into a "new covenant" which will be no longer external to the hearts of people (Jeremiah 31:31-34). This motif was not used by post-exilic traditions, which preferred the image of the "renewed covenant." But the motif emerged with a prophet who spoke of the "new covenant in my blood" (Matthew 26:28). Fifth, the exile will not be permanent; it will end after 70 years (Jeremiah 29:10-14). The math for 586-539 BCE does not yield 70 years, but Jeremiah may have alluded to the symbolism of a person's full lifetime--70 years. The returnees would be a completely separate generation; the old generation had to die off completely. (Jews rededicated the Second Temple on the 70th anniversary of the fall of Jerusalem, 586-516 BCE. Maybe that was the reason for the number, or perhaps they waited until 516 BCE to fulfill Jeremiah's oracle.). Sixth, Jeremiah bought land of a deceased relative, the field at Anathoth, and paid the full price for it. During the siege of Jerusalem, he probably could have paid much less, but he chose to pay full price to demonstrate the land would someday be worth that value again (Jeremiah 32:6-15).

# Conclusion

Judah moved tragically toward its own self-destruction as Israel had done more than a century prior. Deuteronomic Reform sought to change the country, but the people turned their backs on that movement. For all of Jeremiah's warnings the nation ultimately fell. The vision of Jeremiah weeping upon the walls of Jerusalem is tragic, for his mission failed, and his people were destroyed. But he had sown the seeds of hope with his later oracles, and his message and tragic life would become a symbol to be remembered for millennia. His powerful message and tragic experiences suffered for the sake of his message became an inspiration for religious spokespersons throughout the ages. Pre-exilic Yahwism would transform into post-exilic Judaism; Israelites and Judahites would become Jews, and monotheism would triumph.

During or after exile people recalled the Deuteronomistic traditions. Deuteronomy and the Deuteronomistic History were expanded, respected by Jewish leaders and the people, and became the first corpus of sacred literature for the Jews. Within a short time the books and Genesis, Exodus, Leviticus, and Numbers were placed before the Deuteronomistic History as an introduction. The books of Joshua through 2 Kings functioned as a political or national history, but with the addition of the first four books of the Pentateuch the entire collection became the history of a people, a "salvation history." Today we call entire complex of Genesis through 2 Kings the Primary History.

# Bibliography

Joseph Blenkinsopp. *A History of Prophecy in Israel*. Rev. Ed. Louisville, KY: Westminster John Knox, 1996.

Richard Elliott Friedman. *The Exile and Biblical Narrative*. Harvard Semitic Monographs 22. Chico, CA: Scholars Press, 1981.

Steven McKenzie. *The Trouble with Kings: The Composition of the Books of Kings in the Deuteronomistic History*. Supplements to Vetus Testamentum 42. Leiden: Brill, 1991.

Mayes, A. D. H. *The Story of Israel Between Settlement and Exile*. London, 1983.

Richard Nelson. *The Double Redaction of the Deuteronomistic History*. Journal for the Study of the Old Testament Supplement Series 18. Sheffield, Eng.: JSOT Press, 1981,

Brian Peckham. *The Composition of the Deuteronomistic History*. Harvard Semitic Monographs 35. Atlanta, GA: Scholars Press, 1985.

Leo Perdue and Brian Kovacs, eds. A Prophet to the Nations. Winona Lake, IN: Eisenbrauns, 1984.

David Petersen. *The Prophetic Literature*. Louisville, KY: Westminster John Knox, 2002.

Gerhard von Rad. *The Message of the Prophets*. Trans. D. M. G. Stalker. New York, NY: Harper and Row, 1967.

Moshe Weinfeld. *Deuteronomy and the Deuteronomic School*. Winona Lake, IN: Eisenbrauns, 1992.

# *Chapter* **6**

# The "Settlement"

Reading: Joshua 1-11,24,Judges 1-12,17-21

## Entrance into the Land

The people Israel needed land to become a nation and fulfill the ancient promises to the ancestors. Entrance into the arable land of Palestine naturally followed the Exodus and was likewise a sign of divine grace. Israel recalled the settlement of the land in the books of Joshua and Judges. In Joshua the conquest process was characterized as violent and swift, as the Israelites first conquered Jericho and Ai, then experienced victories in the south and the north of Palestine. Joshua distributed the land to the tribes and commissioned them to finish the process of conquest.

This ideal picture of a conquest, however, is undercut by many hints in the biblical text. Israel's settlement occurred more with the assimilation of various peoples, and the book of Joshua recalls the absorption of the Gibeonites, the Shechemites, and even the family of Rahab the harlot in Jericho. Canaanites in the land and the in-coming Joshua people slowly blended into a single people, the Israelites. Joshua probably led only a small group; the vast majority of later Israelites were descended from folk already in Palestine who slowly and unconsciously become Israel. The majority of the people in Palestine in the early years did not really know who they were other than being members of their local village and the tribal region around them. Hence, we should be cautious about contrasting Canaanites with Israelites, since they are the same people. Canaanite actually was the term used by the biblical authors to describe those people in the land and their religious customs, and the biblical authors wished for later Israelites to distinguish themselves from that culture. "Canaanites" would be people who held to some form of the old values of the second millennium BCE Palestinian culture. These people generally lived in the lowlands, not the highlands, and were not devotees of Yahweh. Canaanite was a term sometimes used by Egyptians and Mesopotamians to describe anyone who lived in the land of Palestine. Lowland Palestinians did not use the term to describe themselves; they characterized themselves often by city allegiance. We often use the term Canaanite to compare so-called "Israelite" and "Canaanite" cultural and religious values of the first millennium BCE, but we are really describing the worldview Israel left behind (Canaanite) as they became increasingly monotheistic (Israelite).

Archaeologists have given us much to consider as we speak about the invasion or the settlement process. Since the early 1980's more than three hundred small agricultural villages in the highlands of central and northern Palestine have been studied with special attention to those levels that represent the 13th through the 11th centuries BCE. These villages were built next to good farmland and water sources on virgin sites. Prior to 1200 BCE most people lived in the lowlands, but after 1200 BCE population increased dramatically in these highland villages. The population of Palestine, as deduced from the increased number and size of these villages, appears to have grown from 12,000 in 1200 BCE to about 75,000 by 1050 BCE. Notably in these sites pig bones are lacking, an indicator that these people were either Israelites or some form of proto-Israelites. The age prior to 1200 BCE is called the Late Bronze Age (1550-1200 BCE), thereafter we call it the Iron Age. Small temples, shrines, sanctuaries, and religious objects depicting divine beings appear in sites (mostly in the lowlands) in the Late Bronze Age, but they disappear in the Iron Age. Thus, these villages exhibit simple religious practices, and perhaps were "aniconic," that is, they made no images of god (or seldom did, we may have a few examples). They may have been aniconic because they were poor. Nevertheless, prohibition of images of God could be a sign for us of Israelite identity.

The material dwelling of these people can be characterized. They lived in four room homes, sometimes two levels, with a U shaped courtyard. Animal shelters were on the first level; the humans lived on the second level. Houses were grouped by twos, threes, or fours. This indicates to archaeologists that a single building housed a nuclear family, the collected buildings contained the extended family (bet-ab, "house of the father"), and the entire village might constitute a clan. The houses were all the same size, indicating that no one family was elite; egalitarianism was the pattern of social existence. The same distinctive pottery appears in all the villages; most often we find collar rimmed jars, which are used for food storage. These were simple farming villages, engaging in domestic production with little or no trade with outsiders. The villages lacked walls or any defenses, implying that their existence was primarily peaceful or that they did not fear war. The society appears acephalous, that is, there were no leaders, and no real classes.

Greater numbers of people were able to live in the highlands due to new technological innovations. These highlanders plowed the ground in terraced fashion, which made it possible to farm highland soil without erosion. Cisterns were plastered or coated with lime, which meant they could go deeper to get down to the water table up in the hilly regions. Slowly at first iron made its appearance in these villages, and by 900 BCE iron was more common. Iron on plow tips made farming the rocky highland soil much more feasible and permitted population growth concomitant with food production or "agricultural intensification." An interesting item of discovery was an abecedary from the highland village of 'Izbet Sartah. Someone could write in this early period. The presence of an alphabet indicates we have an exercise tablet that implies some form of instruction occurred already in this early period. Some scholars believe that this means written literature might have been possible already in the monarchic period after 1050 BCE.

All this evidence feeds into the debate concerning the nature of Israel's settlement, and the evidence favors a primarily peaceful process. The archaeological evidence also dovetails nicely with descriptions of life provided for us with the accounts in the books of Judges and 1 Samuel. So, in general, archaeology is helpful is fleshing out of the life of the people recalled in those narratives.

**The Old Palestinian ("Canaanite") View of Reality:** Religious beliefs and practices tell us much about a society's view of the world. Second millennium BCE Palestinian religion provides insight for us into the overall cultural worldview of the people in Palestine, whose descendants would evolve into Israelites. They worshipped El, the father of the gods, and Asherah, his consort, as well as Ba'al or Baal, the god of fertility, and Anat, his sister and consort. People associated these gods with forces of nature and the dynamics of agriculture. Baal was god of the storm that brought the much-needed rain in the spring. He resembled the storm god, Indra in India, as well as Enlil and Marduk in Mesopotamia. Anat was the goddess of war and love (the two go together in goddesses), comparable to Kali in India and both Inanna and Ishtar of Mesopotamia.

Myths discovered at Ugarit in north Phoenicia (modern day Lebanon) from the second millennium BCE provide several stories, one of which related how Baal fought Yam (the sea, the rainy winter season) and won, and then he confronted Mot (the desert, death, the underworld, the dry summer). Baal was taken to the underworld (perhaps reflecting how the vegetation of the spring gave way to the arid summer), but eventually he was rescued by Anat when she cut up Mot in a process of winnowing, which appears to be the act of fall harvesting. The stories either depicted the seasons or long periodic cycles of drought and fertility over several years. These stories reveal the cyclic pattern of the heavenly realm that affects or predetermines the cycles of life here on earth. Sedentary people often view reality in such cyclic terms.

Religious ceremonies re enacted the great events in the realm of the gods to insure fertility on the earth. The sexual activities of the gods were repeated in the cult to maintain contact with the divine realm so as to bring strength, fertility, and knowledge. Devotees participated in sexual activity with other people (some of whom were slaves) and even animals, who symbolized various deities in the divine realm. Such activity brought participants into "contact" or communion with the divine power and thus released the forces of fertility. Sacrifice offered with these rituals strengthened their power and effectiveness, and the most powerful sacrifice was human sacrifice. This worldview typified thought in ancient Egypt, Mesopotamia, India, China, and the New World. This worldview began to weaken after 3000 BCE with the rise of the state and literacy, and it declined especially by the late second millennium BCE among intelligentsia, but many of its intellectual assumptions were still accepted when the Israelites appeared on the scene. Scholars debate the extent to which such sexual practices and human sacrifice were practiced; a few critical scholars aver that sexual activity was not as frequent as biblical and later classical texts imply. But the biblical historians made this an important part of their critique of the older religious practices.

The old view of reality saw great fixed patterns in nature and society repeating in pre-determined fashion like the seasons. Human social order was viewed as fixed by the gods from eternity, including social classes. As the gods in the heavens were arranged in three hierarchical classes, so people were placed into similar castes or classes on earth and they had to accept their status in life. The lives of individuals also were fated in terms of personal destinies and could be predicted by the appropriate forms of divination. This deterministic view of society and humanity also began to break down by the beginning of the first millennium.

In the ancient world, but particularly in Palestine, the king and the warrior caste constituted the upper class along with the priests. (In India, the Brahmin priests rose to higher status than the nobility so that there were four castes in India.) Class identity was hereditary with virtually no upward mobility, though you could fall into debt and lose class status. Kings collected wealth by taxation and controlled distribution from a central storehouse in the city or fort. In times of famine, distribution was provided for the poor, but usually the king and his warriors lived in sumptuous style off of this stored wealth. Chariots and bronze or iron implements of war were owned exclusively by the warrior class, thus assuring the king's position of power. Palestinian cities were fortified citadels located in the fertile agricultural valleys. The king, his warriors, city bureaucrats, traders, artisans, priests, and other professionals resided inside the city walls, while the peasants lived in un-walled villages or "daughter-villages" in the surrounding land. The king controlled the surrounding land because he offered protection to the villages from outsiders, bandits, and foreign elements, and the villages supplied agricultural surplus for life in the walled city. A small middle class in the cities composed of merchants and craftsmen provided the king with additional revenue through taxes on their trade. Such merchants could become wealthy or bad economic times might force them into the lower classes or debt-slavery, just as the village peasants might experience. There was downward social mobility in these societies, but no upward mobility, until ultimately the society would collapse.

From 1550 to 1150 BCE Egypt ruled and imposed heavy tribute upon Palestinian cities in the lowlands. Egyptians took many prisoners of war back to Egypt, as well as native populations, and resettled them there to prevent rebellion against Egyptian rule in Palestine. Added to this were slaves the Egyptians demanded from Palestinian princes as tribute. In the 15th century BCE alone Pharaoh Thutmosis III claimed to have taken 7300 prisoners from Palestine, and his son, Amenhotep II, claimed 89,600. Some of these people returned to Palestine in the Moses-Joshua group and probably in many other groups that escaped from Egypt over the years. They merged into Israel and identified with the Exodus narrative told by the Joshua group. Egyptian rule and harsh rule of local city kings in Palestine eroded the middle class and forced many people into debt-slavery. This weakening of Palestinian society paved the way for the success of the Joshua people. Palestinian peasants paid heavy taxes to the city lords, who in turn provided tribute to Egypt. Peasants were subject to military conscription, their land could be seized, and when they took out loans from the temple or the palace, interest rates ranged from 33%

to 67%. (Interest rates were high, because when merchants took out loans their high rate of profit enabled repayment.) Unable to repay a loan for seed or tools, the poor peasant sold members of his family and ultimately himself into debt slavery to the king, priests, or rich merchants. Children might become servants in the king's palace, or ritual prostitutes in the Temple, as perhaps Rahab of Jericho might have been (which would explain her willingness to join the Joshua movement).

When peasants could no longer endure this situation, they might flee to the hills or the lands east of the Jordan. Neither area could sustain a large population, for farming was difficult and only pastoralism was feasible in the highlands or the arid steppe lands. Runaway peasants uprooted from their land were called "Habiru" or "Hapiru," especially when they engaged in outlaw activity. The term referred to social status, not ethnic identity, so we do not equate them with later Israelites. They preyed upon the trade caravans and weakened cities with raids. Some of them "retribalized" to become pastoralists, that is, they assumed the characteristics of tribal groups with kinship structures. We believe many of them slowly merged into Israel. In fact, the Moses-Joshua group was just such a people, escaped slaves who "retribalized" under Moses in the wilderness. Their story of escape from pharaoh very likely appealed to peasants in Palestine who also experienced Egyptian rule, and sometimes fled from it into the highlands or across the Jordan River (which would remind them of the sea crossing of the slaves). Also attentive to the Exodus story would be Palestinians returning from Egypt in other small refugee groups. The Moses-Joshua group attracted many allies. The name Israel may have belonged to a group already in Palestinian who became allies with the Moses-Joshua people, for the name of the god El was in the name Israel. The biblical authors simply projected the name Israel back earlier into history and attributed it to the Moses-Joshua group before they came into the land. We debate whether there is any connection between the word, "Habiru" and "Hebrew." "Habiru" means "freebooter," while "Hebrew" means "one who crosses over." (Could this have meant "cross" over the Jordan River as a refugee or one entering the land?) However, occasionally "Hebrew" denoted a poor, landless person, especially in the early texts. That lends supports equation of the two terms.

The Moses-Joshua group was small in relation to the various Palestinians who joined the movement over the years. Cultural artifacts found by archaeologists in early Israelite villages, for the most part, reflect a great deal of continuity with the prior cultural material of the Bronze Age and the older Palestinians or Canaanites. But the Moses-Joshua group, or some group of people coming into the land, brought in a few distinctive characteristics. Archaeology indicates that in those early highland villages where "Israel" arose one may observe the following: 1) lack of pig bones, which most conspicuously distinguished these people from lowlanders, 2) a distinctively constructed and simple four-room house, which archaeologists variously suggest may have come in from outside the land, or may have originated out of older lowland dwellings, or may have been inspired by pastoralists who already lived in the land, and 3) a fairly distinctive type of clay pottery, which may have been brought into the land or may have evolved out of predecessor pottery types within the land. Though there may be debate over the origin of some of these cultural characteristics, they do blend together to create the typical archaeological evidence that earmarks a village as Israelite in the early Iron Age (1200-1050 BCE). Archaeology indicates a tremendous growth in population in this era, perhaps from 12,000 to 75,000, which indicates not only that living conditions in the highlands created a population expansion, but also that some new people did enter from outside the land.

Overall, most Palestinians living in the valleys were a sedentary people who lived either in walled cities or villages and farms around the cities, though a few lived in the highlands as pastoralists. In the valleys trade and taxation produced surplus wealth for the upper classes, the king theoretically owned all the property, taxed the people, and imposed tariffs upon trade caravans passing through the region. There was a gap between rich and poor, and Egyptian wars and rule over Palestine widened that gap. By the end of the Bronze Age (1200 BCE), society was crumbling, ready to give way to the newly emerging Israelite society. Israelite society arose in the highlands with some cultural distinctiveness, although in many ways it maintained continuity with the old culture.

**Israelite View of Reality:** Israel emerged with different perspectives and values, though six centuries passed before they took the form we find in the Bible. Old Canaanite culture slowly evolved into the Israelite culture, and the new worldview emerged among Jews only by the time of the Babylonian Exile. In this new Israelite worldview, human events, such as the Exodus and Sinai experiences, were more paradigmatic than the forces of nature and the great cyclic patterns of the world. Israelites did not ignore nature, for Yahweh was still viewed as a storm deity as well a social deity. The Israelites and Jews saw human events as singular and non-repeatable, so if events did not repeat endlessly, then society was not fixed and determined. Instead, humans lived in a world with freedom to make decisions and were morally obligated to take responsibility for their actions. Laws emphasized social ethics and morality as more important than sacrifice and cult. Legal codes indeed contained cultic regulations, but the practices were "historicized." Thus, old agrarian Palestinian festivals took on historical meaning for Israel: Passover and Unleavened Bread festivals recalled the Exodus, the spring harvest festival became the Festival of Weeks and recalled the entrance into the land, and the fall harvest festival became the Festival of Tabernacles that recalled the wilderness wanderings. The older law-code in Exodus 34, the Ritual Dodecalogue, used the old agrarian names, but in Deuteronomic Law, the later historical names were used. Overall, fertility rites decreased in importance for the emerging Israelite culture, as social rather than cultic behavior was seen to be important.

Israelites idealized pastoral cultural values, even though most people who joined the Israelite movement were originally farmers, and in later years the economic life-style of most Israelites was sedentary farming. It is worth reviewing human cultural evolution at this point. Prior to 9000 BCE people were hunters and food gatherers. After 9000 BCE in the Neolithic Era people settled into small villages and farmed in the highlands of the Near East, and by 6000 BCE they slowly moved into the river valleys of Egypt and Mesopotamia for access to water for irrigation. Pastoralism developed out of village populations only after animals had been domesticated. Pastoralists or semi-nomads withdrew from settled society into marginal areas, arid steppes, or rocky highlands with their flocks increasingly after 4000 BCE. Unlike true nomads, who had no livestock, pastoralists often maintained trade connections with villages and cities. If they moved in circumscribed fashion around cities, we speak of them as "enclosed nomads." Urban leaders often tried to coerce pastoralists to settle down under the control of the urban center so they could have access to the meat, milk, and hides of pastoralist flocks. This is what the people of Shechem wished Jacob and his sons to do in Genesis 34. City dwellers often took economic advantage of the pastoralists in trade. Pastoralists would chaff under this control and silently sneak away from the city environs, which may have been the actions of some of the pastoralist groups who came out of Egypt to join Israel.

Pastoral society was built on tribal or kinship structures, so that the language of familial structures was used to describe society. They had tribes instead of states in their society. New people could be absorbed into this large "family." Unlike the territorially based old Palestinians or Canaanites of the second millennium BCE, the Israelites had tribal bonds that could transcend geographic limitations. While Canaanite regions were limited to the valleys in Palestine, Israelite tribal groups linked up throughout the highlands and across the entire country. Hence, Israelites unified Palestine, while the old Canaanites never did. In tribal groups significant wealth (land, flocks, water rights) was held in common by the whole community, at least in the early years. Theft would be the selfish use of communal goods! There was little job specialization, hence no class of soldiers, craftsmen, or merchants existed in pastoral society, all took part in conflict, even women, and the daily tasks of life were shared equally by all. Equality existed between all people, and women had greater rights. Gaps between rich and poor did not exist; wealth was shared by people in the community, first according to need and then according to accomplishment. We suspect that people withdrew from valley cities to the Israelite pastoralist and village communities in the highlands for the benefits of this lifestyle.

Early Israelites were highland pastoralists, escaping slaves, independent villagers living in a few highland villages free from urban control, and people newly escaped from the Palestinian cities in the lowlands. They all were hostile toward the urban cities with their social structures and ready to hear the message of the Moses-Joshua group. Social values of emerging highland Israelites communities probably appealed to more people than the religious values did. In the first six centuries of their existence, Israelites were held together more by a loose social identity than a religious identity. During the Babylonian Exile the religious self-definition became important, and from that time onward these people would be defined by their religious beliefs. Hence, we call them Jews (religious identity) after the exile, while they are Israelites and Judahites (political identity) before then. As Israel emerged in the highlands out of various groups, they maintained a pastoral identity. They used kinship terminology (the "tribes of Israel"), lived in unfortified villages, maintained an anti-urban polemic, distinguished themselves from those people in the lowlands (whom they later called Canaanites), and their oral legal tradition reflected the pastoralist goals of political, social, and economic equality. The laws in the Covenant Code in the 8th century BCE tried to recall those early values.

# The Conquest

Joshua 1-12 and 23-24 contained idealized views of the conquest as a total defeat of the various peoples of the land by Joshua. This portrayal reflected the values of the Deuteronomists, but those same historians included enough memories in the biblical texts for us to sense that the conquest process was more complex. The Deuteronomists portrayed the conquest as a violent war, but it really was a symbolic description of the conflict between old Canaanite culture and the new ethos of Israel. Joshua eradicated the Canaanites in the story, but the narratives really encouraged a spiritual holy war in the hearts of later Judahites and Jews in exile. Canaanites symbolized old social and religious values that the audience must leave behind to embrace the Law of Yahweh, monotheism, and a just society. Joshua narratives do not deceive; they idealize a small invasion into a symbolic conquest of all Palestine. For too many years American Christians have appealed to imagery in the Bible, especially the Joshua conquest, to justify militarism, especially wars with American Indians. The intent of the biblical authors was to describe symbolic spiritual war, not real war. Critics of the Bible point to the primitive morality of Joshua's "holy war." But the morality is primitive only if the text describes actual warfare, which it does not.

**The Joshua Traditions:** In the narrative Joshua and Israel crossed the Jordan, which had stopped flowing, in similar fashion to Moses and the sea crossing, which was a literary attempt to unify the two memories of Exodus and land entrance. Joshua's troops took Jericho and Ai in dramatic fashion and then won battles over coalitions of their Canaanite foes in raids to the north and the south (Joshua 10-12). Joshua assigned the conquered land to the tribes and commanded them to finish the conquest, but the book of Judges depicted the failure of Israelites to do this.

A careful reading of the Joshua accounts reveals that Joshua's conquest was not national, but local, for all the conquered sites mentioned lie in the tribal area of Benjamin. The Joshua story may spring from local tribal memories, and it may have been one of the few times when there was combat. Joshua was idealized perhaps by the Elohist and later by Deuteronomists to be the ideal king who foreshadowed kings like David, Hezekiah, and Josiah. Josiah was king when the Deuteronomistic History was crafted, and perhaps the audience was supposed to see his connection to Joshua. The Joshua group was very small, for when 36 men died in the battle at Ai, they mourned a great defeat. These are small casualties for a large army, unless Joshua's army was really only around 600 to a 1000 people, the same size as the exodus group under Moses. Archaeological research implies that Jericho and Ai were not inhabited when Joshua's people arrived. Perhaps, these cities were held by small forces from another city. The name Ai means "ruin," which was not a real name for a city. Since the site was in ruins since 2200 BCE, the original name had been forgotten. Joshua's conquest probably was a large razzia or raid against small military forces. It has been suggested that the memory of the destruction of the city in the third millennium BCE may have endured as a separate tale woven into the Joshua traditions at some stage in the development of these accounts.

The narratives spoke of people joining the Joshua movement, including both the cities of Gibeon (Joshua 9) and the larger city of Shechem (Joshua 24). Shechem was reported to the Egyptians two centuries prior as a renegade town to which Habiru outlaws fled. (This may be evidence of a connection between Habiru and Hebrew.) People in Shechem could relate to the Joshua group. In Joshua 24, Joshua made a covenant with Shechem and spoke of their common patriarchal ancestry, but he made no allusion to the Exodus, since the people of Shechem did not share that experience. Even at Jericho some citizens came over to Joshua's side. Rahab and her family may have been a few of the many individuals over the years who joined the Israelite movement.

Interesting tensions abound between the books of Joshua and Judges. Joshua's significant battle with general Sisera and Jabin, king of Hazor (Joshua 11), was attributed to Deborah and Barak years later (Judges 4). Areas taken by Joshua were not controlled by Israelites in the book of Judges. The narratives in Judges show no awareness of Joshua. In Judges, the Israelites were not only dis-unified, they battled each other on occasion. The distinction between Israelites and other people in the land appears more blurred in the book of Judges. One suspects that Joshua presents an idealized view of those early years, while Judges may reflect more the actual state of affairs.

**Modern Historical Reconstruction:** Scholars have tried to reconstruct the fuller story of what happened, recognizing that the book of Joshua is an idealistic interpretation, but acknowledging that Joshua and Judges contain authentic memories of that era.

Three theories have been proposed in the past century: 1) German scholars in the 1920's and 1930's believed that peaceful pastoralists infiltrated Palestine from the Transjordan, then after a number of years they became militarily aggressive, and conflicts gave rise to the memory of military actions recorded in Joshua. 2) In the 1940's and 1950's American archaeologists argued that the conquest was a unified military operation by people from the outside the land, as described in Joshua, and that more cities were taken than the biblical text recorded. 3) In the 1960's and 1970's American scholars used sociological and anthropological models to suggest that Israel arose as Canaanite peasants revolted against their urban kings and withdrew to the highlands. Of these, only the first model is compelling to a few contemporary scholars.

Since 1980, Israeli, American, and German archaeologists excavated a great number of small highland villages, in contrast to earlier archaeological expeditions that excavated the larger walled cities. These villages were more typical of Iron Age Israel (1200-1050 BCE), whereas the large walled fortresses were generally Canaanite cities (Hazor, Shechem, Migiddo, Gezer, and Bethel). Archaeologists and scholars perceived a great continuity between Canaanites of the Late Bronze Age (1550-1200 BCE) and Israelites of the early Iron Age 1200-1050 BCE), with only a few differences to distinguish them at times. They concluded that the vast majority of Israelites emerged gradually and peacefully out of the old Canaanite population. The small Joshua group probably introduced early Yahwistic religion and the name, Yahweh, into the land, but the national name Israel was built upon the divine name El, which implies a possible Canaanite origin for that name and perhaps the earliest form of the tribal confederation. The biblical authors simplified the story by calling the Moses-Joshua people Israelites well before they would have recognized the name. Israel evolved primarily out of a Canaanite population peacefully. Biblical authors had to transform the limited conflict of Joshua's people to a grand, national story for symbolic reasons.

There are several proposed variations on this model: 1) Perhaps, Canaanites peacefully migrated from worn-out cities in the valleys to the highland villages (Peaceful Withdrawal Theory). 2) Perhaps, highland pastoralists settled down to farm once lowland cities collapsed and no longer traded agricultural produce with the highlanders (Internal Nomadic Theory). 3) Perhaps, the Israelite population in the highlands gradually increased under good economic conditions while lowland population decreased (Peaceful Transition

Theory). 4) Perhaps, a gradual merger of pastoralists, bandits (such as in Shechem) or Habiru, and incoming people, such as the Joshua group and others, created the Israelite people (Peaceful Transformation Theory).

All these variations appeal to our current knowledge that the Palestinian highlands of Iron Age I (1200-1050 BCE) could support a larger population due to technological breakthroughs such as highland terracing, lime-coated cisterns, and the eventual use of an iron plowshares. Iron became more available after 900 BCE, and the population of the entire country then began to increase. We must not place too much emphasis upon these technological innovations, as though they were primarily responsible for the emergence of Israel in Iron Age I. Terracing and lime coated cisterns were known in Middle and Late Bronze Age times (2000-1200 BCE), they simply were not used extensively by people living in the valleys. Also, the introduction of iron tools actually came rather late in the settlement process (after 900 BCE), so its initial impact upon Israelite culture was minimal. Highland settlement was not motivated by technology; rather, highland settlement caused the emergence of alternative technology in the ensuing years.

From archaeological evidence and the biblical accounts, we can sequence a number of "events" in our theoretic historical reconstruction:

1. According to Egyptian texts, Habiru were causing trouble for Canaanite cities allied to Egypt around 1400-1350 BCE. One such group of folk was at Shechem, a city that would become allies of the Joshua group in later years.

2. From the book of Judges, we learn about the Kenites, Othnielites, and others, who moved into Judah from the south but were not connected with the Joshua group (Judges 1). Ultimately they became part of the tribe of Judah. They may have entered the land prior to Joshua, and since they were separate from the northern Joshua group, this might explain why Judah and Israel were naturally divided in later years.

3. In 1286 BCE, the Egyptian army under Ramses II was weakened by an indecisive battle with the Hittites in Syria at Kadesh on the Orontes. Egyptian control over Palestine became weaker for the next century, thus possibly permitting the entrance of new peoples into the land and the emergence of new social entities, like Israel. The Egyptian pharaoh, Ramses III (1184-1153 BCE), struggled a century later to prevent Sea Peoples from invading Egypt from Palestine. The Sea Peoples weakened Canaanites along the coastline as they moved southward, and they weakened Egypt's ability to intervene in Palestinian affairs in years thereafter, making it possible for highlanders to develop their communities and expand.

4. According to archaeologists, gradual peaceful infiltration of pastoralists into Galilee occurred between 1225 and 1175 BCE, creating the small Galilean tribes of Asher, Zebulon, Naphtali, and Issachar, although old Egyptian records referred to the tribe of Asher in that region well before that time. It is not clear whether the settlers infiltrated from the steppe land of the Transjordan or withdrew from the valley area where the large city of Hazor was located.

5. The Joshua group seized the tribal area of Benjamin, perhaps bringing the Yahweh worship that eventually unified the diverse groups in Palestine. The covenant in Joshua 24 fits in with the image of such gradual unification.

6. Highlanders in Galilee united with the Joshua tribes a century later, and better connection was possible after the defeat of the king of Hazor at the battle of Megiddo in the valley of Esdraelon. Judges 4-5 recounts the victory by Deborah and Barak, while Joshua 11 claims the battle for Joshua. A few scholars suggest there were two battles a century apart against two kings named Jabin and two generals named Sisera. More logically the battle was attributed to Joshua because elements of Joshua's people united with Deborah and Barak against the lowlanders. This union may have been the beginning of the Israel in the north. Judah and Israel eventually united politically only under David.

7. Sea Peoples from the Aegean and Turkey invaded the coastal regions of Palestine in two waves around 1200 and 1100 BCE and evolved into the Philistines. The Sea Peoples weakened Egyptian control over Palestine and wreaked havoc on Palestinian urban centers. (This may be the destruction in archaeological sites that American archaeologists attributed to incoming Israelites.) Some of these Greek and Anatolian peoples merged into Israel. Because of its name and its movement from the coastal area in the southwest (near Philistia) up to Galilee, the tribe of Dan may have come from the Sea Peoples.

This complex history was not recalled by the Deuteronomists, who simplified the memories and spoke only of Joshua's heroic campaigns, thus making theological, not historical observations. Joshua was projected as a hero to tell a later generation to cast off elements of Canaanite religion and politics in their age as a former generation supposedly once did. The Deuteronomistic account testified to Yahweh's presence with the chosen people of Israel. The crossing of the Jordan paralleled the sea crossing under Moses and was portrayed as a liturgical procession. Jericho fell after the Israelites liturgically paraded around it for seven days. The conquest was "Holy War," which meant that God, not the people did the real fighting. "Holy War" declared that an Israelite should not be tempted by the religion, society, or politics of old Palestinian or Canaanite culture, either in Joshua's age or a later age. That was the sin of Aachen, who took wealth from the fallen city of Jericho, when it was all supposed to be destroyed. The command to destroy everyone and everything was a symbol for changing one's attitude toward life. In real war the Israelites would not have killed everyone, for many people would have joined the Israelite movement. The Deuteronomists called for a "Holy War" of the spirit, which they projected into their past.

# The Judges

Deuteronomists recalled early heroes in Israel called judges, and the Hebrew word for judge, "*sophet,*" meant one who brings justice. It could refer to an elder who rendered legal decisions at the gate of a village, but in a broad sense, it could be someone who heroically brought justice for the oppressed and the nation. Some of the personages in the book seem to have been village elders (Tola, Jair, Ibzan, Elon, and Abdon), and scholars call them "minor judges." Others were military heroes who saved Yahweh's people from foreigners; these were the "major judges." The latter were charismatic warriors, mercenaries, temporary rulers, and, sometimes, foreigners or half-breeds (like Jephthah). After the Deuteronomistic introduction (Judges 2:6-3:6), the book gave great attention to warriors such as Ehud (3:12-30), Deborah and Barak (4:1-5:31), Gideon (6:1-8:35), Abimelech (9:1-57), Jephthah (10:1-12:7), and Samson (12:1-16:31). Of course, the warriors had exciting memories associated with them, unlike courtroom judges. Similar sounding words for "judge" in other Near Eastern languages referred to human rulers at the early second millennium BCE city of Mari in north Mesopotamia, as well as to leaders in first millennium BCE Moab, Phoenicia, and Carthage (a colony of the Phoenician city of Tyre). These "judges" were judicial figures, kings, or ruling members of a council.

**The Book of Judges:** Judges related the story of Israel from the conquest to the monarchy. Scholars believe that the portrayal of Israelite life in Judges was more historical than the book of Joshua. In Judges the Israelites appeared disorganized; they even engaged in civil war. A Deuteronomistic refrain in the book stated, "There was no king in Israel; everyone did what was right in his own eyes," referring to strife and a lack of morality. This probably reflected life in Israel in those early years. We cannot reconstruct the historical sequence of the narratives, since many heroes probably overlapped in time. Othniel's entry into the land (Judges 1:11-13) may have been prior to Joshua's entry, and the victory of Deborah and Barak was the same as that of Joshua 11. There was no clear distinction as who was an Israelite. Shamgar, who worshipped Anat as his name indicated, was a Canaanite who fought the Philistines, a common foe (Judges 3:31). Jephthah, who lived in the Transjordan, was half Israelite and knew little of Israelite values.

The book brought together many types of literature: There were ancient tribal memories, such as the migration of the tribe of Dan (Judges 17-18) and the entrance of small tribal groups into Judah (Judges 1). We have tales of bawdy and humorous heroes, such as Samson who killed Philistines and loved women, Ehud who treacherously assassinated Eglon while he sat on the toilet, Gideon who went into battle with only foolish soldiers who let down their guard when they "lapped like dogs" with their heads in the water, and Jephthah who made an oath and subsequently sacrificed his daughter. There were serious memories of important battles: the victory of Deborah and Barak, and the more sober account of Gideon's defeat of the Midianites with a sizeable army. There was a memory of one who would be king (Abimelech), but failed. His name ("my father is the king") implied that his father, Gideon, was king. Gideon said, "I will not rule, but Yahweh will rule you." Maybe this really meant that Yahweh was the ruler of Israel through Gideon, who was the earthly king. The book of Judges suppressed that memory a little. Judges recalled when human sacrifice was acceptable, for Jephthah made a vow requiring the sacrifice of his daughter. Such a custom would be condemned as hideous among Israelites in later years. This story may have provided for the Deuteronomists an example of the chaos of the era. Some of these stories were put in Judges because the historians could not fit them into the idealized version of the settlement told in Joshua. These tales, such as in Judges 1, help us understand the fuller settlement process.

**Theology of History:** Deuteronomists sequenced the narratives in the book of Judges and provided editorial comments before and after the heroic tales. Their view of history in Judges reflected their understanding of all Israel's history. Judges 2:6-20 described how history moved through five stages: 1) people lived in divine grace with peace and prosperity; 2) they sinned and "did evil in the sight of Yahweh," primarily worshipping other gods; 3) Yahweh brought an oppressor, who conquered them, seizing the land that was Yahweh's gift to them; 4) they repented and called to Yahweh for deliverance; and 5) Yahweh raised up a deliverer who freed them from the enemy and returned them to a state of peace. This pattern was not really located in the actual narratives, but in the editorial framework around each account.

This artificial framework provided commentary on the plight of the Jews exiled in Babylon. They were in Babylon, not because Yahweh was impotent to protect them from Babylonian armies and the Babylonian god, Marduk, but because they had sinned against Yahweh. Yahweh, not Marduk, was responsible for their exile. Deuteronomists recorded a history of the nation that stressed how unfaithfulness brought punishment and foreign conquest of the land. Exile in a foreign land was the ultimate form of conquest. But the narratives held out the hope that as Yahweh had saved them in the past after repentance, repentance and faithfulness again might deliver them from exile.

Even though there is theological agenda in the book of Judges, the material has historical value. It reflected the spirit of the age better than the book of Joshua in its portrayal of anarchy, civil strife, and the lack of Israelite identity. We find hints about the social and economic processes operative in Iron Age I (1200-1050 BCE). The historians led the readers to recognize the need for a king, and how David ultimately met that need. The book described the on-going settlement process, and how unification of the people required the strong authority of a king. The biblical text implied that the Philistines were the greatest threat to Israelite identity, and they could be countered only by a king leading a military force. Hence, David finally subdued the Philistines only after Saul failed. But social historians also point out that early state formation develops for economic reasons, too. Archaeologists sense that Israelites were developing trade relationships with each other at this time. Both economic competition between tribes and the trade connections that pulled them together caused social-political development. As trading links became more well developed, the emergence of a strong chieftaincy or state was necessary to protect and facilitate trade, as well as to avoid outside interference with this economic activity. A foreign power, like the Philistines, might look enviously upon a developing economic area and seek to control it. Archaeologists have discovered evidence of a Philistine presence deep in central Israel at this time. The rise of a king was the necessary corollary of national identity formation.

# Conclusion

The complex process of conquest can be recovered partially as we peer behind the theological agenda of the Deuteronomists. When we penetrate the veils obscuring the past, we identify with the people and the circumstances of their age. We understand better the Deuteronomistic reinterpretation of history; we can focus on why certain traditions and perspectives were recorded. The Deuteronomists were no less astute than we, and their insights into the nature of the divine and the human condition still merit consideration in our age. Conquest traditions spoke of God's presence with an ancient people, if they made the ultimate commitment to that deity. The strength of a people was measured by their faith in God and the caliber of their intellectual and moral values. Failure came when they trusted in themselves rather than in God. Archaeology and a critical reading of the biblical text aid us in reconstructing the history. Israelites arose peacefully; they were an amalgamation of diverse peoples willing to begin anew out of the ashes of the Late Bronze Age. Openness to each made the creation of this new people possible, even though the Deuteronomists chose not emphasize that perspective. We can appreciate how the Israelite ethos arose gradually in the hills of Palestine, and monotheism and fuller Jewish religious values did not arise until the Babylonian Exile.

# Bibliography

Gösta Ahlström. *Who Were the Israelites?* Winona Lake, IN: Eisenbrauns, 1986.

Albrecht Alt. "The Settlement of Israelites in Palestine." *Essays on Old Testament History and Religion.* Trans. R. A. Wilson. Garden City, NY: Doubleday, 1966.

William Dever. *Who Were the Early Israelites and Where Did They Come From?* Grand Rapids, MI: Eerdmans, 2003.

Robert Gnuse. "Israelite Settlement of Canaan: A Peaceful Internal Process." *Biblical Theology Bulletin* 21 (1991): 56-66, 109-117.

David Hopkins. *The Highlands of Canaan.* The Social World of Biblical Antiquity Series 3. Sheffield, Eng.: Almond, 1985.

Philip King and Lawrence Stager. *Life in Biblical Israel.* Library of Ancient Israel. Louisville, KY: Westminster John Knox, 2001.

Paula McNutt. *Reconstructing the Society of Ancient Israel.* Library of Ancient Israel. Louisville, KY: Westminster John Knox, 1999.

Victor Matthews and Donald Benjamin. *Social World of Ancient Israel 1250-587 BCE.* Peabody, MA: Hendrickson, 1993.

Leo Perdue et al, eds. *Families in Ancient Israel.* The Family, Religion, and Culture. Louisville, KY: Westminster John Knox, 1997.

Hershel Shanks, ed. *The Rise of Ancient Israel.* Washington, D.C.: Biblical Archaeology Society, 1992.

# The United Monarchy

Readings: 1 Samuel 1-31, 2 Samuel 1-20, 1 Kings 1-2

## Unified Rule

The Bible presents the history of the monarchy as a sermon to teach moral responsibility to people. Samuel and Kings were a compilation of oral and written traditions brought together in the Deuteronomistic History, and each of these traditions had its own peculiar message, each worth special consideration. Since the Deuteronomistic History as a unified literary work communicated several messages, we must ask how each individual unit fits into the message of that larger work. The monarchy was a necessity brought upon Israelites by economic, social, and political forces, but they saw it as the unfolding of the divine will in tension with human will. Biblical historians knew that monarchy brought both good and bad results. They were interested especially in the conflict between authoritarian kings and idealistic prophets.

The reigns of David and Solomon were an era in which Israel enjoyed a brief period of political unity. In the ancient Near East their regime was relatively small, but for them it was their only moment of glory, and in their theology they anticipated a future age that would restore the golden age of David and Solomon. Yet at the same time the biblical text honestly admitted the evils and limitations of that first unified monarchy.

The United Monarchy arose due to a power vacuum in the political world of the 11th and 10th centuries BCE. The great empires were weakened as the Late Bronze Age ended (1550-1200 BCE). The Hittite Empire in Asia Minor (Turkey) was overrun by invading Sea-Peoples, and Egypt was weakened internally by attacks of those same Sea-Peoples. In Mesopotamia both Assyria and Babylon endured a series of weak kings and the general economic disorder that existed everywhere. Movements of peoples in Greece, Asia Minor, Palestine, and Mesopotamia toppled old regimes and created new centers of economic development. Much of this chaos may have been caused by prolonged drought, which led to crop shortages, famine, and disease. The era from 1200 to 1050 BCE was one of transition when a small kingdom in Palestine could carve out a temporary niche.

Archaeology provides some limited insight into the history during this period. Strangely, very little data comes from the time of David and Solomon; hardly any comes from Jerusalem, where we would expect it. Two answers are given: 1) Levels wherein archaeological remains might be found from the Davidic-Solomon era have been destroyed by later generations of people who reused the material. 2) The Davidic-Solomon kingdom was far less important than the biblical text seems to indicate, Jerusalem was a small center of power for a very insignificant kingdom (some extremely critical scholars have suggested that maybe there was no historical David or Solomon).

Some finds for this era suggest that the kingdom was significant in scope. 1) There were the city gates at Gezer, Hazor, and Megiddo, each with four entry gates in a row and casemate or double city walls. Building these sophisticated structures required a strong central government with resources, especially at all three sites. However, some archaeologists suspect the gates might come from the next century. 2) The description of the Temple in 1 Kings 5-6 conformed closely to 30 other temples unearthed from the 10th and 9th centuries BCE in Syria, Phoenicia, and Palestine. All these buildings exhibit the classic "long room" shape, with two pillars in the front, interlaced wood beams in the stones, and typical artistic features which included the portrayal of cherubim, palm trees, and lion thrones. In many temples the deity was portrayed as enthroned invisibly on the lion thrones, and in the Jerusalem Temple Yahweh was supposedly enthroned invisibly above the cherubim on the Ark of the Covenant. 1 Kings 5 stated that Solomon had the Temple constructed with the help of Hiram of Tyre and his Phoenician workers. This style of temple was unique to this period, so it appears that the description in 1 Kings 5-6 was historically accurate. 3) The Gezer Calendar, an inscription that described the agricultural seasons in Palestine, implies that writing was a skill practice in this era. 4) In the past, archaeologists thought that the stables in the city of Megiddo and the port of Ezion-Geber on the Gulf of Aqaba were built by Solomon. Now we suspect that they were built in the next century.

The story of Saul, David, and Solomon was recalled in the books of 1 and 2 Samuel and the beginning of 1 Kings. Oppressed by the Philistines, Israelites banded together under a king to obtain economic and political independence. The highlands and the coastline of Palestine were economically developing, and the Philistines on the southwest coast sought to control the interior with its developing agricultural wealth. Agriculture was bringing highlanders together in trading relationships and uniting them. Political and military pressure by the Philistines caused the Israelites to draw closer together in political alliance.

Saul was the first king of Israel according to the biblical text. Prior to him, Gideon may have ruled like a king over part of central Israel. Gideon's son, Abimelech, failed miserably as a king, and the kingdom created by Gideon fell apart. The biblical authors probably wished to forget that experience, so they relegated those stories to the book of Judges and made no mention of Gideon's royal rule. Instead, Saul was perceived as the first person to unite Israelites. He was a dauntless hero, like one of the judges, but he was destined to fail, because Israel needed a professional rather than a charismatic leader. With a professional army, an awesome ability to lead, and political savvy, David united Israel and Judah into a political entity. Solomon inherited the empire forged by his father. Despite the memory of Solomon's great wealth and wisdom, he burst the bubble with his ruthless aggrandizement of wealth and building projects.

Kings brought Israel wealth, unity, and security, but also the oppression typical of ancient Near Eastern monarchs. Taxes, forced labor conscription, and expropriation of familial lands became frequent, all the evils their ancestors had fled, both from Egypt and the valleys of Palestinian city-states. Solomon even armed some of the old valley cities, Megiddo, Gezer, and Hazor. Did these sites defend against foreign enemies or the Israelites themselves (since David had several revolts against his rule)? Upon Solomon's death, the northern tribes revolted against his son, Rehoboam, and the land returned to the natural division of Judah and Israel as separate countries. Later Israelites and Jews recalled David's rule as a golden age, and they believed that a future golden age would bring back the glories of David's empire and a "new David" would arise. The United Monarchy inspired many symbols for the vision of a "messianic age," and eventually this imagery would be inherited by Christians, who spoke of Jesus as the new David.

# Kingship as a Social Institution

The period of the judges demonstrated the need for central authority. Economic development brought the need for ruling authority to coordinate economic and political activity. A new Israelite identity was emerging that was different from second millennium BCE Bronze Age Canaanite culture, though Israelites were not conscious of this. Kingship would contribute to the evolution of this new Israelite identity. The Philistines who sought to rule Palestine were different from the old Bronze Age city-states, which relied on their walled cities for defense and did not seek to expand their political influence beyond a well-defined geographical region. Against these old city-states and their armies, charismatic warriors like Deborah and Barak could prevail, but volunteer militia could not battle Philistine forces in prolonged campaigns. This was why Saul and his volunteer army fell in battle, but David prevailed with his professional and mercenary soldiers.

In the past scholars attributed state formation to the United Monarchy. Prior to the monarchy Israelites were loose, dis-unified tribal elements in the highlands of Palestine. Saul's rule appeared to be an early stage of state formation, what anthropologists call a "chieftaincy" rather than an actual state, held together by the commitment of regional leaders to Saul. The kingdom of David and Solomon was considered an actual "state" with bureaucratic structures. But more recent authors prefer to describe the rule of David and Solomon as advanced "chieftaincy," for their kingdom looks more like a feudal lord's rule over a large area with military force. The Bible described Solomon's kingdom as having administrative structures and bureaucracy. But we suspect that his rule was more like a second millennium BCE Bronze Age city state with a bureaucracy only in the capital city, Jerusalem, and which ruled a rather rustic surrounding kingdom with force. The real emergence of a true state leaves archaeological records, such as written inscriptions with economic records, which is evidence of well-developed trade and taxation. We find that evidence only by middle of the 9th century BCE for the northern state of Israel and the late 8th century BCE for the southern state of Judah. Only then do the names of Israel and Judah appear in the records of other foreign nations. The emergence of true states among the Israelite people was late, prior to that time rulers were more like feudal lords. The kingdom of David and Solomon, however, prepared the way for the emergence of more highly developed states in those later centuries.

If we read the biblical text of 1 Samuel, 2 Samuel, and 1 Kings carefully, we discern that the rule of David was rustic. He was the supreme judge for legal appeals for the entire country. His control over the country was very tenuous, as evidenced by several revolts against him. He may have ruled only those cities and towns in which he had garrisoned soldiers. Solomon was remembered for building projects, but they primarily were confined to Jerusalem (the Temple and the royal palace). Buildings previously attributed by archaeologists to Solomon (stables at Megiddo, gates in fortress cities, and a port at Ezion-Geber in the south), now appear to be the work of 9th century BCE Israelite kings in the north, such as Omri and Ahab. David and Solomon ruled a simple kingdom and governed Palestine with a loosely administered rule, but they may have been the first local rulers in Palestine to control in limited fashion both highlands and lowlands.

# Biblical Narratives of the United Monarchy

Scholars have often separated the biblical text into separate cycles of literature that may represent sources used by the Deuteronomists: 1) Samuel and Saul--the Rise of the Monarchy, 1 Samuel 1-15; 2) The Rise of David, 1 Samuel 16-31, 2 Samuel 1-8; 3) The Succession Narrative, 2 Samuel 9-20, 1 Kings 1-2; and 4) the Court History of Solomon, 1 Kings 3-11. Scholars debate the exact division of some of the chapters listed above. All of these cycles may have used royal court annals along with the folk memories.

**Rise of the Monarchy (1 Samuel 1-15):** This section appears to be composed of distinct sources identifiable by their particular perspectives. Each source has seams enabling us to separate and analyze specific ideological and religious perspectives. Perhaps the Deuteronomists wove these received sources, either oral or written, into the larger work of Joshua through Kings. They added material to give a distinct interpretation of the era. As a unity 1 Samuel 1-15 leaves us with an overall impression that Saul was inadequate and David met the needs of the people more effectively, for Deuteronomists portrayed David as the model for a future ideal king.

*Pro-Monarchial Source (1 Samuel 9:1-10:16, 11:1-15, 13:1-7, 16-23, 14:1-52):* These chapters contained an old source that portrayed Saul as a charismatic king similar to the judges. The source may have emerged within a century or so after Saul lived. He was the important personage; Samuel was only a local seer. Saul was a hero, acclaimed king by the people, and old Samuel showed no reluctance to make him king. This source contained archaic memories of the era, especially about Samuel as a seer. These traditions about Saul may have been attached to an early cycle of tales about the judges or "saviors" of Israel, for the language in these chapters is strikingly similar to stories in the book of Judges. The texts reflect early, positive views toward kingship in general. Since the stories recalled how Saul was made king three times, once by Samuel, once by national election, and once after his victory over the Ammonites, there may be sources even within this source, and probably much oral tradition has been lost.

*Ark Narrative (1 Samuel 4-6, 2 Samuel 6)*: These separate fragments about the story of the Ark of the Covenant appear archaic and may have been recounted as a unified tale at some point in time. They may date from a time not long after the Saul traditions. They have been separated into the two different books of Samuel, probably by the Deuteronomistic Historians, and they show how David brought the Ark to a place of honor. The traditions contained an ancient Near Eastern narrative motif about how a national deity may desert his or her people to punish them for sin, usually the failure to properly observe the cult (the "divine abandonment" motif). In the Israelite story the sin was moral failure rather than mere cultic misdemeanors.

The Ark was the sacred box that contained the tablets of the Law and fragments of manna from the wilderness. On the lid of the Ark were cherubim, which in these early years were probably images of winged bulls. Cherubim were viewed as the throne for the invisible presence of Yahweh (though too often Israelites saw Yahweh in the cherubim). In the post-exilic period a reconstructed Ark in the Temple may have used human figures. In the early years the Ark was carried into battle by Israelites as a war-palladium to bring the presence of Yahweh as a divine warrior into the fray and insure victory. The sons of Eli took the Ark into battle to manipulate divine power, so Yahweh let them be defeated and the Ark fell into Philistine hands. The ancients believed that when your sacred objects were captured, your gods were angry and punished you by leaving your country.

The Ark Narrative proclaimed judgment upon Israel. 1 Samuel 1-3 described the sinfulness of Eli and his sons, and by placing these chapters before the Ark Narrative, Deuteronomists emphasized the loss of the Ark as punishment. The portrayal of Hophni and Phineas in the Ark Narrative was not as negative as in 1 Samuel 1-3, so the sequencing done by the historians created the impression of judgment upon the Elides. In turn, Samuel appeared more righteous than the priests, even as a little boy. The Ark caused great havoc and plague among the Philistines, and this motif did not occur in other ancient Near Eastern accounts of "divine abandonment." This motif emphasized Yahweh's power over the other gods and hinted at monotheism. The Ark even caused a pagan god (a statue) to fall off its pedestal. The narrative contained humor, and a falling statue of a foreign god was early monotheistic humor. The Philistines sent the Ark back into Israelite territory where it resided in a small town for years. Finally, David brought it to Jerusalem with a grand ceremony that celebrated the march of Yahweh as ruler and perhaps even divine warrior into the land. By locating the Ark in Jerusalem (2 Samuel 6) David assured that Jerusalem would become the religious center of Israel, and thus enhanced his own position of power. The narrative testified against the sin of manipulating God as well as describing the transfer of its power to David and Jerusalem.

*Samuel Idyll (1 Samuel 1-3)*: This narrative may be dated anywhere in the 8th or 7th centuries BCE. It portrayed the little boy Samuel and his mother, Hannah, as ideal examples of piety. Hannah was barren, and she prayed at Shiloh for a child whom she would dedicate to Yahweh. After Samuel was born, she sang a thanksgiving hymn (1 Samuel 2:1-10), which later inspired the New Testament Magnificat (Luke 1:46-55). True to her promise, she brought Samuel to Shiloh to serve under the old priest, Eli. She named her little child Samuel and said his name meant, "asked of the Lord" (1 Samuel 1:20). Actually, his name meant "name of God," for "asked of the Lord" alluded to Saul's name. This was a little joke, a word pun, by our author, who thereby hinted Samuel would be in authority over Saul, even to the point of stealing his name. As Samuel made and unmade Saul as king, so prophets throughout history should be the authoritative voice of God, not the kings.

Samuel's piety contrasted with the two greedy sons of Eli, whose abuse of their priestly duties was presented as justification for Shiloh's fall and the loss of the Ark (1 Samuel 4-6). A nameless prophet even proclaimed a word of judgment against the house of Eli (1 Samuel 2:27-36) in a section inserted by the Deuteronomists. In Samuel's prophetic call experience, which was recorded in the form of an auditory dream message (1 Samuel 3:1-21), the house of Eli was condemned. The reader senses that the great Samuel, who was a prophet already as a child, would stand as the true authority over Saul. These events justified the eventual transfer of power from Shiloh to Jerusalem, as David made the latter city the new religious center. By placing one set of traditions (1 Samuel 1-3) before another (1 Samuel 4-6), the Deuteronomists spoke about sin and the punishment it brought. They also foreshadowed the destruction of Jerusalem and the Temple by reference to the implied destruction of Shiloh and loss of the Ark.

Samuel was seer, prophet, judge, war leader, and priest, for in those early days, a leader like Samuel did many things, and later traditions projected back to him many institutional offices, as with Moses. Some roles attributed to Samuel did not exist at that time; the Deuteronomists even noted in 1 Samuel 9:9 that the term "prophet" was not used in those days. On the other hand, Samuel performed activities that later would be considered unacceptable: as a seer he engaged in clairvoyance (1 Samuel 9:6-8, 19-20), and he offered sacrifice, which only priests should do. He trained students to be professional prophets (1 Samuel 10:9-13, 19:18-24), whereas the later prophets usually felt their office to be a call from Yahweh, and receiving professional training to induce oracles from Yahweh was considered divination. These traditions about Samuel recall diverse and archaic memories.

*Anti-Monarchical Source (1 Samuel 7-8, 10:17-27, 12, 15)*: These chapters viewed Saul and the institution of kingship in a negative fashion, probably reflecting the bitter experience with Israelite kings over the years. This source was later than the Pro-Monarchical Source, and probably reflected Deuteronomistic editorializing. The people prevailed upon Samuel and Yahweh to give them a "king like the nations," and in so doing, they rejected Samuel and especially Yahweh. Samuel warned the people of the evils of kingship to no avail. Deuteronomistic style permeated these speeches (1 Samuel 8, 12), and they provided theological commentary for the greater Deuteronomistic History.

Like Greek historians in the 5th and 4th centuries BCE, Deuteronomistic Historians communicated essential ideas through artificial speeches spoken by great leaders. Speeches only vaguely recalled what the historical person said; they were vehicles for historians to make editorial comment upon the events of that age. A comparable speech was Solomon's prayer in 1 Kings 8. (The New Testament author of the book of Acts did this with the speeches of Peter, Paul, and Stephen.) The central message of these biblical books was communicated through the speeches.

In this source Samuel was foremost a prophet to whom Saul should be obedient. Samuel served Israel as warrior, judge, prophet, and priest; the popular desire for a king was unnecessary. Saul became king, but his refusal to obey Samuel led to his ultimate downfall, and Saul's disintegration occurred with the inevitability that we observe in tragic Greek figures. The texts hinted at why David had to be the chosen one, for he alone could succeed where Saul failed. The texts also implied that Israel would go into exile someday, if they chose despotic kings over Yahweh's rule.

**The Rise of David (1 Samuel 16 to 2 Samuel 8)**: The second major cycle of stories contained loosely woven legends about David's rise to power. Though we have different versions of the same accounts, scholars cannot separate them into clearly defined sources. Davidic court annals may have been woven together with well-known oral folk tales about the heroic deeds of David. There are doublets, or duplicate accounts, of David's introduction to Saul and Saul's attempts to kill David. But we speak of the cycle as a whole, because we cannot separate the stories as with 1 Samuel 1-15, nor can we observe different theological agenda in the various parts. The stories justified why David succeeded Saul. Parallel narratives in the ancient world justified the usurpation of the throne by an outsider. We find remarkable similarities in a Hittite work entitled, "The Apology of Hattushilis III" (circa 1200 BCE) and a Syrian work entitled, "The Apology of Idrimi of Alalakh" (1450 BCE or later), both of which may have influenced the creators of the Davidic tales (or the original Davidic court annals used by our biblical narrative). In these court writings the rise of the hero to the status of king was justified by indicating that the person destined to become king had divine support. The hero assumed rule without self-interest and was innocent of shedding the blood of members in the previous royal house. He was a friend to his royal predecessor, but he was betrayed, whereupon he went into exile, until gradually he seized the power of the central government. Hattushilis made every move after receiving directions from the goddess Ishtar in dreams. Perhaps Davidic annals imitated this international stereotypical account of royal usurpers, and then these annals were cannibalized by the biblical author and worked together with folktales about David's rise. One also could point out that similar accounts by usurpers come from the 6th century BCE. The Chaldean Babylonian ruler, Nabonidus, overthrew Labasi-Marduk in 556 BCE, and the Persian ruler, Cyrus the Great, overthrew Nabonidus in 540 BCE, and both rulers issued proclamations declaring that: 1) their predecessor was no longer desired by the Babylonian god, Marduk, 2) Marduk sought a pious new king, 3) Marduk found such an individual in Nabonidus/Cyrus, 4) Marduk willed the takeover, 5) people accepted the takeover, and 6) political and religious peace resulted. Some scholars, who date the total creation of the literature in the books of Samuel to the 6th century BCE Babylonian Exile, suspect that our biblical author also knew these two accounts.

These stories of David were charming tales in which David appeared as a hero, rogue bandit, lover of women, great warrior, brilliant leader, and champion of the oppressed.

This portrayal contrasted vividly with the image of David in the next section of literature, wherein he appeared weak and indecisive. As in real life, people are complex, and both portrayals of David were probably true to some degree.

Though the narratives were crafted with theological agenda, these collected traditions provide us with insight into the historical reasons for David's rise to power. He gathered an experienced cadre of mercenaries (many of them foreign), thus creating an effective fighting force against foreign powers and troops loyal to him in revolutions (such as Absalom's). He ingratiated himself with disenchanted people who lived on the periphery. He was a clever strategist who played his enemies against each other; he knew when to betray his Philistine overlords and defeat them in battle. Marriages contributed greatly to his rise. Michal, daughter of Saul, gave him a claim to the throne, Abigail brought him wealth, and other wives were princesses of neighboring kingdoms. Members of Saul's family and Saul's allies often met with assassination, but David was never directly responsible for shedding Saulide blood, and he appeared to mourn their deaths. The fact that people came to David seeking a reward for killing his enemies implies to us that someone put out the message that there were rewards for assassination.

David gradually assumed rule over Israel by first establishing control in the city of Hebron to rule Judah, then making a covenant with northern Israelite tribes, and finally, making a covenant with all Israelites. He stopped the pretense of being a Philistine vassal and defeated them. With his enemies subdued, he created of a new capital city, an act that typified the rule of great conquerors who began dynasties. This city had to be in neutral territory between the antagonistic regions of Israel and Judah, so that it would be free from pre-existing governmental structures, such as the tribal elders of Israel or Judah. Instead of building a city, like Sargon who built Akkad in Mesopotamia (2400 BCE) or Menes who built Memphis in Egypt (3100 BCE), David seized the city of the Jerusalem from the Jebusites (2 Samuel 5:1-10). Henceforth it was David's city, a free city responsible only to the Davidic family, having separate "elders" and governance. Moving the Ark of the Covenant to the city gave Jerusalem religious importance, for it then became a place of pilgrimage in addition to being a bureaucratic center. Perhaps, the appearance of Zadok as the high priest under David may really have been David's selection of a Jerusalem Jebusite priest. The word "zedek" is associated with pre-Israelite Jerusalem in the names of its leaders (Melchizedek, a priest in Genesis 14:18, and Adonizedek, a king according to Joshua 10:1). If so, names of the Jerusalem Jebusite god(s) (El-Elyon, El-Shaddai, etc.) might have become other names for Yahweh at this time. Zadok appeared to replace Abiathar, the old high priest, and perhaps in this way David secured the loyalty of the Jebusites in Jerusalem. It has been suggested that maybe even Nathan was a local Jerusalem prophet taken in by David. The final legitimation of David came with the dynastic oracle in 2 Samuel 7, in which Nathan declared that Yahweh would establish David's dynasty forever.

Our present biblical text contains folk tales and memories from David's annals. We can hypothetically reconstruct the social and political agenda of David's emergence, even though biblical authors were not interested in recording that kind of information. Our ability to make such observations implies that biblical authors did recall some real social and political aspects of David's rise. A few scholars, however, believe we are making too much out of this information, which may be more romantically fictionalized.

Deuteronomists legitimated David's rise to power by adding comments like "Yahweh loved David" and "Saul decreased while David increased." David appeared justified in overthrowing Saul, for "Yahweh departed from Saul and an evil spirit took possession of him." Though he was a deserter, an outlaw, and even a Philistine mercenary, David was recalled in heroic fashion. His rise to power was willed by Yahweh, and the very first narrative in the cycle of tales recalled how Yahweh sent Samuel to anoint this lowly shepherd boy to become king. The image of a prophet elevating such a poor member of society to be king, while a king still reigned, is a very radical statement about the authority of prophets. Deuteronomists did not add too much to these texts in comparison to their additions in 1 Samuel 1-15. The memories about the rise of David suited their purposes, so their editorial activity consisted merely in creating the narrative sequence and including some accounts while excluding others. The final message was that David was God's choice for king, and a future king like David would be an ideal king.

**Succession Narrative (2 Samuel 9-20 and 1 Kings 1-2):** This unified novelistic narrative evidences little Deuteronomistic editing. It explained why Solomon, of all David's sons, succeeded David. Our author may have used Davidic court annals supplemented by a very creative portrayal of characters and dialogue. So real is the narrative that some scholars suggest that the author was an eyewitness, perhaps even a woman in the court. Most believe that it was a creative story told a century or more after the events to justify Davidic rule over all Israel. It may have circulated in the north as religious propaganda to encourage reunification (850-800 BCE). Some, however, feel that the narrative was created much later, perhaps after 700 BCE, after the fall of the northern state, and still others date it to the Babylonian Exile. There is also disagreement as to where the narrative begins; some scholars variously begin the story with the promise to David in chapter 7 or the lament of David over the Saulides in chapter 1.

In the Succession Narrative claimants to the throne of David eliminated themselves by folly (Amnon, Absalom, and Adonijah) until only Solomon was left. The once heroic David became an old, indecisive ruler, relying on his general, Joab, to make the necessary decisions. Mistakes and past sins, such as the affair with Bathsheba, haunted him. His sons shared his vices in their sexual lust and quest for power, and David was unable to reprimand them, as when Amnon raped Tamar. His love for Absalom was pathetic, for he could not deal with him, even when Absalom militarily rebelled. By contrast, Solomon systematically and without emotion eliminated his potential opponents, even Joab.

The lively characterization, unity of plot, infrequent allusions to Yahweh and divine activity, and an emphasis upon human emotions, wisdom, and folly make this narrative appear secular and humanistic. Years ago some scholars suggested that the Succession Narrative might be wisdom literature, a novelistic form of teaching material comparable to the book of Proverbs. Though we now are less inclined to call it wisdom literature, we still acknowledge the presence of generic wisdom literary motifs, which may reflect the common discourse in telling popular tales. The Succession Narrative may also be the earliest example of the short story or novel that emerged in the post-exilic period.

Perhaps the narrative has re-arranged the memory of the events of an earlier story. When David remained in Jerusalem during the war with Ammon and seduced Bathsheba, he appears to us to be an older man. During the later Absalom revolt, he appears to be younger. During that revolt, when so many people turned against him, the ruler of Ammon helped him (2 Samuel 17:27), which sounds strange if the war with Ammon had occurred prior to that. When David spoke of the loyalty of a prior king of Ammon (2 Samuel 10:2), he might have been speaking of loyalty during the Absalom revolt. If this is correct, then Absalom's revolt occurred before the Bathsheba incident. Why has our biblical author switched the stories? The Bathsheba affair was paradigmatic for the Succession Narrative, because David's adultery was paralleled by the sins of sexual weakness of his sons, which led each of them to destruction. Ammon desired Tamar and feigned illness to lure her to his bedroom and rape her; Absalom subsequently killed him (2 Samuel 13:1-38). When Absalom seized Jerusalem during his revolt, he had sex with David's concubines in public to indicate that he was the new king (2 Samuel 16:21-22). Adonijah asked for the pretty young girl who slept with David but did not have sex with David because of his impotence. His request was seen by Solomon as a potential claim to the throne, so Adonijah was executed (1 Kings 2:13-25). David's sin with Bathsheba foreshadowed the weaknesses exhibited by his sons, which led to their elimination. Only cold and passionless Solomon deserved to be king, for he did not have a weakness for the pretty ladies. Later Israelites knew that Solomon was cold and methodical, and they hated him for it. The Succession Narrative played this theme to say that Solomon's personality actually was the reason he deserved to be king rather than his brothers. The movement of the Bathsheba account to the beginning of the narrative set up the entire story to make this point clearly. (Critics of this theory of narrative displacement point out that it is hard to reconcile the ages of the sons with the historical actuality, especially Solomon, who was Bathsheba's second son, if the Bathsheba event happened later in David's life. But perhaps numbers can be modified, too!)

Like the narratives in the "Rise of David" cycle, there appears to be very little or no editorial additions by the Deuteronomists in the "Succession Narrative." Apparently they liked the plot line as it was, and it added to the overall message of their own history. That is interesting, because the very negative portrayal of David in this account would seem to contradict the overall ideal picture of David as a foreshadowing of the future ideal king that we find in the rest of the Deuteronomistic History. It would seem that the Deuteronomists had a realistic portrayal of human beings, even the good ones, and recognized that people stood before God as finite and in need of grace. Perhaps, more significantly, was the memory that David repented after his sin with Bathsheba. For the Deuteronomists the need to repent was a theme that permeated their material. Only after people have repented will God save and deliver them from their enemies. David became a paradigm for the people of Israel and Judah, for they needed to repent of their sin and obey God just as the great David had done. The need for proclaiming this message of penance in the Babylonian Exile was exceptionally great.

**Court History of Solomon: 1 Kings 3-11**: This material resembled court histories created by pharaohs in ancient Egypt. They typically began with a dream in which a deity acclaimed the new pharaoh as the legitimate ruler and promised success in his reign. The report was followed by a boastful recounting of the pharaoh's later accomplishments in trade, war, and building projects. The dream report in 1 Kings 3 began Solomon's reign with quite similar promises (and language), and the rest of the court history portrayed

Solomon as powerful, wealthy, and wise, listing his accomplishments in trade and building projects. (Solomon, however, never engaged in war; his father built the empire.)

Egyptian court histories praised the king's wisdom in romantic fashion, and we find this also in the biblical narrative when Solomon tricked two women into revealing who was the true mother of the living child (1 Kings 3:16-28). God told Solomon to request a gift, and when Solomon asked for wisdom, God gave him the other gifts also. The contest in the court demonstrated this wisdom. However, the text also allows us to perceive that Solomon's wisdom was really passionless and cunning. Solomon methodically killed all those who would have been a threat to his rule. Would he really have cut the baby in half? Yes! He bluffed the women, and if his bluff failed, he would have saved face by killing the baby. Many of his actions in the narratives betray the image of a cold, calculating monarch. The Deuteronomists may have expanded these stories as they portrayed Solomon as a tyrant in contrast to his father, David.

Perhaps the stories that praise Solomon's wisdom may be later additions. Scholars now suspect that the flowering of wisdom literature in the royal court may have occurred not with Solomon, but under king Hezekiah of Judah (circa 710 BCE), who was credited with collecting the sayings in the book of Proverbs (Proverbs 25:1). Hezekiah's scribes may have attributed the beginnings of wisdom study to the time of Solomon in order to create a venerable and ancient past to this endeavor. Henceforth, Solomon's name appeared on subsequent literature even down to the 1st century BCE. Proverbs, Ecclesiastes, Song of Songs, Wisdom of Solomon, and the extra-canonical Psalms of Solomon all bore his name. Thus, 1 Kings 3-11 may have been expanded secondarily to include wisdom references, such as the Queen of Sheba story. Years ago scholars spoke of the reign of Solomon as an "enlightenment," which produced a flowering of great literature, especially Wisdom Literature, such as Proverbs 9-31, the Succession Narrative, and the Joseph Novella in Genesis 37, 39-50. Now, however, we date this literature to later periods, to the Babylonian Exile and later. Solomon probably had scribal activity that merited the projection of a wisdom tradition to his court by the scribes of Hezekiah, but we now suspect that Solomon's kingdom was more rustic than we used to think.

The Court History narrative declared that this was an era of national unification, economic growth, and vast building projects, but the text may have exaggerated all these things. Solomon most likely increased royal trade that brought wealth to the kingdom, and he imposed tariffs on foreign trade caravans that passed through his kingdom, all of which brought him wealth. His wealth may have been significant for that era, but not really great in comparisons to later ages. He engaged in several building projects: the Temple in Jerusalem, the royal palace in Jerusalem, and a landfill to unite the two parts of Jerusalem. However, we can perceive a darker side to his reign in hints found in the biblical narrative, which may be Deuteronomistic additions designed to contrast him with David. Some negative narratives sound archaic and may be from old sources. The accumulation of royal wealth and servants, increased taxes, forced labor or corvee (mandatory work on the king's building projects, as was done in Egypt), the replacement of tribal boundaries with newly created administrative districts, and the creation of a Jerusalemite bureaucracy led to the rift between Israel and Judah, especially when the tribe of Judah was exempt from many of the taxes. Solomon even attempted to sell Israelite land to foreigners, a thing unthinkable in Israel. Solomon displayed the characteristics of a traditional ancient Near Eastern monarch, comparable to the old Bronze Age Canaanite kinglets of the second millennium BCE. Born into the palace in Jerusalem, he never understood the common people.

David in contrast was remembered as a man of the people, who began as a shepherd boy, a man of passion--noble in victory, loyal to his friends, a lover of women, generous to friend and foe alike, a man who could dance naked before the Lord (and Israel) when the Ark arrived in Jerusalem. Whether he was these things or not, we can never be sure, but that is the way he was remembered. He was a soldier who built up the country, while Solomon never left the comfort of the palace. David had the passion to commit adultery and the ability to repent profusely; Solomon did neither. David had compassion; Solomon forever lacked it. The Deuteronomists portrayed David and Solomon in classic contrast as a good king and a tyrant.

# The Nature of Monarchy

Kingship came at a price, as was evident under Solomon, but the process had begun with David. Even though we see Davidic and Solomonic rule as "chiefdoms" rather than full states, the problems of the later states were already evident. Monarchy gradually brought central control and power back to the old walled cities, the old centers of Palestinian Bronze Age culture. Highlands were under control of the valleys once more, and this returned Israelites to the patterns of social and economic existence of the Late Bronze Age. Tribal, clan, and familial structures began to erode, and this occurred with increasing speed after 750 BCE, when more organized state structures emerged in both Israel and Judah. Local kinship structures surrendered activities. For example, village elders lost their judicial authority to courts created by the king, and frequently people appointed to the courts came from the rich and powerful families of the urban areas. (The Bible recalls that the first royal courts in Judah were mandated by king Jehoshaphat around 880 BCE to defend justice--2 Chronicles 19:5-11--but in time corruption crept into the courts.)

Central government sponsored trade between the various regions of the country and with outside foreign contacts, especially with an increased population requiring more food, agricultural intensification, and agricultural specialization of the various regions of Israel. Israelite farmers lost their regional independence; they slowly developed an interlocked economic structure. The chiefdom and the later state were needed for regulation. Mercantilism arose in urban areas due to trade and bureaucratic expansion. Rich families used their wealth to garner more wealth, often at the expense of highland families. The process increased over the years, until the 8th century BCE witnessed great disparity between the urban rich and the highland poor.

The royal court sponsored a religion in which Yahweh was the national high god, but the worship customs followed the traditional West-Semitic patterns of Baal devotion. David's appointment of Zadok over Abiathar appears to be a state sponsored religious compromise, for scholars suspect that Zadok was a native of Jerusalem before David's conquest, and this act put a Jebusite devotee into the office of high priest. Solomon was admonished for introducing foreign religions into Jerusalem, done in the name of good international politics. In particular, he built shrines to foreign gods for his foreign wives, since those marriages were part of important political treaty relationships. Ahab in Israel (850 BCE) gave his wife, Jezebel, the power to sponsor the devotion to the Baal of her native city of Sidon, for she was a high priestess of Baal. There was tension between royal ideology and the social and religious values of the Yahwistic highlanders; kings acted pragmatically and tried to offer a wide range of devotion to various gods, while the highlanders, though not monotheistic, were into a slowly emerging Yahwistic piety. The policies of many kings were a threat to this emerging Yahwistic piety.

Kings did bring blessings. They provided national defense, increased trade, a beautiful Temple, and other blessings that insured the continued existence of these people through the years. Even though the monarchs introduced the worship of foreign gods and often were polytheists in their own personal convictions, they did endorse Yahweh as the national deity, and thus they laid the foundation for the eventual emergence of monotheism among the masses. Certain kings like Hezekiah and Josiah, with their exclusive devotion to Yahweh, probably engaged in activities that seriously laid the foundation for the people to become monotheistic. Also, the institution of the monarchy generated images that inspired later priests, prophets, sages, and scribes. Even critics of the monarchy, like the Deuteronomists, took royal imagery, such as the Messiah, to craft a meaningful message of hope for the future. The ancient Near Eastern notion of the ideal king spoke of a monarch who mediated between this world and the gods, upheld justice, defended the weak, and brought prosperity to the land by his upright behavior. Though kings usually fell short of these values, the image remained as an inspiration. Israelite thinkers used these images in their prophetic oracles and post-exilic visions of the future, and finally Christians applied them to Jesus. Concepts such as "Messiah," "Day of Yahweh," "Age of Peace," "Son of David," "Prince of Peace," and many others were drawn from royal theology.

# Conclusion

The books of Samuel and Kings give us different angles by which to view the institution of kingship. Sources inherited and shaped by the Deuteronomistic Historians were diverse, for some were positive about kings, and some were negative. The Deuteronomists looked back from their era (620-550 BCE) and saw kingship as generally negative. They portrayed both Saul and Solomon in rather negative fashion, as foils for David. Except for David, and later kings like Hezekiah and Josiah of Judah, all other kings were critically assessed. Kings brought war, a gap between rich and poor, and ultimately the destruction of the nation in 586 BCE. But a king could be a good ruler, if he was subordinate to the will of God and heeded the words of the prophets. Saul should have listened to Samuel, and fortunately David did heed the words of Nathan. The historians have given us not so much a history, as a sermon. David became the image of the ideal king who would come to lead Jews not only politically but also morally.

The kings were portrayed heroically, but also as fallible individuals who stood under the demands of God. Saul was a hero whose actions were worth emulating, but he became a tragic figure who failed to heed God and the prophet Samuel. David was a romantic hero, warrior, and lover, but his weakness for the women brought him low, and he became an ineffectual father. David set the image for all humanity by being a person capable of repenting of his sin and beginning anew. Solomon could be the noble person who asked God for wisdom in his dream revelation, but he became the tyrant who oppressed his people and let in foreign gods with his foreign wives. One may see here the biblical theme of how we are all a mixture of good and evil; people are sinners in need of divine grace and guidance. These different images of the monarchs came from different sources, but in their final form the narratives cast an image of the ambiguity of human existence, the complexity of the human personality found in each of us.

# Bibliography

Albrecht Alt. "The Formation of the Israelite State in Palestine." *Essays on Old Testament History and Religion.* Trans. R. A. Wilson. Garden City, NY: Doubleday, 1966.

David Gunn. *The Story of King David: Genre and Interpretation.* Sheffield, Eng.: JSOT Press, 1978.

Baruch Halpern. *David's Secret Demons: Messiah, Murderer, Traitor, King.* Grand Rapids, MI: Eerdmans, 2001.

Hans Hertzberg. *I & II Samuel.* Trans. John Bowden. Old Testament Library. Philadelphia, PA: Westminster, 1964.

Dale Launderville. *Piety and Politics: The Dynamics of Royal Authority in Homeric Greece, Biblical Israel, and Old Babylonian Mesopotamia.* Grand Rapids, MI: Eerdmans, 2003.

Kyle McCarter. *I Samuel.* Anchor Bible. Garden City, NY: Doubleday, 1980.

Kyle McCarter. *II Samuel.* Anchor Bible. Garden City, NY: Doubleday, 1984.

Steven McKenzie. *King David: A Biography.* New York, NY: Oxford University Press, 2000.

Leonhard Rost. *The Succession to the Throne of David.* Sheffield, Eng.: Almond, 1982.

# Chapter 8

# The Divided Monarchies

Reading: 1 Kings 3-22,2 Kings 1-11,18-20,22-23

1 Kings 12-22 and 2 Kings 1-8 recalled the early years of the divided monarchies and the early prophets. Though Deuteronomists used the term "Israel" for all the people after the reign of Solomon, the people actually reverted to their natural political configuration of two separate countries, Judah and Israel. Israelites were less unified throughout their existence than a quick reading of the Deuteronomistic History might lead us to perceive. The books of Kings were a theological interpretation of history, a sermon by prophetically inspired historians who sought to understand their past and make sense of it for the believers of their age.

Judah in the south was called the "two tribes," and Israel in the north was the "ten tribes," but the division was not so neat. Judah absorbed the tribe of Simeon and the secular tribe of Levi (which may have been distinct from the Levites, the religious tribe). Benjamin was claimed by the south, but often controlled by the north. The other tribes composed the "ten tribes" of the north. The biblical text recorded tensions and strife between the two regions in the early years. Jerusalem, the capital of Judah, lay on the border between the north and the south, and thus Judah attempted to control the tribe of Benjamin to maintain a buffer to the north of the city. Our biblical texts come to us from the scribes in Judah and favor the southern perspective, but since some of the biblical traditions came from the north, their perspectives were not altogether eliminated. Israel was politically, economically, and socially the more powerful of the two kingdoms. Israel ruled the central plains, the northern Galilean highlands, and most of the Transjordan, the area east of the Jordan. Judah controlled the southern highlands and occasionally some of the Transjordan to the east of the Dead Sea. In war Israel usually prevailed. The Israelite king Omri made Judah into a vassal in the middle of the 9th century BCE, and two of his descendents ruled both countries for a time. Israel may have dominated Judah also during the reign of Jeroboam II in the early and mid-8th century BCE. The biblical text was reluctant to admit how often Judah may have fallen under the sway of Israel, since the final form of the narratives reflected the perspective of Judah.

Israel held land straddling major trade routes from the coast to the interior regions; thus, revenue came from the tariffs imposed upon trade caravans and state sponsored trade. Israel was more exposed to international culture than Judah, which was advantageous, but foreign culture had great impact upon Israel's politics and religion. Because Israel was the larger state, it was a target for military invasion by major powers like Assyria and Chaldean Babylon. It was easier to defend smaller Judah in the highlands of the south. Thus, the larger and stronger state, Israel, fell to Assyria in 722 BCE, while Judah remained until Chaldean Babylon devastated it in 586 BCE.

In the century after the division the people were afflicted by a major Egyptian invasion, wars between Israel and Judah, and wars between Israel and Syria. However, in the 8th century BCE, there was cooperation between Israel and Judah, especially under the powerful rule of Jeroboam II of Israel, and an age of prosperity dawned for both states. Wealthy classes arose in Samaria, the capital in the north, a city built by Omri a century prior. Culture and art flourished in both Jerusalem and Samaria, but with wealth came a widening gap between urban rich and highland peasants. Peasants in the highlands were displaced by the rich, who created large farms run by servants rather than family farms, and many people became debt slaves and servants living in the cities. Those who remained on their farms lost direct ownership of the land and became sharecroppers or simply slaves. Archaeologists have unearthed wealthy homes in Samaria, with beautiful ivory beds that once had inlaid gold, while in other parts of the city high occupational density indicated the presence of poor people, displaced from their farms, living in extremely crowded conditions. Such disproportion of wealth was extremely high for this small state, and that meant a potentially unstable society. This was the age when the 8th century BCE prophets proclaimed judgment against both religious and economic abuses.

Significant archaeological discoveries offer additional insights into the dynamics of life and society in this age. In the late 10th century BCE Pharaoh Sheshonk or Shishak of Egypt invaded Palestine and wrought havoc in both Israel and Judah. Historians have used his list of destroyed cities with the archaeological testimony of burn levels at many sites to reconstruct his path of devastation. The burn levels at cities, including Hazor, Megiddo, Tirzah, and Bethshan in the north as well as Gezer in the south, to name only a few of the sties which experienced destruction, have become benchmarks for archaeologists to date various levels in these sites. His extensive destruction indicates that he believed that Israel and Judah were political forces worthy of attacking and weakening. In the city of Megiddo, in the northern state of Israel, we have unearthed what appear to be stables or storehouses built in the 9th century BCE, apparently by king Ahab. (Years ago we thought these stables were built a century earlier by Solomon.) We observe that Samaria was built with a strong citadel fortress, which the biblical text attributed to Omri. The northern city of Hazor also had strong fortifications, presumably under Omri or Ahab. This tells us that the work of Omri and Ahab in strengthening the state of Israel was more significant than the biblical text allows us to hear. A dramatic discovery was the inscription from Tel-Dan which refers to the "house of David," the only archaeological or ancient testimony to the rule of David. This inscription was the proclamation of a Syrian king, who claimed to have killed both kings of Judah (Ahaziah) and Israel (Joram), when the biblical text attributed both deaths to Jehu the general (2 Kings 9). Other interesting finds include the very expensive carved ivories unearthed at Samaria from the late 9th and 8th centuries BCE testifying to tremendous wealth in the hands of a few, implying a great disparity between the rich and the poor.

From the 8th century BCE we have some dramatic archaeological discoveries. Over 100 ostraca or broken potshards from Samaria contain writing, business records, which help us reconstruct the evolution of the Hebrew language. Two sites in the deep south, Kuntillet 'Ajrud and Khirbet el-Qom, both contain inscriptions that refer to Yahweh and "his Asherah," which in the opinion of many scholars indicates that common Israelites viewed the goddess Asherah as a divine consort for Yahweh. (Some believe "Asherah" refers to an emblem and not a goddess.) In the late 8th century BCE Hezekiah, king of Judah, built a water tunnel in Jerusalem as part of his preparations for an Assyrian siege of the city. We discovered this tunnel and an inscription describing the building process over a century ago. Excavations revealed the tremendous destruction of the city of Lachish, a fortress city designed to help defend Jerusalem, by the Assyrians in conjunction with the invasion of Judah by Sennacherib in 701 BCE. In Nineveh the Assyrians created a carved wall mural to celebrate their conquest of Lachish. In this same era, south of Jerusalem, we found a fortress site with a temple in the city of Arad, thus demonstrating that the Temple in Jerusalem was not the only viable site for sacrifice.

We discovered interesting things connected to the last days of Judah's existence from the late 7th and early 6th centuries BCE. There are letters from Lachish, more than 20 in number, written to leaders in Jerusalem telling them of the successful advance of the Babylonian army under Nebuchadrezzar. We also have a seal that belonged to a scribe named Baruch, who may have been Jeremiah's scribe responsible for writing the early editions of the book of Jeremiah and perhaps even the Deuteronomistic History.

From Assyria we have recovered royal annals that refer to Israelite and Judahite kings, thus helping us cross reference rulers of all three countries and create synchronistic chronologies. Assyrian annals referred to Israelite kings such as Omri (876-869), Ahab (869-850), Jehoram (849-842), Jehu (842-815), Joash (801-786), Menahem (745-738), Pekah (737-732), and Hoshea (732-724), and to Judahite kings such as Ahaz (735-715), Hezekiah (725/715-687), and Manasseh (687-642). Chaldean Babylonian annals referred to Josiah (640-609) and Jehoiachin (598) of Judah.

In addition to these artifacts and texts listed above we have many other archaeological finds, including levels at various city sites that reflect housing and fortifications, objects, such as pottery fragments, seals, religious objects, and other examples of writing found on small objects. All of these finds help us reconstruct the culture and the history of this period. In general, we have much more archaeological evidence from the era than the earlier periods of Israelite history, which leads critical historians to take these narratives in the biblical text more seriously in terms of their historical content.

# History of Israel

**Jeroboam I of Israel**: Solomon's son, Rehoboam, ascended the throne in either 931 or 922 BCE and was asked to be more lenient than Solomon had been (1 Kings 12:1-19). We learn that corvee, forced labor conscription on royal building projects, had been imposed on Israelite citizens as well as the native Canaanites (who alone were mentioned in the Court History of Solomon). Taxes, conscription, and other forms of royal oppression fell upon all the Israelite tribes, except Judah, so that northern money had funded the lavish court of Jerusalem in tax-exempt Judah. The elders of Israel had just grievances, but Rehoboam refused to hear their demands, believing that to show weakness to the people would erode his authority, as has been the opinion of rulers throughout history.

The northern tribes subsequently revolted and picked Jeroboam, a former corvee official who fled to Egypt, to be their king (1 Kings 12:20-33). His biography, especially the image of Jeroboam fleeing the role of taskmaster, reminds us of Moses, except that Jeroboam fled to Egypt instead of from Egypt before he returned as the hero. He liberated his people from the rule of Jerusalem kings, as Moses liberated slaves from pharaoh. In addition, he built golden bulls for the worship of Yahweh, which reminds us of Aaron. Scholars opine that the author of the book of 1 Kings may have used a romantic or political story of Jeroboam designed to make him appear to be another Moses. Jeroboam assumed rule of the northern tribes, but unfortunately, he engaged in the policies of authoritarian monarchs. He set up a capital in a walled city, levied taxes, and created a compromise government that respected the values of both highland Israelites and other people in the land (especially devotees of Baal and El). This was most evident with his erection of the "golden bulls," or "calves" as the biblical text called them.

The bull or cherubim was an old, acceptable Yahwistic image, viewed as the throne on which Yahweh was invisibly seated. But many in Palestine viewed it as the icon for both El and Baal (as well as for Israelites who worshipped El and Baal in addition to Yahweh). The bull was a strong and virile farm animal, so for years people used it as an image for their deities (El and Baal especially). El and Baal were seen to be a divine presence in the statue; Yahweh devotees envisioned Yahweh to be invisible above the bull (or least, they were supposed to see it this way). The Temple in Jerusalem had bull statuary in the courtyard (called cherubim by the biblical text, where they were respected images). Hence, a clever ruler could use this image and appeal to the religious sensitivities of everyone. The result, however, was a compromise state religion that corrupted Yahwism.

Jeroboam set up rival shrines in the north at Dan and Bethel to keep pilgrims and wealth from going down to the Temple in Jerusalem. In those sanctuaries he erected golden bulls and proclaimed these were the "gods" who brought them out of Egypt, a clear reference to Yahweh. Since the word for gods, "elohim," is ambiguous, it can be understood in the singular or the plural, Jeroboam thus appealed to the various beliefs of people. For lowland folk, their gods, El and Baal, were in the bulls, and for highland Israelites, Yahweh was invisibly enthroned above the bulls. While trying to please all religious parties in the land, Jeroboam sponsored Yahwistic piety indistinguishable from other forms of West-Semitic religion.

Most people in Palestine in this age were not clear about their religious identity. We speak of so-called lowland Canaanites and highland Israelites from our modern perspective, but most of them did not really know who they were and what they really believed. Most continued to practice the religion that had been done in their villages for years. The distinctions between traditional polytheism of the Late Bronze Age and the new devotion to Yahweh were very fuzzy, since most Israelites were really Canaanites in the slow process of transformation. From Jeroboam's perspective as a king, he felt that he was acting correctly. His creations corresponded to popular piety, for his people had not yet evolved into the Yahwists of a later age. We should not characterize Jeroboam's activity as a deliberate mixture of Yahwistic and old Canaanite belief, for it probably reflected what people believed. Ultimately Jeroboam's "practical" political move caused most Israelites over the years to see Yahweh in the calves rather than enthroned invisibly above the calves. It was good "politics" in his age, but Jeroboam drew the ire of later prophets and Deuteronomic reformers, who judged Jeroboam by later standards.

**House of Omri:** Around 875 BCE Omri, a general of non-Israelite descent, won a three-way civil war and created a strong dynasty. Though the Deuteronomists dispensed with his reign briefly (1 Kings 16:21-28), Assyrian texts inform us that he was one of Israel's strongest kings, and his political activities shaped Israel for the rest of the country's existence. He built Samaria to be a permanent capital city, replacing the previous transitory centers of rule. The city was close to the sea and the coastal plain (25 miles) and not too far from the highlands. Located on the main trade route in central Israel, Samaria attracted trade for its merchants. Caravans journeyed from Mesopotamia and Syria to Egypt, and this strategic location enabled the king to levy tariffs on caravans and amass wealth. This brought Samaria to the peak of its prosperity in the age of Jeroboam II (750 BCE), who controlled the trade routes in the Transjordan, and the wealth of Jeroboam II may have been greater than that of Solomon's. Samaria was a strong defensible military site, which enabled Omri to fend off the rising power of Syria to the northeast and create a strong military and trade alliance with Phoenicia to the northwest. When the city finally was destroyed in an Assyrian siege (722 BCE), it held out longer than any other city (three years) before the Assyrian armies. It fell only because the siege had followed years of political and economic weakness.

Tribal elders in other cities could be strong political adversaries to the king. But Samaria, like Jerusalem, was a royal city free from tribal structures. Omri purchased the land and built the city on the site. The "elders of Samaria" became a distinct entity from the "elders of Israel." In fact, Jehu, the general who overthrew Omri's dynasty, had to seek confirmation for his rule separately from the "elders of Samaria" and the people and "elders of Israel." Samaria was loyal to the family of the king alone, especially since most of the citizenry probably came from the lowland and coastal areas, where highland Israelite values were relatively meaningless. Omri created a "free city state" within Israel, a domain exempt from the laws of Yahweh. Years ago scholars even suggested that Omri created a "dual monarchy" of Israelite highlanders and non-Israelite lowlanders, in which two capitals, Samaria and Tirzah, functioned as the dual administrative centers.

Omri perhaps created a new economic polity for Israel (scholars debate this issue greatly). His purchase of the site for Samaria may have legitimated the notion of private property and the sale of land, which highland Israelites did not acknowledge. They believed that Yahweh gave the land to all the people, and it would remain in the hands of families permanently. Omri may have paved the way for the general sale of land, property aggrandizement, and the eventual displacement of poor highlanders from their village farmlands in the next century. Samaria's new class of nobility had so much power that they victimized the highland peasants in the next century and inspired Amos and Hosea to speak their words of judgment.

**Yahwist Opposition:**  Omride religious and economic practices encountered opposition from Israelite Yahwists.  Omri's alliance with Phoenicia, especially Tyre, brought a greater foreign presence and new ways of dealing with Israelite society.  Ahab, the son of Omri, executed Naboth and seized his vineyard, as Jezebel, the wife of Ahab, engineered this plan.  She was the daughter of the king of Sidon and a high priestess in the cult of the Phoenician Baal, she proselytized Baal worship aggressively, and she may have come from a culture in which kings had the power to purchase and seize land.  Israelites were ruled by a regime that disregarded their religious and economic values.

Economic oppression and the aggressive Phoenician Baal cult brought many highland Israelites, and maybe even polytheistic lowlanders, into an alliance against the Omride family. We believe that the veneration of the new Phoenician Baal alienated both Yahwists and Palestinian El devotees. The key leaders of this resistance movement were Elijah and Elisha. Elijah's name meant, "My El is Yahweh," a clear statement in opposition to worshippers of the foreign Baal. The equation of El with Yahweh in the name of Elijah perhaps reflected that El worshippers were merging with the highland Israelites in their opposition to Omri's family. This might have been a significant point in the development of Israelite monotheism, for El and Yahweh came to be seen as the same god by a greater number of people.

The frequent allusion to "poor" people in the stories of Elijah and Elisha may indicate that economic factors were involved in this struggle.  Both Elijah and Elisha helped widows, a classic symbol of poor people.  Elisha more frequently helped the poor, which may be recalled because it was part of the memory of his opposition to the kings. Whereas monarchs took the sons of widows to serve in their armies, Elijah raised a widow's son from the dead (1 Kings 17:24); whereas monarchs taxed and drained the resources of peasants, Elisha gave endless oil for sustenance (2 Kings 4:1-7).

One might notice also that the prophets were portrayed in a way to affirm the life-giving power of Yahweh over against the fertility deity, Baal.  The prophets were empowered by Yahweh to bring life to dead people (both Elijah and Elisha raised someone from the dead, 1 Kings 17:17-24, 2 Kings 4:8-37), to control the weather (the drought ended under Elijah, 1 Kings 18:41-46), to provide healing (Elisha healed Naaman, 2 Kings 5:1-19), to provide fertility (Elisha told the Shunammite woman she would have a son, 2 Kings 2:8-17), to provide food (both Elijah and Elisha provided food for women with jars that supplied endless food or oil, 1 Kings 17:8-16, 2 Kings 4:1-7; and Elisha multiplied 20 loaves of barley and grain for 100 men to eat, 2 Kings 4:42-44), and to purify water and food (Elisha purified water and stew, 2 Kings 2:19-22, 4:38-41).  In all these instances Yahweh, the god of Israel and the Exodus, usurped the domain of Baal, the god of fertility and rain, who may have been seen by some as a dying and rising vegetation deity.  If the last statement is true, the ability to raise people from the dead was most significant. Elijah's sarcasm to the prophets of Baal that perhaps their god was sleeping or on a journey may refer to Baal's seasonal descent into the underworld at the hands of Mot (1 Kings 18:27).

Prior to Elijah and Elisha, there had been ecstatic seers, charismatic figures upon whom the Spirit of Yahweh descended, people like Samuel and other early figures, who functioned in what would be recognized by later generations as a prophetic mode. But with Elijah and Elisha prophecy may have evolved significantly. Conflict between the prophets of Baal and Elijah on Mount Carmel (1 Kings 18:20-40) somehow vindicated the Yahweh party and related prophetic movements over against Baal movements. (We notice that in the story the prophets of Baal were killed, but nothing was said about the prophets of Asherah who also were there. Asherah was the consort of El, and if El and Yahweh were being merged at this time, the Asherah prophets escaped execution.) Elijah and Elisha set the tenor for the development of later prophets and monotheism itself. Elijah's experience on Mt. Horeb (1 Kings 19:4-18) may have provided later generations with the image for how the "word of the Lord" was communicated to prophets. It came "in a still, small voice" instead of the natural phenomena experienced by Moses at Sinai, and this subsequently became the mode of revelation for later prophets.

The Yahwist party prevailed over the Omrides. After the Naboth vineyard seizure by Ahab, Elijah proclaimed a curse on the family of Omri and Ahab (1 Kings 21). When Jehu destroyed the Omrides (2 Kings 9), this curse came true. Later prophets and the Deuteronomistic Historians recalled this curse and its fulfillment, for they saw the conflict as symbolic of any conflict between kings and prophets. The house of Omri collapsed in 842 BCE, as Jehu, a general in the Israelite army, was anointed by Elisha to rise in revolt. Jehu killed Joram, king of Israel, and Ahaziah, king of Judah, who was part of the Omride clan. Thus, Omride control over Judah was broken by this revolution in Israel. Jehu also killed the priests and supporters of the Phoenician Baal in Samaria. But to gain control of Samaria, Jehu had to compromise with "the elders of Samaria," which probably entailed keeping the mercantilistic economic system. Jehu came to power with the support of the Yahwistic prophets, but from the Yahwistic perspective it was a half-finished revolution. Powerful families of Samaria increased in political and economic power until the time of Jeroboam II (750 BCE). Later classical prophets, like Hosea, remembered Jehu quite negatively for his bloodshed of the Omrides (Hosea 1:4), and perhaps because of his compromise with powerful leaders of Samaria.

The Phoenician Baal was gone and El and Yahweh were being merged, but Yahweh worship was not monotheism in the minds of most people. Yahweh was adored by many as a typical fertility deity, like Baal, especially at the royal shrines of Dan and Bethel. The later prophets condemned the people who believed that sacrifice to Yahweh was the most important part of the religion, and they condemned the fertility customs practiced in Yahweh worship. The prophets demanded that people return to the customs of highland Yahwism, but their rhetoric actually led to a new monotheistic Yahwism, since the vast majority of Israelites were polytheists throughout their history.

**Fall of Israel:** International events determined Israel's fate. Jehu's successors had war with Syria or Aram, because they lost the Phoenicians as an ally after the revolution

(Jehu killed Jezebel, a Phoenician princess). Syrian pressure abated when the Assyrians attacked various Syrian states consistently after 800 BCE, and this paved the way for economic development under Jeroboam II of Israel (786-746 BCE). Israel's glory days were numbered, for the Assyrians gobbled up the Syrian city-states and moved southward toward Israel. Israelites lived as though they would not be conquered, an attitude of overly self-confident people. They felt that with Yahweh on their side, they would never fall (a familiar refrain in history).

Classical prophecy arose late in the reign of Jeroboam II and in the time of his successors, when Amos and Hosea appeared. Amos condemned the rich and powerful people of Israel and Samaria for mercantilism and the oppression of the village highlanders. While economic abuses such as land seizure and debt enslavement occurred, rich Israelites worshipped Yahweh dutifully at Bethel. For Amos such religious observances were an act of sin when the same worshippers oppressed marginal people (Amos 4-5). Hosea proclaimed that Israel ought to return to Yahweh, but he saw little hope for such repentance, so he predicted the end of the nation (Hosea 9-14). People scoffed at the prophets, for never had times been so good; but no one scoffed when the Assyrian king, Tiglath-Pileser III, made his devastating attack on Syria and Palestine in 734-733 BCE. Israel was reduced to vassalage along with other nations. In 725 BCE Israel revolted against Sargon of Assyria, but after a three-year siege, the new Assyrian king, Sennacherib, destroyed Samaria and Israel in 722 BCE.

# History of Judah

**The Early Kings:** Unlike Israel with its frequent dynastic changes, Judah enjoyed relative political stability with a long succession of Davidic kings. Judah was smaller, easier to defend and less prone to dynastic upheaval. Judah was more likely to be absorbed by Israel through dynastic intermarriage (as with the Omrides) or through economic domination (as with Jeroboam II). After Jehu killed king Ahaziah, a member of the Omride family, Judah was relatively free. When the Judahites later executed queen Athaliah, the last of the Omrides was gone. Under king Uzziah (783-742 BCE) Judah prospered in conjunction with Israel. Wealth accrued in the urban center of Jerusalem, and this tempted the rich to use their new affluence to manipulate the economy and seize farmlands from the highland peasants. As in Israel, prophets arose in the south to condemn these practices.

Isaiah received a dramatic call to be a prophet (Isaiah 6:1-13), and as a court prophet he pleaded with the kings of Judah to trust in Yahweh and not foreign alliances. King Ahaz of Judah (735-715 BCE) ignored Isaiah's warning (Isaiah 7), allied Judah with Assyria, and thus brought the attack of Tiglath-Pileser III upon both Syria and Israel. Israel's destruction did not really help Judah, for Judah realized that alliance with Assyria was no better than vassalage. King Hezekiah of Judah (715-687 BCE) was seen by Isaiah to be more faithful to Yahweh than his father before him. He reformed Temple worship (1 Kings 18:4), perhaps removing cultic objects placed there by his father Ahaz, who may have appeased the Assyrians with these cultic changes. Hezekiah undertook religious and political reform to separate from Assyrian rule. He closed shrines outside of Jerusalem, some of which were for deities other than Yahweh, and he removed images like the Nehustan, the bronze serpent of Moses, which people may have worshipped as a manifestation of Yahweh.

Deuteronomists viewed him as a forerunner of their own reform a century later (2 Kings 18-21); however, some modern historians think he may have done this only to prevent religious objects from falling into the hands of the invading Assyrians. Nevertheless, in the Deuteronomistic History only David, Hezekiah, and Josiah were viewed as good kings in either Israel or Judah because of their devotion to Yahweh. Hezekiah probably was not a monotheist, but he advocated exclusive allegiance to the national deity, Yahweh, and so he contributed to the evolution of monotheism. Some historians think he advocated an exclusive national religion, elevating the national deity, Yahweh, very highly, and to later generations he appeared monotheistic.

Hezekiah's revolt against Assyria brought tremendous destruction by Sennacherib in 701 BCE, for all of Judah except Jerusalem was devastated. Jerusalem almost fell in the siege, but a plague in the Assyrian army caused Sennacherib to withdraw, taking only tribute from Hezekiah. (1 Kings 18:14-16 mentioned tribute, as did Assyrian records.) Historians debate whether the Assyrians actually surrounded Jerusalem or simply were advancing upon the city. Some scholars even suggest that there were two invasions, one in 701 BCE and the other in 688 BCE. The two-invasion theory states that tribute was paid during the first invasion (1 Kings 18:13-16), but plague drove the Assyrian away after the second invasion (1 Kings 18:17-37, 19:1-37). It would explain how Tirhakah of Egypt was involved in the political machinations according to 1 Kings 19:9, when he became pharaoh only after 690 BCE, and why Sennacherib's assassination in 681 BCE would be mentioned in 1 Kings 19:37, as though it happened shortly after the invasion. Most scholars still prefer the one invasion theory, however. During the siege Isaiah declared that the city would not fall, so that after Assyrian withdrawal Isaiah was seen as a great prophet. This dramatic success probably is why his oracles were remembered and later written down, and why so many of his motifs influenced later prophets. The deliverance of Jerusalem in 701 BCE was like another Exodus in the minds of the people. Hezekiah remained on the throne, but only as an Assyrian vassal. His son Manasseh was a faithful vassal of Assyria, whether through coercion or willing submission is debated, and he persecuted prophets who criticized his program of syncretism (687-642 BCE).

**Josiah's Reform:** Judah was a submissive vassal under Manasseh until Assyria declined in the late 7th century BCE. When Josiah became king (640-609 BCE), Judah experienced respite from Assyrian domination, so Josiah undertook political reform to garner some independence. No Assyrian response was forthcoming, so Josiah undertook increased activity, including religious reform and the removal of the Assyrian gods. During his reign a copy of the Law was discovered in the Temple, which further inspired his own efforts (2 Kings 22:1-23:30). We suspect this Law was the basic core of Deuteronomy 12-26. Not only did these laws seek to remove the abuses attacked by the prophets, the laws called for consolidating worship at the Temple in Jerusalem. With this reform a move toward monotheism became more possible than ever before.

Josiah attempted to recreate David's Empire by reclaiming northern territory. After the destruction of Samaria in 722 BCE, Israel was resettled by foreigners who merged with the remaining Israelites to produce the Samaritans. Actually, the new people were still Samarians or Israelites, since there were numerically more Israelites hiding in the highlands outside of Samaria than imported foreigners. But the upper and middle classes of Israel had been deported, and that degraded the national self-identity of the people significantly. Josiah destroyed the shrine at Bethel as a token rejection of the old northern cult and a statement of his rule over the area. But Josiah was killed in a battle fighting Pharaoh Necho of Egypt (or was executed by him), who also wanted to claim the northern territories for his own new Egyptian empire (609 BCE). With Josiah's death, Deuteronomic reform came to an end, many people reverted to polytheism, and an age of political incompetence began which lasted until the destruction of Jerusalem in 586 BCE.

**Fall of Jerusalem:** In 605 BCE Babylonian armies defeated Egyptian forces at Carchemish in the far north and thus claimed Palestine. Judah passed over to Chaldean Babylonian control after four years of Egyptian rule (609-605 BCE). King Jehoiakim, who was made ruler by Pharaoh Necho in 609 BCE, remained on the throne, perhaps by convincing the Babylonian king of his loyalty. In 597 BCE Jehoiakim and Judah revolted, and Babylonians under king Nebuchadrezzar took the city of Jerusalem. Many leading citizens were dragged off into exile, including the newly crowned king Jehoiachin and the prophet Ezekiel. This first exile removed many significant leaders, and their loss caused some of the political chaos in Judah for the following eleven years.

A major revolt by the Judahites under king Zedekiah led to a total destruction of the city in 586 BCE and the exile of most of the leading citizens. As in the northern state of Israel more than a century prior, so also in Judah, a majority of the population remained in the land, but they were the poor village peasants outside the cities. Some of them moved into Jerusalem and became squatters, so that returning exiles displaced them in the late 6th and 5th centuries BCE, which created an abjectly poor group of people. When the urban dwellers, the upper and middle classes, were exiled from any country, the national identity of that region was destroyed. That was why Assyrians and Babylonians moved people around so extensively, and the policy of deportation and resettlement continued even under the Persians, Greeks, and Romans. The bulk of the Jewish exiles lived Babylon (586-539 BCE) until the Persian king Cyrus granted them permission to return. But most Jews never returned to Jerusalem again; they remained in exile all over the world. The Greek word "diaspora" ("the scattering") refers to this dispersal. From this time onward, we call these people "Jews" rather than Israelites or Judahites. A new age had begun.

# Conclusion

The books of Kings provide us with different perspectives by which to view the history of kingship, in part, because the sources contained their own message, and the Deuteronomists sought to craft the sources with new perceptions. For the most part, the Deuteronomists saw the story of the kings in rather negative fashion as a tragic history. Only Hezekiah and Josiah of Judah were seen as good kings, not because of their political acumen, but because of their religious devotion to Yahweh. Kings were responsible for the worship of other gods, the oppression of the poor, and the ultimate destruction of the state in 586 BCE. Only if a king subordinated himself to God and to the words of the prophet, would a nation be blessed, as was the case when Hezekiah listened to Isaiah and Josiah followed the advice of his contemporary prophets. The Deuteronomistic History was not a history by our understanding, but it was a theological interpretation of history that called upon people to obey God and the prophets.

Overarching the messages of the various literary units in the Deuteronomistic History was a proclamation of divine justice and retribution. Obedience to God brought blessing and peace to the land; disobedience brought disharmony, chaos, and punishment. There was the clear message that obedience to God was owed by king and peasant alike. Today we fail to appreciate how revolutionary the language of the Bible was when it stated that kings are under the law and moral demand of God like anyone else. Herein we see the roots of our own democratic thought and notions of equality for all people.

The age of the divided monarchies was painful for the people of Israel and Judah. Politics and religion were interwoven in a way that we can recover only partially. The narrative tells us that the mistakes of the people and their leaders came back to haunt them, ultimately with the Babylonian Exile. The stories preached that people needed to obey God, and when they erred, they had to admit their mistakes, repent, and try to live obediently once more. That was the message of the Deuteronomists, especially in the second edition of their history around 550 BCE. They essentially said, "If we repent, like David, perhaps God will restore our land." Indeed, when the return to Palestine occurred after 539 BCE, the Deuteronomistic History was vindicated.

# Bibliography

Albrecht Alt. "The Monarchy in the Kingdoms of Israel and Judah." *Essays on Old Testament History and Religion*. Trans. R. A. Wilson. Garden City, NY: Doubleday, 1966.

Michael Coogan, ed. *The Oxford History of the Biblical World*. New York, NY: Oxford University Press, 1998.

Robert Gnuse. *No Tolerance for Tyrants: The Biblical Assault on Kingship*. Collegeville, MN: Liturgical Press, 2010.

John Gray. *I & II Kings*. 2nd Ed. Old Testament Library. Philadelphia: Westminster, 1970.

John Hayes and Maxwell Miller. *Israelite and Judean History*. Old Testament Library. Philadelphia, PA: Westminster, 1977.

Richard Lowery. *The Reforming Kings*. Journal for the Study of the Old Testament Supplements 120. Sheffield, Eng.: JSOT Press, 1990.

Marvin Sweeney. *I & II Kings*. Old Testament Library. Louisville, KY: Westminster John Knox, 2007.

# Chapter 9

# Exilic Prophets

Reading: Ezekiel 1-3,16,23,27-28,34,37,Isaiah 40-55

olitics of the age destroyed the people of Judah. The kings of Judah, Jehoiakim and Zedekiah, allied themselves with Egypt to gain independence from the Chaldean Babylonians. These attempts failed, and the Judahites paid the price by being attacked and exiled by Nebuchadrezzar of Babylon. In the first exile of 597 BCE the leading citizens of Jerusalem were captured and resettled in Babylon in an effort to break the spirit of resistance in Judah. Jehoiakim died before the attack and his successor, Jehoiachin, found himself exiled to Babylon after only one month of rule. He was imprisoned for 37 years before the Babylonian king released him to serve in the Babylonian court. In later years Jehoiachin may have become the symbol of the good king who suffered for the sake of his people, and he may have inspired, in part, the image of the suffering servant in Second Isaiah. Ezekiel also was taken in this first exile. Zedekiah was placed upon the throne by Nebuchadrezzar to be a loyal vassal. But he, too, revolted, and his revolt crushed in 586 BCE. Jerusalem was destroyed, the Temple burned, and Babylonians took into exile as many of the citizenry as they could seize.

## Tragedy of Exile

In reality, the Babylonians did not depopulate the land completely, for that would have been impossible. They seized many people in the urban centers, which constituted only one-tenth of the total population. But these people included the upper and middle classes, the leaders, and basically the people who gave a national identity to the region. By removing the leadership, foreign powers of that age sought to break the identity and spirit of resistance in a province that rebelled. People remained in the countryside of Judah, but very few remained in Jerusalem. However, some scholars suggest that there were a significant number of people in Jerusalem, and perhaps they generated the Deuteronomistic History. Perhaps people from the countryside moved into Jerusalem and squatted on land, and they were displaced by returning exiles in later years. These displaced people might have become the extremely poor Jews of the post-exilic era.

Because exiles included intelligentsia and the religious leadership, including many religionists leaning toward a monotheistic perspective, modern scholars believe that significant biblical literature was generated among these exiles. After the exile the religionists who came back to Jerusalem from Babylon brought sacred literature, as Ezra did in the next century, and they may have brought a developed concept of consistent monotheism. Prior to the exile monotheistic expression may have called for exclusive devotion to Yahweh, but among the exiles the idea arose that Yahweh was the only god who existed. Thus, returning exiles had to convert the Jews who had remained in the land of Judah to their newly defined form of Judaism with its stricter monotheism.

The exile caused a religious and intellectual crisis for these people. Survivors in Babylon lost family and friends in the siege and destruction of Jerusalem, and the forced march to Babylon caused even more deaths. They were physically and psychologically devastated. According to ancient Near Eastern understandings their defeat by the Babylonians implied either that their god was too weak to defeat the Babylonian god, Marduk, or their god had deserted them. Now they found themselves in a foreign land and obligated by the logic of defeat and their persuasive Babylonian neighbors to worship Marduk. After their trauma it was easy to consider such a transformation, especially for Judahites who had been polytheistic back in Palestine. Switching to worship the gods of the land in which they were now located was logical. The ancients assumed that different gods ruled in the various lands, and it was wise to know the gods of the land to which you had moved and to propitiate them. Perhaps more than half of the Jews in exile gradually became Babylonians, worshipped gods like Marduk, and disappeared into the greater population, as the Israelites of the so-called "lost ten tribes" had done in northern Mesopotamia more than a century prior.

If they chose to worship Yahweh, the god of their land and their ancestors, they had to justify this decision. They had to conclude that they could worship Yahweh, if he were still present in their midst. If Yahweh were present with them, it implied that Yahweh was in control of the land of their exile. The pre-exilic tendencies toward monolatry, the worship of Yahweh that ignored the other gods, transformed into pure monotheism. Yahweh ruled over them in Babylon, because Yahweh was the only deity who existed. Thus, they retained their traditional religious and social identity. Or, to put it another way, those people who survived the exile and returned to Jerusalem, were those with exclusive religious convictions and a strong Jewish identity.

By way of reference, we usually call these people Israelites up until the time of the exile. More specifically, we might call them Israelites (from the north) and Judahites (from the south). But during and after the exile we call them Jews. Israelite and Judahites were political and national distinctions. You could be an Israelite without being a Yahweh devotee. The word Jew, which came from the word for Judah used by the Persians in the post-exilic period, denoted a person who was Jewish by virtue of religious conviction.

You could be a Jew in any part of the world, so your religious identity became more important than political identity. The tendency to define themselves by religious identity was forced upon Jews by two reasons. First, most of them were scattered around the ancient world, and especially in the area of Babylon, so that political identification tied to a particular land was impossible. Second, Judah would be a province in someone else's empire for 600 years. Only for a short time, under the Maccabees, would they have their own independent state. That, too, made it impractical to have a self-definition that was national or political. In our textbooks they are called Israelites before the exile and Jews afterward; they evolve from being a political entity into a religious movement.

Jews lived around the city of Babylon in Mesopotamia where they had been marched by their conquerors. No longer could they sing the psalms and offer sacrifice in the Temple of Jerusalem, as the lament in Psalm 137 bemoaned. But ironically in later years, when exiles were permitted to return (539 BCE), many chose to remain in exile. We estimate that only one-eighth of the exiled Jews returned to Palestine. Many migrated to other lands that contained more promise than desolate Judah. Other Jews fled to Egypt during and after the fall of Jerusalem, including Jeremiah who was taken there in 580 BCE. This was the beginning of the worldwide *Jewish golah*, the "scattering" or "dispersion," also called by the Greek term *diaspora*. With the Roman destruction of Jerusalem in 70 CE, all Jews would experience permanent diaspora that lasted until this century.

The dispersion of Jews all over the world paved the way for new and creative ideas to enter Judaism. Jews in Egypt spoke Greek and created the Septuagint, the Greek Old Testament used by Jews and extensively by later Christians. Jewish communities all over the world became steppingstones for the expansion of Christianity in its early Jewish missionary phase. For in those communities Jews made converts among the Gentiles for many years prior to the arrival of Christianity, so Christian missionaries built upon an existing missionary impulse already in Judaism.

**Religious Themes in Exile:** During the exile Jewish intelligentsia had to address several intellectual and religious questions. The result was the emergence of brilliant and creative individuals whose efforts created early Judaism and much of what would become the Hebrew Bible. Social crisis often breeds a great intellectual and spiritual response. Jewish theologians had to address intellectual and spiritual needs of people that satisfied them meaningfully. Issues that needed to be addressed included:

*Punishment for Sin and Forgiveness*: They had to explain why military disaster befell the Jews. Did it mean that Yahweh was too weak or had deserted them? As hideous as it may sound to us, their answer was the only one they could offer in a polytheistic setting. Theologians maintained that Yahweh willed this horrid destruction, for to say otherwise would grant power to another deity. They concluded that Yahweh willed the destruction as punishment for the sin of the people of Judah, so the gods of the nations were in no way responsible for the destruction. Jews were being punished for their sins of social injustice and the worship of other deities. Such was the response of prophets like Ezekiel, and those who crafted written texts of the pre-exilic prophets and the final edition of the Deuteronomistic History. They remembered the words of earlier judgment prophets who declared destruction might come for their disobedience. Deuteronomistic literature once more received respectful consideration, and we suspect that exilic expansions to the history included allusions to future exile and more serious words of judgment in the mouths of pre-exilic personages. Exiles were called upon to accept this divine judgment, so that they might repent and pray for forgiveness.

If harsh judgment from Yahweh was accepted by the listeners, then the theologians had to communicate subsequently a message of forgiveness. They had to reassure the audience that Yahweh still loved them. This message had to be dramatic because it needed to match the emotional pain of accepting the judgment. As prophets like Ezekiel gave messages of judgment with dramatic flair, so also the message of hope had to be comparable. Perhaps, the most hope oriented of all prophets during the exile was Second Isaiah, who spoke no words of judgment and proclaimed grand images of hope.

*Future Hope:* After encouraging people to realize that their God had caused the exile for the purpose of chastisement, the theologians had to offer some message of future hope. For otherwise, a message of pure judgment in the exile would have caused despair and wholesale alienation from Yahwism. Some of the exilic theologians spoke of the divine presence of Yahweh in the midst of the exiles. This was emphasized by Ezekiel and implied in the Priestly traditions. This divine presence could accompany Jews wherever they went in the world. Most exilic theologians also provided some implicit or direct expression that Jews might someday return to the land. This was true of Ezekiel and Second Isaiah, as well as the edited corpus of pre-exilic prophetic oracles created and written down in the exile. The editors of that prophetic corpus may have inserted hope messages into the traditions of various pre-exilic judgment prophets, like Amos 9:11-15, which referred to the fallen tent of David or Judah which would be raised up, and Micah 4, 5, 7, which contained exilic-sounding hope oracles. Judgment oracles predominated in the prophetic corpus, but existentially hope oracles were the final message.

*Preservation of Traditions:* Traditions of the past had to be remembered, and this might explain why so much literature was written in the exile, including perhaps most of the pre-exilic prophets, the Deuteronomistic History, the Yahwist Epic, and the Priestly traditions. The Priestly traditions, in particular, took special pains to recall the customs and the appearance of the sacred paraphernalia from the Temple that had been destroyed. The Priestly traditions symbolically portrayed the Temple as the Tabernacle in the days of Moses, and other religious paraphernalia and customs were projected into the Mosaic period as objects created and used by those Israelites. By creating this fiction, the Priests extended important Temple imagery back into the foundational period of Israelite existence under Moses and thus lent it a great antiquity and religious authority. From a practical perspective the Priestly texts in Exodus became a repository for the memory of the Temple cult. This enabled Jews after the exile to reconstruct some of those objects in the Second Temple. Priestly editors expanded the story of Moses, attributed the creation of sacred objects in the Temple to him, and did not render a narrative of the Monarchy when those religious realia were really created. Nor did they have to acknowledge that Solomon built the Temple and created the objects precious to them. Solomon represented kingship, an institution that priests despised in the post-exilic era.

*Monotheism:* Most important of all, the affirmation of monotheism and the need for exclusive devotion to Yahweh was stressed during the exile. Earlier prophets and theologians proclaimed practical monotheism, or monolatry. For Israel, there was only one God to be worshipped; the existence of other gods was not denied, but only considered irrelevant for Israelites. Once in exile, Jews were surrounded by people who worshipped other deities, so Jews had to come to a conclusion about the status of other gods. Past traditions portrayed Yahweh as Lord of human affairs, and if this were so, then Yahweh was master of the destinies of those other nations. Hence, the biblical theologians concluded that Yahweh was the god of all peoples. Yahwists had to speak of Yahweh being the creator of the world more directly, whereas formerly they made only loose allusions to this effect. Surrounded by Babylonians who worshipped Marduk as the great high creator god, it was especially important to describe Yahweh as a creator deity and thereby usurp Marduk's role. Second Isaiah and the Priestly traditions especially portrayed Yahweh as creator of the universe. All of the exilic traditions testified to monotheism, but in particular Second Isaiah and the Priestly tradition made extremely strong monotheistic statements, implying the folly of people was great when they worshipped other gods. Because of the efforts of these exilic spokespersons, Jewish identity received a strong boost, and when Jews returned from the exile, they were already on a trajectory to classic Judaism.

*Jewish Identity:* Jewish intellectuals relied on religious traditions as a unifying theme, especially referring to those customs that set priests apart from the general population back in Palestine. Old customs were recorded in the book of Leviticus to become binding for all Jews, so that Jews symbolically became priests, or a "holy people." This was practical, for the observance of such priestly food and clothing customs made a person appear very strange to foreign neighbors. If you are perceived by your neighbors as unusual or distinct, this perception will affect how you think about yourself. Similar folk bond together and isolate themselves from others. As Jews kept the priestly laws, so the customs preserved Jewish identity and religion.

Three priestly customs became extremely important: 1) Before the exile Sabbath was a day of rest, but in exile it also became a day of religious observation. Jews refrained from work every seventh day, and this distinguished them from others in society. Babylonians did not have a concept of the week, but rather worked with a month long unit of time with various days of misfortune on which they would not work. 2) Kosher food laws created even clearer lines of demarcation. Before the exile food only priests observed food guidelines, but in the exile they became the dietary standard for all who remained Jews. Jews could no longer eat in the homes of foreigners; they had to seek out a gathering of other Jews for common meal gatherings. Additionally, a person had to live in neighborhoods where Jewish merchants provided kosher food. This forced Jews frequently to live together in communities, so that the common identity of all was strengthened, and Jewish children would more likely marry each other. 3) Circumcision was not a public sign, like the first two, but it was permanent. Every Jewish male carried the constant reminder of his Jewish identity, and if he were tempted to pass as Babylonian, the mark of circumcision would always remind him of his Jewish roots.

Who were the Jewish intellectuals who addressed these issues and wrought tremendous social and intellectual transformations? Most were nameless scribes who creatively wrote down large segments of the oral traditions. Scribes usually remain anonymous, for they view themselves as handing down the work of great predecessors, the true authors.  Thus, Baruch probably prepared Jeremiah's oracles in written form, but he would not put his name on the collection.  Baruch was the writer, but Jeremiah was the author, for the author is the person who spoke the words.  Pre-exilic prophetic oracles were written down, as well as traditions of the Yahwist Historian and Priestly Editors.  If these texts were not generated in the exile, they were written in the years shortly after the return from exile.  There also were prophets who stood out for their contributions, particularly Ezekiel and the anonymous prophet we call "Second Isaiah."

# Ezekiel

The first deportation engineered by the Babylonians in 597 BCE carried off artisans, craftsmen, intellectuals, and political leaders to Babylon, including a priest named Ezekiel who became a prophet in exile.  Like Jeremiah, with whom he overlapped ten or more years, he spoke words of judgment prior to the fall of Jerusalem, but when the city fell, he became a prophet of hope.  Since Ezekiel proclaimed oracles for years after the fall, there were more hope oracles in his book than in the book of Jeremiah.

Ezekiel has been called "bizarre" by commentators because of his unusual imagery and violent, sensual, brutal language.  Some of his motifs were used by the later apocalyptic writers, for his visions readily inspired imagery that portrayed the end of the world.  A connection existed between Ezekiel and the material in Zechariah 9-14, Isaiah 24-27, Daniel 7-12, and the New Testament book of Revelation.  Ezekiel acted out some of his oracles in a manner that convinced many ancient listeners and modern commentators that he was insane.  Perhaps he was really very clever, for his bizarre behavior was effective in grabbing the attention of exiles numbed by their horrible experiences.

**Message of Judgment:** Prior to Jerusalem's fall Ezekiel impressed upon his audience that the impending destruction of the city was punishment for sin.  In the early years after the deportation of 597 BCE, Judahites in exile and in Jerusalem expected Yahweh to save the exiles and return them to Judah.  Both Jeremiah and Ezekiel sought to disabuse their listeners of this belief.  Jeremiah wrote a letter to exiles in Babylon telling them that exile would last for many years (Jeremiah 29), and Ezekiel symbolically acted out the fall of Jerusalem in several oracles.  Ezekiel lay on his side for 430 days to symbolize the combined exile of Israel and Judah (Ezekiel 4:1-8).  As a symbol of life in exile he cooked food with dung (Ezekiel 4:9-17), an especially odious thing for a priest to do.  He cut off his hair, burned some of it, cut some of it, and threw the rest into the air, indicating death by siege, battle, and exile for those who remained in Jerusalem (Ezekiel 5:1-17).  He built a mud wall and crept repeatedly through a hole in it, symbolizing refugees fleeing Jerusalem (Ezekiel 12:3-16).

Ezekiel stressed divine justice behind the inevitable and imminent fall of Jerusalem.  In his call experience (Ezekiel 1-3) he envisioned the glory of the Lord leaving Jerusalem to come into exile, and he described Yahweh leaving the Temple in the "wheels within wheels" oracle (Ezekiel 10).  Only late in his ministry did the prophet describe the future return of Yahweh's glory (Ezekiel 43).  Allegorically he portrayed Judah as a deserted baby girl left at birth to die, reared by Yahweh to become a wife, who then played the harlot as an adult (Ezekiel 16).  The allegory of the sisters, Oholah and Oholibah, who also were harlots, represented the unfaithfulness of Israel and Judah (Ezekiel 23).  Both allegories were sensual and brutal in their imagery, so that English translations soften these passages, and the texts are not to be read publicly or before children according to the Jewish tradition. Ezekiel depicted the abominations in the Jerusalem Temple worship, which justified Yahweh's destruction of the city (Ezekiel 8-9), and he described the leaders of Judah as bad shepherds who exploited the sheep (Ezekiel 34).

**Message of Hope**: Ezekiel 33-48 envisioned the future restoration of the nation in numerous oracles. The parable of the shepherds (Ezekiel 34) began with the image of bad shepherds or kings, but ended with the hope that good shepherds would come in the future. A famous passage was the vision in the valley of dry bones (Ezekiel 37) wherein the nation was portrayed like skeletons on an old battlefield, perhaps Megiddo where Josiah died. The prophet was told that Yahweh had the power to bring the nation back to life by resurrecting the skeletons into human bodies once more. The vision was a statement about national resurrection or restoration, not a promise of individual afterlife. But it was the first articulation of the possibility that Yahweh had the power to make dead people alive. It ironically inspired the development of the concept of afterlife and resurrection in the Jewish tradition. Jews and later Christians would use the metaphor of the resurrected body to speak of the hope of an afterlife.

Ezekiel 40-48 described the national restoration of the twelve tribes, Jerusalem, and the Temple. The description of the Temple interests scholars because it differs from the one given in the Pentateuch. Some suggest that Ezekiel's memory was older and a more complete description than the one in the Pentateuch; others suggest that his was merely a fanciful vision unconnected to the real appearance of the Temple. The king would reign over a reunited Israel (Ezekiel 48), rendered fertile by the sacred river flowing from the Temple (Ezekiel 47). This river is like the river in Eden (Genesis 2), and elsewhere, Ezekiel used imagery from Genesis 1-3 and other parallel traditions otherwise lost to us.

Judgment oracles against the nations were really hope oracles for Judah. Ezekiel 26-28 condemned the king of Tyre with imagery drawn from Genesis 3 combined with some apparently pre-Israelite myths unknown to us. Perhaps Ezekiel used a version of the Genesis 3 story older than our present biblical text, for it placed the garden on a mountain and has no reference to a woman with the man. Ezekiel 38-39 spoke of how "Gog," king of "Magog" would be destroyed by Yahweh. "Gog" symbolized either Chaldean Babylon or the empire, be it Lydia or Media, which would destroy Babylon and subsequently be destroyed by Yahweh. ("Gog" sounds like the name Gyges, who was a great king of Lydia a century before Ezekiel lived.) The motif of foreign nations destroyed outside of Jerusalem would be developed by Zechariah, Daniel, and Revelation. This is a good example of symbolic imagery that would fire the imagination of later Jewish authors. Ezekiel (593-573 BCE) gave exiles not only self-understanding of their predicament, but more importantly, the hope of a return. He was also an early example of the transformation of prophecy into apocalyptic literature.

# Second Isaiah

Around 550 to 540 BCE an anonymous prophet in exile either proclaimed or more likely wrote oracles found in Isaiah 34-35, 40-55. Perhaps for fear of the Babylonian authorities, he spoke with anonymity; thus, his oracles were included in the book of Isaiah, with whom he had strong theological connections. Cyrus, the newly emergent king of Persia and Media, conquered lands on the east and north of Chaldean Babylon. He provided a large measure of local rule within his empire and often he let political exiles return home. This differed from the old policy of the Assyrians and Babylonians, so that resistance to his military advance was weakened. Second Isaiah saw Cyrus as the divinely anointed one, the "servant of the Lord," sent by Yahweh to free Jews (Isaiah 44:24-45:13). However, in later years, the prophet believed the servant to be someone other than Cyrus. Second Isaiah proclaimed that Babylon would fall to Cyrus and that Cyrus would let the Jews return home and rebuild their city and Temple. Probably many Jews in Babylon felt that the prophet was crazy to dream such an impossible dream, for imperial Babylon appeared to be too strong and newly emergent empires simply repeated the policies of the past by keeping deported peoples in exile and sending even more conquered peoples away from their homes. However, when in 539 BCE Cyrus defeated the Babylonians at Opis, near modern day Baghdad, and took Nabonidus prisoner, he entered the city of Babylon. Babylonian priests wisely proclaimed Cyrus king of the city and heralded his arrival to avoid bloodshed in the city. Within a year Cyrus initiated a new policy of rule by allowing people who were exiled to return home and by giving them a limited amount of autonomy within the parameters of Persian rule. We discovered the famous "Cyrus "Cylinder" in 1879 in which Cyrus declared himself the representative of the Babylonian god Marduk, who was chosen to seize Babylon to restore the true worship of Marduk and return people to their homes. These events probably vindicated the prophet in the minds of many Jews in Babylon.

**Message of Hope:** Second Isaiah (or Deutero-Isaiah) was the most hope-oriented prophet among the classical prophets, for indeed the Jews needed to hear a message of forgiveness and hope (Isaiah 40:1-2). According to his vision the exiles will depart on a triumphal procession to their homeland, the desert will be prepared for them, and God will create a smooth highway by filling in valleys and grading down the mountains (Isaiah 40:3-5). This may be an allusion to the Persian policy of building roads for fast troop movement. The idea of return would not have appealed to many Jews, since the forced march to Babylon in the previous generation claimed many lives. But the prophet emphasized that this return would be a wonderful experience; the route would be shorter because Yahweh would lead Jews across the desert rather than following the long, circular route from Babylon to Palestine.

Second Isaiah was the first radical monotheist that we can identify. He ridiculed the gods of the nations and portrayed their devotees as foolish as the blocks of wood and metal they fashioned into gods (Isaiah 41:21-29, 44:9-20, 45:20-46:13). He radically declared that Yahweh was the deity who created the world. Prior to this time, Israelites and Jews spoke of their deity as a redeemer god who delivered them in the Exodus and at other times in their national existence. But Jews now lived in a land where the primary god was Marduk, a creator god, and the temptation existed for them to worship Marduk in addition to or instead of Yahweh. Second Isaiah stole Babylonian motifs to describe Yahweh as creator, and so usurped the significance of Marduk in the minds of the Jews.

In the Babylonian myth, the Enuma Elish, Marduk killed Tiamat, the monster of the deep who represented primordial chaos. By cutting her body in half, Marduk created the waters above and below the firmament, and then Marduk created the world in between the waters. Second Isaiah claimed instead that Yahweh cut the beast in half (Isaiah 51:9-11), and the prophet drew a parallel between the cutting of waters at creation and the cutting of waters in the crossing of the Sea of Reeds. By this combined metaphor, Second Isaiah portrayed Yahweh as both a creator deity, who made the world, and a redeemer deity, who saved Israel at the sea. Usually, ancient peoples viewed the creator deity as a high and distant god, while the redeemer deity was more immanent and personal. Second Isaiah combined both images and made the theoretic concept of monotheism possible.

As Yahweh cut the waters at the creation of the world and the waters at the Sea of Reeds, so Yahweh would "cut" the desert for the return to Jerusalem. By this triple metaphor, Second Isaiah implied that the return to Palestine would be both a "new creation" and a "second exodus" experience. The return would be an event comparable to the creation of the world and the Exodus, which constituted a rather dramatic event (Isaiah 43:15-21). Yahweh who did the "former things" of creation and Exodus would now do a "new thing" or the "latter things," wherein Israel would be recreated and saved once more. To proclaim the return to be comparable to the creation of the world was a grand promise. It also foreshadowed eschatological imagery in the post-exilic prophets and apocalyptic literature. This "new thing" would include rebuilding the city, homes, and the Temple, and Yahweh would dwell in their midst.

The fulfillment of Second Isaiah's hope for a return and rebuilding vindicated this prophet and assured the inclusion of his oracles in the emerging prophetic canon of that age. But the vision did not come true completely in the way Second Isaiah gloriously portrayed it. Later prophets, such as Isaiah 56-66, implied that the vision was coming to greater and more complete fulfillment in the future. Each succeeding generation captured the vibrancy of the images and developed them some more, heightening the imagery in ever-grander fashion. This would be why the post-exilic prophets were so eschatological in their oracles and why eventually they evolved into apocalypticists.

Second Isaiah stated that the foreign nations would recognize Yahweh (Isaiah 42:1, 10-13; 45:22-24; 49:1, 6-7; 55:5). We are not sure whether this implied that foreigners would be converted to the exclusive worship of Yahweh. Christians later believed the prophet anticipated the conversion of many Gentiles to Christianity. Or did the prophet mean that foreigners would revere Yahweh without necessarily rejecting their own religious beliefs? Cyrus sacrificed to the various deities of the peoples whom he conquered as a way of appeasing the populace. With the seizure of Babylon, Cyrus worshipped at the shrine of Marduk, and he also acknowledged the deities of all the other peoples, presumably including Yahweh. This vindicated the prophet, but whether it was what Second Isaiah envisioned, we do not know. Perhaps Second Isaiah expected more of Cyrus, and that is why the later "servant" hymns did not view Cyrus as the servant. Modern scholars believe Second Isaiah's references to the Gentiles meant that foreigners would respect Yahweh as a great deity and acknowledge the exalted position of the Jews. Second Isaiah at least expected respect for Yahweh in the minds of people everywhere.

**"Suffering Servant"**: The Suffering Servant of the Lord image was found in four hymns in Isaiah 42:1-4, 49:1-6, 50:4-9, 52:13-53:12. If these hymns are removed from their literary context, the remaining text of Isaiah 40-55 reads more smoothly. It appears as though these hymns were inserted into our present text at a later stage either by Second Isaiah or his students. They redefined the "servant" in a greater way, as someone other than Cyrus, who otherwise was called the servant outside the hymns. Theologians have discussed for years what the "servant" was meant to represent in the hymns. Christians see Jesus as the ultimate fulfillment of these hymns, but the question remains for scholars as to the original meaning intended by Second Isaiah or his disciples.

The passages described someone who was wise like a sage, brought justice like a king, was called and proclaimed a message like a prophet (allusions to Jeremiah are quite evident), and above all, in the last hymn, suffered for the people. Commentators suggest various individuals. Isaiah used wisdom language and supposedly was martyred. Jeremiah was called in the womb like the servant, proclaimed a sharp message like the servant, and suffered for his prophetic mission. King Jehoiachin suffered in prison for the sake of his nation, and were he to have ruled as an ideal king, he would have brought justice and compassion. King Josiah brought reform and justice, and he died for the sake of the people at Megiddo. Even Moses, who was ruler, sage, prophet, priest, and lawgiver, suffered for Israel and even offered to die for the people in the wilderness when Yahweh threatened to destroy them. Perhaps Second Isaiah described some unknown teacher in the exile who fit these qualities. Perhaps Second Isaiah himself was the suffering servant, especially if he were thrown into prison by the Babylonians. The last hymn in Isaiah 53 might have been composed by his students. Maybe Second Isaiah envisioned a contemporary prophet who was to appear on the scene. What is haunting is that all of these options make good sense, and each of them fits certain characteristics in certain allusions in the text. To this author it seems that Second Isaiah painted a composite of many great individual heroes of the faith.

Many commentators have suggested that Second Isaiah's suffering servant was a corporate figure, the Jews themselves. The only clear identification made in the hymns (Isaiah 49:3) was with the people of Israel. (Israel or Jacob was casually called God's "servant" in Isaiah 41:8, 44:1, 48:20). Israel also was described as a "light to the nations" in texts outside the hymns (Isaiah 42:6, 51:4) as the servant was deemed to be within one of the hymns (Isaiah 49:6), and hence Israel was a "prophet" to the people of the world as the "servant" was portrayed in the hymns. In the patriarchal narratives and elsewhere, stories alternated between individual and corporate imagery when describing actions of a hero. Such polyvalent poetic usage would befit Second Isaiah as we have seen with his imagery of the return. Jewish tradition has maintained that Israel was the suffering servant, suffering for the nations who did not worship the true God. Like the five righteous people in Sodom, if they had existed, could have saved the city, so Jews saved the world by their faithful worship of Yahweh, even though the world persecuted them. This would have made make good sense in the exile where Jews were told that they must worship Marduk and partake in the New Year Akitu festival in order to prevent the evil goddess Tiamat from destroying the world with water, presumably an allusion to potential spring floods from the Tigris and Euphrates Rivers. The Jew could respond that world order was preserved not by sacrifice to Marduk, but by ethical obedience to the Law of Yahweh, especially Sabbath and kosher food. If Jews suffered for Gentiles as the servant, it would imply that Second Isaiah's universalistic allusions to the nations worshipping Yahweh might have the sense of true worship. Some modern commentators have modified the corporate interpretation by suggesting that the Jews who were the suffering servants were actually a minority of Jews, those faithful Jews who adhered to the customs of Yahwism throughout the exile and especially suffered for their convictions. If so, they suffered not for all people in the world, but for other Jews. Thus, the "righteous remnant," spoken of by the prophets, was the "suffering servant," and not all Jews.

A third major theory maintains that Second Isaiah intended the image to represent a composite of all the various individuals and also collective Israel. That the prophet could metaphor both is suggested by how creation, Exodus, and the return were woven together by the prophet in the imagery of Yahweh "cutting" a path in the waters/wilderness. Prophets are poets, and a poetic symbol can have many levels of meaning. If God wishes to communicate a powerful message to people, what better means is there than a polyvalent metaphor? Christians saw the image of Jesus in the servant, especially the fourth hymn in Isaiah 52:13-53:12. But if one considers this final theory advocated by scholars, an interesting insight emerges. If the suffering servant is both individual and corporate for Second Isaiah, could it not have been likewise for the first Christians? If Jesus was the individual who suffered, then the corporate group that suffers would be all Christians, who were called upon to suffer as Jesus did.

# Conclusion

The prophets and other scribal theologians (including those who created the final edition of the Deuteronomistic History around 550 BCE) provided a message to sustain and give hope to Jews in exile. In so doing, they created the ideology and the literature that would create Judaism. During the Babylonian Exile Jewish theologians produced their greatest works and ideas. They spoke of how punishment was deserved, but how repentance would bring restoration. Jews heard that God was present with them in exile and anywhere they wandered, because their God was the only God in the universe. Jews at last became monotheistic. Or better said, those among the exiles who became monotheistic, survived as Jews. Jews heard that Yahweh had not deserted them, but loved them, forgave them, and would bring to fulfillment all the promises. Their response led them to the exclusive worship of Yahweh and faithful obedience to the Law.

# Bibliography

Joseph Blenkinsopp. *A History of Prophecy in Israel*. Rev. Ed. Louisville, KY: Westminster John Knox, 1996.

Walther Eichrodt. *Ezekiel*. Trans. Cosslett Quinn. Old Testament Library. Philadelphia, PA: Westminster, 1970.

H. McKeating. *Ezekiel*. Old Testament Guides. Sheffield, Eng.: JSOT Press, 1993.

David Petersen. *The Prophetic Literature*. Louisville, KY: Westminster John Knox, 2002.

Gerhard von Rad. *The Message of the Prophets*. Trans. D. M. G. Stalker. New York, NY: Harper and Row, 1967.

Daniel Smith-Christopher. *A Biblical Theology of Exile*. Overtures to Biblical Theology. Minneapolis, MN: Fortress, 2002.

Roger Whybray. The Second Isaiah. Old Testament Guides. Sheffield, Eng.: Sheffield Academic Press, 1983.

Walther Zimmerli. *Ezekiel 1*. Trans. Ronald Clements. Hermeneia. Philadelphia, PA: Fortress, 1979.

Walther Zimmerli, *Ezekiel 2*. Trans. James Martin. Hermeneia. Philadelphia, PA: Fortress, 1983.

# Chapter 10

# Yahwist Historian

Reading: Genesis 2-11

As the Jews languished in exile, intelligentsia among them felt the need to recall the national traditions (Joshua, Judges, Samuel, Kings), laws, and prophetic oracles and place them into written form. They also saw the importance of recalling the foundational stories of their existence, since many of those accounts provided the framework for presenting their laws. Thus, narrative accounts in Genesis, Exodus, and Numbers may have taken final written shape during or soon after the exile. (Realize that a Jewish scribe might have written these traditions in 500 BCE, and if he were in Babylon, he would still be "in exile.") These stories spoke about ancestors who lived in an era when there was no national state; they lived as pastoralists in the land of Palestine (the patriarchs) or as liberated slaves wandering in the wilderness under Moses. Such narratives would have spoken meaningfully to exiles in Babylon, for they, too, lived as wandering exiles in a land that was not their own. Like their ancestors, they, too, looked forward to a day when they would return to the land that they believed was theirs.

Scholars diverge greatly in their of assessment of the origin of the literature in Genesis, Exodus, and Numbers. Some date the narrative material early, attributing it to the time of the United Monarchy and the Divided Monarchy, and see a fair degree of authentic historical memory in the accounts. We call them maximalists. Others believe the bulk of these narratives arose during the late pre-exilic era and exile, or even late in the post-exilic period. These authors propose that although there was some historical memory in the accounts, most of the narratives were fiction with a theological message. Some narratives may contain veiled allusions to historical and social events of later era, maybe even post-exilic experiences. We call them minimalists. Increasingly scholars favor the minimalist perspective, but in a cautious fashion. Most scholars would suggest the exile as the time of origin for the narratives, but would be reluctant to suggest the late Persian period (539-332 BCE) or even the Hellenistic period (332-164 BCE), as some extreme minimalists do. This textbook sides with the moderate voices that posit exile and shortly thereafter as the time when Pentateuchal narratives underwent formation.

# Epic Literature

In the Babylonian Exile, or shortly thereafter, the Yahwist and Elohist narratives may have been written down. Among authors who see the exile as a time of formation for the epic literature, there are still various models to explain the extent of this development. This is a highly debated issue, but it seems to many that there are exilic themes in the epic traditions, especially in the Yahwist. Some believe the Yahwist drew together very fragmentary pre-exilic oral traditions (including the Elohist fragments) in a fairly original written composition. Hence, they discuss the Yahwist only from an exilic social and historical perspective. Some scholars suggest that the epic traditions were evolving oral traditions from the time of the monarchy down until the exile, and in this process they precipitated from loose oral traditions into larger oral cycles (like Homer's *Iliad* and *Odyssey*) and then into written form during the exile. Thus, we might talk about the meaning these oral traditions had over the years before they took final written form.

In past generations scholars argued for an early date for when the traditions took shape. They posited that the Yahwist arose during the time of Solomon (950 BCE) and the Elohist emerged some time during the Divided Monarchy (930-720 BCE). They suggested that the oral Yahwist and Elohist cycles were combined at the time of Hezekiah (700 BCE) into an oral JE Epic (J stands for Yahwist and E for Elohist). Either during or after the exile the Priestly Editors worked with this material, and the edited JEP narrative was placed at the beginning of the written Deuteronomistic History. Only a very few scholars still use this model.

If the Yahwist took shape during the Babylonian Exile or early post-exilic age, we should be able to observe evidence of this in the accounts. In the narratives we find names that make sense for people in exile. Abraham's migration to Palestine through Ur of the Chaldees and Haran makes sense only after the rise of the Chaldean Empire in 605 BCE, since both cities were religious sites for Chaldean kings. Familial customs in Yahwist patriarchal narratives were closely related to the customs and laws of the Neo-Babylonian or Chaldean laws (550 BCE). Cities visited by the patriarchs in Palestine were inhabited simultaneously only two times in Israel's history, 1050 BCE and 550 BCE, which, of course, points ambiguously to the days of Solomon as well as the exile. The name of Mount Ararat was a place name known to Israelites and Jews only after 750 BCE with the Assyrian wars against Urartu in modern-day Armenia. Traditions about the seer Balaam (Numbers 20-24) have been discovered in the Transjordan, in the city of Deir Alla among a non-Israelite people (perhaps half-Israelite at most), and they date to 750-700 BCE. The Garden of Eden was mentioned elsewhere in the biblical text only in late passages (Ezekiel 28:13, 36:35, Isaiah 51:3, Joel 2:3), as was Noah (Isaiah 54:9). The land of Shinar mentioned in Genesis 11:2 likewise was mentioned in late texts like Zechariah 5:11 and Daniel 1:2. Abraham's journey to Palestine reminds some scholars of the return trip undertaken by exiles after 539 BCE, which points to an early post-exilic era.

Likewise, the story of the Tower of Babel might be a parable on the fall of Babylon and the end of Nabonidus' building projects in 539 BCE. If you argue for an early date for the Yahwist, then you must suggest that names, customs, and some traditions have been introduced into an exilic revision of the pre-exilic Yahwist (plus Elohist) epic, otherwise you posit the 6th century BCE origin.

Theological themes also point to an exilic origin. Abraham's journey to a distant land in the west (Genesis 12) and the promise of divine accompaniment to all three patriarchs makes more sense to Jews during and after the exile. Jacob returned to north Mesopotamia from Palestine and then came home, like the exiles! The promise of children, land, and greatness would be most meaningful to exiles in a foreign land fearful of their ethnic disappearance. In the Primeval History it seems that the Cain and Abel story might have begun the cycle of stories at some point in the development of the traditions, and the story of the man and woman might have been added at a later stage. Genesis 2-3 contained Mesopotamian themes, and the expulsion from the garden reminds us of the exile from Palestine. It is possible that this material was added to an earlier edition of the Primeval History (Genesis 2-11) in exile or shortly thereafter. As the traditions emerged from the hands of the Yahwist Historian and later Priestly Editors, the story of Genesis, Exodus, and Numbers unfolded as a message of hope to exiles in a foreign land and recent returnees. The narrative speaks of landless patriarchs wandering the highlands, slaves in Egypt, and wandering Israelites in the wilderness. Jews in Babylon could identify with these people, and they would recognize Yahweh was a deity who journeyed with landless people.

# The Yahwist

The traditions of the ancestors perhaps were transmitted orally for generations by bards. Oral tradition can recall a vast number of corporate memories and retain them for years. But when wars, famine, forced migrations, or other dramatic circumstances arise, the bards disappear and the stories can be lost. Thus, oral traditions may be committed to some fixed or written form in a period of stress or social change. The Babylonian Exile (586-539 BCE) caused most of the Hebrew Bible to be fixed in written form, and the Yahwist Historian may have written in this same era.

We believe bards recited their tales at shrines during festivals or special occasions. These tales may have been arranged into several narrative cycles: 1) Patriarchs, 2) Exodus, 3) Wilderness Wanderings, 4) Sinai, and 5) Conquest. How well developed these may have been is often disputed. Exodus accounts might have been recalled during Passover in the early spring, Sinai memories during the fall Festival of Tabernacles along with tales about living in "tents" in the wilderness (for "tabernacle" refers to the tents), and conquest memories during the Festival of First Fruits (Pentecost) in the late spring. If we are correct in our assumptions, then the significant accomplishment of the Yahwist was to weave these cycles into one grand epic. If the Yahwist was early, the grand epic was oral, if the Yahwist was exilic or later, the epic was written.

Some believe that the Yahwist broke the cycle of the Wilderness Wandering tales in half and placed the Sinai traditions into the middle. Perhaps this suggests that Sinai and Wilderness traditions were celebrated at separate festivals. By placing the Sinai traditions into the Wilderness cycle following the Exodus traditions, the Yahwist was doing more than simply reconstructing a historical sequence of events. The Yahwist placed the giving of the Law close to the Exodus experience so that obedience to the Law given at Sinai would be seen as a grateful response to divine deliverance in the Exodus. To these five native Israelite cycles of tradition, the Yahwist added a Primeval History, taken from Mesopotamian traditions, to form a prologue. The use of Mesopotamian traditions again implies an exilic setting for the Yahwist.

The Yahwist arranged narratives in chronological or linear order, and though this appears to be the obvious thing to do, it was innovative for that age. It foreshadowed "history-writing," an attempt to see events from a linear human perspective rather than from a cyclic pattern that reflected the seasons, as we find with the Canaanite literature of Baal from Ugarit from the second millennium BCE. Yahwistic "history-writing" paralleled contemporary Greek historiography, which was emerging at the same time. Historiography, as we would define it, arose with Herodotus and Thucydides (450-350 BCE), who were interested in relating human events apart from a connection to the divine realm. The Yahwist epic, like the epics of Homer and various Babylonian chronicles, still spoke of the relationship of the divine and human realm, which meant it was not history-writing in our modern sense of the term. But the Yahwist discussed events from the beginning of time up to his era in a more humanistic mode than in contemporary literature of the ancient world, and thus anticipated later Greek history writing.

**The Primeval History:** Yahwist accounts predominated in the Pentateuch, especially in Genesis, Exodus, and Numbers. When the Yahwist recounted these memories, the stories were too well known to permit extensive reinterpretation. Selection of certain stories and their sequencing was the way in which the Yahwist expressed distinctive viewpoints, such as placing the southern patriarch Abraham before the northern patriarch Jacob and creating passages to link narratives (birth narratives). But with stories and myths taken from the Canaanites and Mesopotamians, the Yahwist could shape a brilliant theological masterpiece. Thus, a critical approach to evaluating Yahwist theology is consideration of the Primeval History in Genesis 2-11 where foreign materials were adapted.

The Yahwist provided us with five accounts: 1) the man and the woman in the garden (Genesis 2-3), 2) Cain and Abel (Genesis 4), 3) the Flood (Genesis 5-8), 4) Noah's blessing and curse (Genesis 9-10), and 5) the Tower of Babel (Genesis 11). There is an observable pattern in these stories: initial divine blessing or grace, human sin, the consequent punishment for sin, and divine forgiveness or blessing. This conveys one of the key themes of the Yahwist: that Yahweh was constantly gracious to a rebellious humanity. This concept ultimately influenced the Christian understanding of divine grace toward a sinful humanity. Close attention paid to Genesis by Reformation theologians, Luther and Calvin, created the very strong emphasis upon the total grace and forgiveness of God in the Protestant traditions (especially the Lutheran).

*Man and Woman in the Garden:* The Man and the Woman did not have proper names until after their expulsion from the garden, for they were symbols of all human beings. They lived in the garden in a state of innocence or simple childhood (Genesis 2:4-25).

Yahweh created the Man or the Adam out of the ground, and the word Adam meant "earth" or more generally it was a generic word for humanity. It was not a real name; it was a title. We are made from "dirt," this stresses our oneness with the earth, yet by breathing in the "breath of life," Yahweh made this creature special.

Because the Adam was lonely, Yahweh created animals from the ground. God created animals just like the Adam, which indicates our human oneness with the animal world and the natural order. No animal could suffice as Adam's friend, so Yahweh created a Woman out of his rib. Once the "female" was created, the Adam was subsequently called "male" instead of generic "man." In the Hebrew the word for "male" was *aesch*, and this word was not used until the "female" (*aeschah*) was created, which means the two sexual identities arose together. It is a misuse of the text to speak of male superiority by saying "male" was created before "female," for both arose together out of the Adam. (Genesis 1:27 actually said the same thing, "God made man, male and female He made them.")

There were two trees in the garden. The first was the tree of the knowledge of good and evil. Over the years commentators have differed over what "good and evil" may mean. 1) Perhaps it meant everything from "good to evil," implying of range of things or the totality of knowledge (i.e., from "soup to nuts" in modern slang). They were thus ready to become fully rational and capable human beings in God's world. 2) Perhaps moral awareness was implied, the ability to discern right and wrong, as when children attain the age of accountability. This might imply that the man and the woman were still children in the garden. But obtaining this knowledge should be good, so why would God be angry, unless the man and the woman thus "grew up" before God was ready for them to do so. 3) Occasionally sexual awareness is suggested by commentators, since shame was mentioned by the man in connection with nakedness. But Gen 2:24 implied that the couple could have sex potentially at some point and thus sex was viewed as positive, so that knowledge of sex was not to be seen as bad. (I prefer the second interpretation.) The tree of life has been seen by commentators as a tree which granted immortality or which brought rejuvenation when people became old. In the former instance one need eat only once, in the latter instance continual consumption would be necessary. Most commentators prefer the former option. Interestingly, live trees in the Temple courtyard (Psalms 52:8, 92:12-13) may have been symbols of this tree of life.

What angered God about their eating the fruit may have been manifold. They clearly rebelled against the divine command; that was serious enough. More compelling, of course, was their reason for eating—they wished to have the knowledge that God had. Of course, they had not a clue what this knowledge entailed; they just wanted it. Commentators have called this an act of extreme hybris, inappropriate pride—desire to be like God or the gods. But there was yet another sin: the refusal to take responsibility for their own actions, and perhaps this was the most serious sin. Had they repented immediately, they might have stayed in the garden (following the logic of the story, one could assume this). However, when confronted by Yahweh, they passed the blame: the man to the woman, the woman to the snake, and the man passed it ultimately back to God. They denied their freedom and responsibility for their actions (a big theme in the Yahwist). They acted like small children who shun responsibility required by adulthood (even as many adults do). This also reflected the mentality of the ancient cyclic worldview that assumed since all things were fated, people need not take responsibility with ethical behavior, but need to offer proper sacrifice to appease the gods in the divinely predestined universe. The man and the woman symbolized human beings of any age who fail to take responsibility for their actions and pass the blame to others

Their punishment, or curse, reflected the many disharmonies in the everyday world: the tensions between men and women (dangers and pain of childbirth), the conflict between people and the animal realm (conflict with the snake), the struggle between people and the earth (the toil of farming), and the alienation between humanity and God (expulsion from the garden). On another level of meaning, the story was a profound parable about leaving behind the innocence of childhood, and shouldering the responsibility and the pains of adulthood. Thus, the story functioned as a negative parable about human rebellion against God and a positive parable about adulthood and the assumption of freedom and responsibility.

Although the curses sound severe to us, they were not the final word in the stories. The theme of grace concluded every Yahwist account. The man and the woman did not die, as God's threat at first indicated; they continued to live. Though they were cast out of the garden, they received names and became true individuals or adults. Until this time, they were symbolically "everyman" or "everywoman"; on another level, they were like children with no real identity of their own. Once the woman received the name "Eve," then "Adam" can be viewed as a name, not a title. Yahweh also taught them how to make clothing so that they might live in the world, and the greatest of all gifts was imparted to them, children of their own. Their story was a double metaphor of falling from grace and the coming to adulthood that accepts both freedom and responsibility. They were metaphors for any individual and the Jews as a people.

In a sense, the ultimate destiny of the man and the woman was to leave the garden, to go forth and till the ground, the task for which they were created, and to develop human culture. Some Jewish and Christian commentators over the years have suggested that the man and the woman were predestined by God to sin and leave the garden so that they could fulfill their destiny as the creators of culture or to experience the grace of God (as some 17th century Christian commentators suggested).

The story invites comparison with some of the earlier myths from the ancient Near East. In making these comparisons, however, we must admit that we are comparing biblical material from the first millennium BCE with ancient Near Eastern texts from the second and third millennia BCE. We should expect the biblical narratives to appear more sophisticated, and we must acknowledge the biblical authors were indebted to the intellectual heritage of the ancient Near Eastern world that preceded them. Hence, we must speak of the biblical ideology not in diametrical opposition to the worldview of the ancient Near East so much as viewing it to be the worldview which grew out of and went beyond the values of the prior ancient Near Eastern culture.

Particular myths that invite attention in this comparison include the following:

1. *Atrahasis Myth and Enuma Elish Myth.* Both of these long Akkadian epics from the second millennium BCE recounted the creation of people, as part of their

longer narration about the origin of the world. In both accounts, creation of humanity was commissioned by the creator deity (Ea or Enki in Atrahasis and Marduk in Enuma Elish), after he defeated the forces of chaos (the rebellious gods in Atrahasis or the goddess of chaos, Tiamat in Enuma Elish). People were made from clay and the blood of a defeated, evil god named We-ilu in Atrahasis or Kingu in Enuma Elish. They were destined to serve the gods by providing sacrifice, and they became slaves of the gods because of their origin. By contrast, the biblical story told how people were made from clay and enlivened with the breath of Yahweh. Hence, they were created good, free, and responsible.

2. *Adapa Myth.* In this short Akkadian myth from the second millennium BCE the hero was Adapa, a priest of Ea (or Enki) in Eridu. While fishing, he calmed the sea by cursing the south wind and breaking its wing. Since the wind then could not bring rain to the farmers, people cried to the gods. Adapa had to appear before the gods, especially Anu. The god Enki, who often befriended humanity, warned him not to eat or drink anything in the divine realm, since it was poison. Before the gods Adapa pled his case as a poor, struggling mortal living on earth, and he won their respect so that they offered him the bread and wine of immortality. Recalling Enki's advice, he declined the offer (mumbling something about his stop at McDonald's on the way up), and thus forever lost the chance of immortality. If he symbolized all of humanity, this story told why people must die. We lost immortality due to bad luck. But there is ambiguity in the story! Was Enki surprised by the other gods' decision, or did he know that such an offer would be made to Adapa. If the latter was the case, did he deceive Adapa out a desire to keep Adapa as his servant, or did Enki believe that mortality was actually good for a humanity that might otherwise overpopulate the earth and thereby suffer? At any rate, the imagery of divine fate in the outcome of the story contrasts with the emphasis in the biblical text upon human free will in choosing to rebel against God and thereby losing immortality.

3. *Gilgamesh Epic.* The Gilgamesh Epic was a lengthy Akkadian composition from the late second millennium BCE, which evolved out of smaller stories reaching back to third millennium BCE Sumerian origins. Early in the Gilgamesh Epic, the hero Enkidu, who would become the friend of Gilgamesh, was transformed from his wild state to being civilized by a prolonged sexual encounter with a sacred prostitute. Afterward his animal friends fled from him, for he had "fallen" into a "civilized" state. Enkidu represented wild, uncivilized humanity and the prostitute represented the civilized culture of the Mesopotamian city with the Temple (where the prostitute worked) as the apex of the city's existence. Thus, sex became the tool by which Enkidu became civilized. In the biblical account the man and the woman did not have sex, presumably, but they attained sexual awareness in their act of rebellion and thus moved from childhood toward adulthood. But the emphasis was upon human will and decisions, not the sexual act.

Toward the end of the Gilgamesh Epic, Gilgamesh lost the plant of youthful rejuvenation while he was swimming in a pond outside of Uruk after his long journey and search for the secret of immortality. The snake ate his plant. Presumably this was a Mesopotamian aetiology for why snakes knew the secret of youthful rejuvenation, medical healing, and sexual potency, skills attributed to snakes due to the ability of snakes to shed their skins and appear as though they became alive after dying. The ancients in the Near East and later Greece revered snake deities and sought these gifts at their shrines through complex rituals and overnight dream incubation. Bad luck wrested rejuvenation and perhaps a form of immortality from Gilgamesh. But in the biblical account a human decision, made in free will, did this.

*Cain and Abel:* The murder in the Cain and Abel narrative was the first true sin, an act of serious violence, for the sin in the garden was also a metaphor for coming to adulthood. Some scholars suspect that in an early stage of the Yahwist epic, this was the first account in the Primeval History. Ironically, in the later Jewish literature which was not put into the Bible, including Enoch 6:1-5, 7:1-6, 15:2-16:1, Jubilees 5:1-6, 10:1-9, the first sin was the activity described in Genesis 6:1-4.

The family setting in Genesis 4:1-2 reflected a state of grace. Eve's statement, "I have produced a man with the help of the Lord" was a proclamation of a woman's success in bearing a son for the household, which was a great source of pride for Israelite women in a culture that always had too few people. Her cry may have been a formula used by women to introduce the newborn baby into the household. Cain's name meant either "strong" or "metal-smith" (and there was a word play with the verb "to acquire," as Eve stated she "acquired" a man from God), while Abel's name meant "puff of smoke" or "vanity" (as in "vanity of vanities" in Koheleth). The text may have portrayed them as brothers born years apart or perhaps more likely as twins born a few minutes apart. One senses that Abel was not going to last very long in this account.

Cain's envy led to murder and showed how inner desires can be the source of equally evil actions. As Jesus rightly said, "Whoever hates his brother is a murderer." Cain's punishment was exile from the land, a severe curse for a farmer. As he was the only living son of the primal couple, he was symbolically the ancestor of all humanity (disregarding Seth, because the Priestly Editors added him). As a murderer, he was the person who introduced war into the world; this was the aetiology for human violence and bloodshed. To stop war and murder, Cain had to be killed, but to kill Cain would be to terminate humanity, for Cain was our symbolic eponymous ancestor. Thus, to end war, Yahweh must terminate humanity. But Yahweh chose another way, and that was the message of the entire Bible! In grace Yahweh kept Cain or humanity and would attempt to teach them with the Law that would come with Moses.

Yahweh's grace was the final word. As a murderer, Cain could not survive in a world in which family members would someday have to kill Cain to avenge the murder of Abel. Cain was a symbol; he must be hunted for endless ages in order to stop the curse of bloodshed and war. Yet to kill him would mean the termination of humanity--what an irony! Yahweh protected Cain from those who forever must seek revenge. Cain was given a "mark," a tribal tattoo for protection during his wanderings (Genesis 4:13-26). We think that this mark is equivalent to the later mark used for blessing, the last letter of the Hebrew alphabet, the tau. This letter looks remarkably like the later Christian cross, because Jewish Christians made the form of the actual Roman cross appear like the tau. It is interesting to observe how Cain's mark of protection or blessing is commonly considered a curse by many today. We speak of the curse on Cain. Too often, our negative or pessimistic piety will not let us see blessings in these stories.

An interesting ancient Near Eastern parallel to this story is found in the third millennium BCE Sumerian myth about Dumuzi the farmer and Enkimdu the shepherd. Both loved the beautiful Inanna. Dumuzi won her, for he did not stink like Enkimdu (blame the sheep for that!), and he represented the more civilized life-style of the river-valley farmer. Dumuzi and Enkimdu then separated their regions of living; Dumuzi got the valleys and Enkimdu received the highlands. The story was an aetiology about the origins of sedentarism and pastoralism with sedentary farmers seen as the good guys by Mesopotamians. Israelites always idealized their origins as pastoralists, so in their version the good guy was the shepherd Abel, and Cain the pastoralist, was the murderer.

*The Flood:* The flood story (Genesis 6:9-8:19) was preceded by a strange vignette about sex between the "daughters of men" and the "sons of God" (Genesis 6:1-4). The Yahwist perhaps adapted an old lost Canaanite myth about the origin of semi-divine ancestors, "the mighty men that were of old, the men of renown" (Genesis 6:4). Canaanites or Phoenicians may have used this story to venerate their semi-divine ancestors, but the story was changed to explain why Yahweh destroyed the world, so these semi-divine ancestors were really very evil beings. Evil permeated both the human and the divine realms. Since the "sons of Gods" were seen as the pantheon of gods by polytheists, the Yahwist was saying to polytheists, "Your gods were so evil that our deity, Yahweh, had to destroy them!" Though this sounds as if the author assumed polytheism, it was really a monotheistic statement to elevate the power of Yahweh and attack polytheism. The Yahwist then introduced another reason for the flood. On the earth "violence" or social injustice (murder, rape, and robbery) increased, so that the human heart was evil "continually" (Genesis 6:5). Yahweh flooded the human and the divine realms. Using water for destruction spoke to people who lived in river valleys, such as Egypt and Mesopotamia, for they saw floods as a return to primordial chaos.

The Yahwist modified accounts of the flood taken from myths of Mesopotamia, the stories of Ziusudra, Atrahasis, and Utnapishtim, whose accounts dated from the second millennium BCE. Ziusudra's tale was told in the Sumerian "Eridu Genesis," which described how people were created, then built cities for Enki, but were condemned to die by Enlil in a 7 day flood. Ziusudra saved people and animals in an ark, offered sacrifice after the flood, and was made immortal and placed on the island of Dilmun, especially after Enki rebuked Enlil for the flood. The experience of Atrahasis was recounted in the Atrahasis Epic, a tale of both creation and the flood. After people were created, they disturbed Enlil with noise and overpopulated the world, so the gods tried to thin out humanity with a plague, famine, a series of disasters, and finally a flood. Enki warned Atrahasis to sacrifice to avert each of these disasters, and finally for the flood Enki directed Atrahasis to build an ark with seven floors and nine compartments on each floor. After the flood Atrahasis sent out a raven, swallow, and dove to check the land. Ultimately Atrahasis and his family were divinized and taken to a distant land, while Enki created people once more and the gods used sterility and stillbirth to limit human population.

In the Gilgamesh Epic, Gilgamesh learned the story of the flood from Utnapishtim, who lived on a distant isle. The gods determined to destroy humanity by a flood because of their noise, and they told Enki not to speak to humanity. But Utnapishtim was warned of the flood by Enki, who spoke to a reed hut in which Utnapishtim was sleeping. He, too, built an ark of the same dimensions as did Atrahasis, endured a flood for seven days, and sent out the same three birds, as did Atrahasis. He offered up sacrifice to the gods, who were hungry and swarmed around the sacrifice like flies (a strange metaphor), and they pleaded with Enlil not to kill humanity again. Utnapishtim was made immortal and lived in the land to which Gilgamesh came seeking the secret of immortality.

The biblical text used many of these details in reconstructing a new narrative. The similarities which the biblical account shared with the Mesopotamian accounts included the following:  1) a divine plan to drown the world and the reason for this action, 2) warning given to an individual including on how to build an ark and its dimensions, 3) animals and people were placed in the ark in order that they might survive, 4) floodwaters covered the earth, including the mountains, and drowned all life, 5) the ark landed on a mountain in Urartu (Mesopotamian name of the region) or Ararat (biblical name of the region) as the water level receded, 6) birds (both versions have a raven and a dove) were sent out to check for dry land, 7) the hero exited the ark and sacrificed, and 8) there was a divine response to the hero after the sacrifice. In the biblical account, however, the motives of Yahweh were much more noble than those of the Mesopotamian deities, who either wished to destroy a "noisy" humanity or to limit population in a crowded world. Yahweh communicated directly to Noah, not having to circumvent the will of other gods by deceitful communication to the flood hero. Yahweh was in total control of the flood (he even closed the ark door and steadied it in the water), while in the Mesopotamian stories the gods were terrified of the flood they unleashed. Yahweh was in control of the ark as it floated, and he brought it to rest on the mountain. Yahweh did not need sacrifice, as did Mesopotamian deities, so Yahweh freely created a covenant with Noah promising never again to destroy people. Finally, Yahweh blessed all of humanity with the promise of stable seasons and no more flooding, while the Mesopotamian accounts limited the blessing merely to divinity or immortality granted to the flood hero.

Ultimately, Mesopotamians also believed that the goddess of watery chaos (Tiamat) could flood them again, so their New Year's celebration was designed to avoid another flood. The Yahwist implied that no such a threat existed with the moral deity of the biblical accounts. One senses the Yahwist has elevated the old Mesopotamian myths with a higher moral consciousness, resulting from monotheistic perspectives. Again, we must not imply that the ancient Near Eastern accounts were intellectually or morally inferior to the biblical narratives. The biblical narratives arose a thousand years later than their ancient Near Eastern antecedents. One would expect greater sophistication. But we must recognize the significance of the advance made by the biblical authors from their ancient Near Eastern roots.

*Noah's Sons*:  Noah and his sons left the ark and lived under divine blessing with the gift of human and animal fertility. The land was blessed and yielded good produce for Noah--grapes which became wine. After drinking his new agricultural blessing, Noah became drunk and took off his clothing, for he was hot after excessive wine consumption.

Many people erroneously think the sin in this story was drunkenness, but the biblical tradition did not see that as the sin, the sin was the activity of Ham. In calling attention to Noah's drunken condition (Genesis 9:22-23), Ham committed three offenses. He offended cultic purity by seeing his father's nakedness. Such prohibitions against viewing a naked relative were to prevent incestuous marriages from arising in small pastoralist or village societies. He committed a social offense by failing to help his father. Ancient proverbs spoke of children's responsibilities to guide their parents home when the parents were drunk, a privilege reserved as one of the few pleasures available to old, retired members of the family. Finally, he heaped ridicule on the father by inviting his brothers to look. The two brothers, however, showed proper respect for Noah. The text also has a word play--"seeing the nakedness" of someone was a euphemism for sex. So the text may hint that Ham took sexual advantage of Noah, which may have polemicized sexual-religious customs of the people supposedly descended from Ham, the Canaanites.

After he was sober, Noah cursed Canaan, the son of Ham (Genesis 9:24-25). The reason for Noah's curse on Canaan became apparent in the list of Canaan's descendants (Genesis 10:15-19); they were the people defeated by Israel, including the Jebusites. The curse was fulfilled by Joshua and David. People today refer to the "curse on Ham," but the expression did not exist in the Bible; it has been made up by people who quote the Bible rather than reading it. The expression was used to justify the enslavement and suppression of African people over the past four centuries, saying that Africans were the descended from Ham. This interpretation is additionally wrong because the table of nations in Genesis 10 listed as the descendants of Ham not only Africans, but also many non-African peoples, such as Philistines, Cretans, Egyptians, and others. Use of the Bible in this fashion typifies the horrible misuse of the Bible that so often occurs when people do not read the biblical text or lack the courage to contradict those who misinterpret the Bible.

Noah proclaimed a blessing upon both Shem and Japheth. Shem's blessing foreshadowed the rise of the David; Japheth's blessing referred to those nations around Israel that prospered from the peace and trade created by David's rule. Since such images foreshadowed the United Monarchy, scholars once suggested that the Yahwist epic took shape under Solomon. Now we believe the biblical author foreshadowed David to suggest to exiles in Babylon that a future David would come again.

*Tower of Babel*: Noah's descendants spoke the same language as they moved into Shinar, the ancient Israelite name for Sumer, southern Mesopotamia, where ancient civilizations arose. Fearful lest Yahweh flood them again, the people refused to disperse and repopulate the world. This sin of distrust was magnified by the sin of pride, their desire to build a tower. The tower would protect them from another flood, but they also believed the tower would enable them to storm the heavens, that is, to become like the gods, immortal and all knowing. This was the same sin of the man and the woman in the garden when they ate the fruit. The Primeval History began and ended with the sin of human pride, or hubris, the desire to be like the gods. Their attempt to storm the heavens and their magnificent technology was ridiculed by the biblical author when Yahweh had to come down to see the tiny, puny thing the people were building. Their punishment was precisely what they sought to avoid. They were scattered abroad over the whole earth, and they lost the ability to communicate with each other.

The story may have been a parable on the rise and fall of great Mesopotamian empires. Often an emergent empire brought together diverse peoples from around the Near East for massive building projects in the central ruling cities. With the demise of the empire and collapse of central government, these peoples sometimes went home or were scattered abroad. Thus, the word "babel" is really a combination of the Hebrew words "balel" ("to rave like a madman") and "babal" ("Babylon"). The building they constructed was reminiscent of the ziggurat or temple structure built by Mesopotamians from 2000 to 550 BCE. Famous ziggurats were build by Ur-Nammu of Ur around 2000 BCE and Kashtiliash of Babylon around 1300 BCE. Several shrine refurbishing projects were undertaken by Nabonidus of Chaldean Babylon around 550 BCE, when the Jews were in exile. Of special interest in this regard were the records of Nebuchadrezzar, the king who destroyed Jerusalem in 586 BCE. He proclaimed that he brought people from all over his empire to work on the Eteminanki, the great temple in Babylon, which was a symbolic sacred mountain (like the ziggurats). Nabonidus also refurbished this same shrine. One might almost suggest that the Eteminanki could have inspired directly the image of the "Tower of Babel." Kings or high priests ascended these symbolic cosmic mountains to sacrifice, because as supreme leaders in society they could approach the gods most closely, and this legitimated their authority over people. Such symbolism offended egalitarian monotheists, such as the Jewish theologians. Most likely the biblical author recalled Nebuchadrezzar's Eteminanki or perhaps Nabonidus, who undertook the building or renovation of numerous shrines in Ur, Uruk, Sippar, Babylon, and Harran to the honor of the moon deity, Sin, many of which were left unfinished when his empire fell to the Persians. Since Jews and others were allowed to return to their homes after Cyrus the Great of Persia defeated Nabonidus, I suspect that Genesis 11 may have been inspired by the collapse of Nabonidus' Babylon, for the "scattering" would refer to the return of the Jews. In particular, directly after the Babel story we are told how Abraham went to Palestine by passing through two cities, Ur of the Chaldees and Haran  (Nabonidus began building ziggurats in both), and Abraham's family supposedly were moon devotees, like Nabonidus. In later Jewish literature (Daniel 4 and "The Prayer of Nabonidus") Nabonidus provided inspiration for the insane Babylonian king, so it would be logical that Genesis 11 could be a parable on him. The story is much more a polemic against Babylonian politics and religion, than the memory of an unfinished building.

The story ended with no blessing, unless it was the repopulation of the world by these people. But we suspect the real blessing intended by the Yahwist was the call of Abram in Genesis 12, who was called out of the city of Ur, where great ziggurats often were built. If so, the Yahwist created a clever literary ploy to link the Primeval History with the cycle of the Patriarchal Narratives. After the failure of humanity, Yahweh began again with the ancestor of Israel, called forth from Ur of the Chaldees. The reference to Chaldeans makes us recall the Babylonian Exile, when Jews were ruled by Chaldeans. Abraham's journey symbolized the return of Jews to Palestine after 539 BCE.

**Theology of the Yahwist,** Yahwist accounts emphasized divine grace and forgiveness. People were finite beings who often sinned against Yahweh. But Yahweh forgave and restored the patriarchs, Israel, and humanity in general. Punishment may come, but grace opens new possibilities for the future. Jacob was called to be the patriarch after he cheated Isaac and Esau and ran from home. Israel was saved in the Exodus.

Yahweh ruled over society and human events. Though Yahweh was creator and lord of nature, it was divine direction of human events from the beginning of time that was most important for Yahweh. This implied that expected obedience should be exhibited in social, everyday terms. Ethics and morality should take precedence over cult and sacrifice. Israel was called to be a people before they had land, so Yahweh was not a deity of a particular country, like the other gods, but a God of people, wherever they might be. This theme was most meaningful for exiles in Babylon (586-539 BCE).

More than any other tradition, the Yahwist stressed the loving, personal nature of God. Yahweh was portrayed physically (the term for this is "anthropomorphism" meaning in the body of a human being), as walking, standing beside people, and even having human body parts. Yahweh also was portrayed as having human emotions (the term for this is "anthropopathism" meaning human pathos, or emotions). The Yahwist was not primitive, as scholars in the 19th century suggested, but these images deliberately stressed the personal nature of God's relationship to humanity. Thus, Yahweh took human form and debated with Abraham over the fate of the evil cities in Genesis 18.

Yahwist narratives were held together by linking motifs, the most important of which were the "Promises to the Forefathers." Yahweh promised the patriarchs that their descendants would have land, be great in number, and be a blessing to other nations. Such promises were fulfilled in the Davidic Empire, but exiled Jews believed the Davidic Empire of the past was a paradigm for the golden age to come, so these promises would come true again. Jews who returned to Palestine after 539 BCE saw themselves walking in the footsteps of Abraham to receive the fulfillment of the land promises again.

The identity of the Yahwist is important in understanding this source. Many stories have the earmarks of the bard's craft--earthy humor, especially in the patriarchal narratives, thus scholars have suggested the Yahwist was a bard. Some authors think the author was a woman because of the frequent ridicule of men, like the patriarchs. However, folktales often glorify the heroics of women, tricksters, and underdogs, such as second born (Isaac and Jacob) and last born (Joseph), but especially slaves, like Israel in Egypt. The author crafted narratives that not only were entertaining but also contained a powerful message about divine grace.

# Conclusion

The Yahwist gave a message to sustain and give hope to Jews in exile. In so doing, the Yahwist created a very significant component of the message that would later characterize Jewish and Christian understandings about human finitude and divine grace. Emphasis upon universal history directed by Yahweh spoke to Jews of how their God was present with them in exile or anywhere in the world, because Yahweh was a universal deity. The message of these texts strengthened newly emerging monotheism among Jews in exile. In these traditions Jews heard that their God, a deity of all people, had chosen them and promised to them a great destiny. This God had not deserted them, but loved them, forgave them, and would bring to fulfillment all the promises made to the patriarchs.

# Bibliography

Joseph Blenkinsopp, *The Pentateuch*. New York, NY: Doubleday, 1992.

Thomas Dozeman and Konrad Schmid, eds. *A Farewell to the Yahwist?* Atlanta, GA: Society of Biblical Literature, 2006.

Theodore Hiebert. *The Yahwist's Landscape: Nature and Religion in Early Israel*. New York, NY: Oxford University, 1996.

Johnson Lim. *Grace in the Midst of Judgment: Grappling with Genesis 1-11*. Beihefte zur Zeitschrift für die alttestamentliche Wissenschaft 314. New York, NY: Walter de Gruyter, 2002.

Gerhard von Rad. *Old Testament Theology*, vol. 1. Trans. D. M. G. Stalker. New York, NY: Harper and Row, 1962.

John Van Seters. *The Life of Moses: The Yahwist as Historian in Exodus-Numbers*. Louisville, KY: Westminster John Knox, 1994.

John Van Seters. *Prologue to History: The Yahwist as Historian in Genesis*. Louisville, KY: Westminster John Knox, 1992.

Bruce Vawter. *On Genesis*. New York, NY: Doubleday, 1970.

Claus Westermann. *Genesis 1-11*. Trans. John Scullion. Minneapolis, MN: Augsburg, 1984.

# Chapter 11

# Matriarchs and Patriarchs

Reading: Genesis 12-36,38

## Ancestral Narratives

The narratives about the ancestors of Israel in Genesis 12-37 might really be called the "Old Testament" of the "Old Testament," for they recall the experiences and religious beliefs of those ancestors who lived before Israel truly came into existence. The history of Israel and the Jews began with the Exodus experience and the giving of the Law at Sinai. In a sense, the Exodus experience is comparable to the resurrection of Jesus in the New Testament. Both events were seen by believers as the dramatic and gracious actions of God in human history to save people and create a worshipping community (election) which will celebrate that foundational event forever (Passover or Easter) and view it as a paradigm by which to understand the deeper nature of God (as primarily gracious) and to anticipate a future event which will culminate world history. In that light, Genesis spoke of a time before the great event and the establishment of the covenant people. Hence, it bore a relationship to the rest of the Hebrew Bible as the Hebrew Bible or Old Testament bore to the New Testament. Crucial in this relationship of Genesis to the later events recorded were promises given by God to Abraham, Isaac, and Jacob which foreshadowed the Exodus, the conquest of the land, and the rise of David.

The narratives of Genesis 12-36, 38, in particular, recorded the memory of Abraham, Isaac, and Jacob, as well as their wives, Sarah, Rebecca, Leah, and Rachel. From the traditions of various people who would become Israel, stories preserved in oral tradition were woven together as accounts of the ancestors of the nation. These accounts were remembered orally for years and preserved some of the cultural memories of that pre-Exodus era. But as editors brought these stories together, important religious messages were imparted to the texts. Much of the imagery in the narratives and the plot line reflected the religious agenda of that later era when the texts were written down, and also later familial customs. The narratives may be studied by us to learn not only about the pre-Exodus era, but also about the era when the stories were cast in written form (6th century BCE exile or later). While the patriarchal narratives were recalled in Genesis 12-36, 38, the story of Joseph in Genesis 37, 39-50 was a post-exilic short story, an expansion perhaps of older traditions. It was placed at the end of Genesis rather than standing alone as an independent book.

Patriarchal narratives foreshadowed God's gracious election and blessing of later Israel. Some of the memories contained in these accounts may have come from the various peoples who eventually merged into Israel. Diverse peoples envisioned the patriarchs as ancestors, so the tales may have been retold over the years and facilitated the gradual merger of various groups. Most Israelites originally were Canaanite farmers and city dwellers in the lowlands or herders in the highlands who either joined the Israelites or gradually became Israelites.

# Historical and Cultural Background

People often wish to know how much historical memory is in the patriarchal and the matriarchal narratives. Scholars suggest that there are ancient memories that recall some elements of pre-Israelite and early Israelite life, but the accounts have been cast in creative story form for theological reasons. Debate exists as to the degree of historical memory. Early in the 20th century some scholars dated the patriarchs as real individuals to the Middle Bronze Period (1900-1550 BCE) in accord with the biblical chronology and by connecting them to the expansion of the Amorites in the Near East. Some current historians date them to the Late Bronze Period (1550-1200 BCE) or early Iron Age (1200-1050 BCE), periods of turmoil in which many of the people who would become Israel made their appearance. They also believe that the patriarchs were not historical individuals, but they were symbols of many people who lived in that era. A growing number of modern scholars suspect the stories really portray rather loosely the lives of people returning to the land from exile after 539 BCE.

**Pastoralism**: What appears to be a significant historical memory was the portrayal of the patriarchs and matriarchs as pastoralists or semi-nomads, people who moved with their flocks from one grazing area to another. This was the historical lifestyle of highlanders prior to the Iron Age (1200 BCE) who gradually merged into Israel. These pastoralists were not nomads; rather, they had regular pasturage areas and when there was sufficient rain, they even practiced farming. Pastoralists generally herd sheep and goats, so when the patriarchal narratives mention cattle (Genesis 12:16, 13:5, 18:7, 26:14), that implies farming, for farmers grow grain to feed cattle. Furthermore, Isaac was said to be successful at farming according to Genesis 26:12-13. So the patriarchs were portrayed as pastoralists who tended flocks and did some farming, as was characteristic of life before 1200 BCE. The contrast in the biblical accounts was not between farmers and shepherds, since the same people would do both activities. Rather, the contrast was between the highlanders who did farming and shepherding and the people who lived in the cities in the valley regions, who did more extensive farming. True nomadism did not emerge until the domestication of the camel after 1000 B.C.E. The patriarchs resembled a form of semi-nomadism called "enclosed nomadism," wherein pastoralists moved in a circumscribed area, maintaining contact with a few urban centers for the sake of trade. Among such "enclosed nomads," a relationship with sedentary peoples or urban centers was often problematic, and we observe this in the narratives, especially in story about Jacob, his sons, and Shechem (Genesis 34). The patriarchal narratives do not give us any indication that the patriarchs moved their flocks great distances with the change of the seasons, thus leaving us with the impression even more that these people were "enclosed nomads," a phenomenon found in Palestine prior to 1200 BCE. (But this same activity may have existed in the years after the destruction of Jerusalem in 586 BCE.)

Pastoralists sometimes were sedentary farmers who withdrew or fled from urban or settled areas to find freedom in the hills, steppe lands, or other fringe areas of civilization. Sometimes they withdrew in times of prolonged drought, which was devastating to extensive farming, and they engaged in the economic activity of pastoralism with limited agriculture, for that was an effective economic strategy during prolonged dry seasons. It is interesting to observe that the Bible recalls how Abraham withdrew from the cities of Ur and Haran to live in the hills of Palestine. Such pastoralist withdrawal occurred in Palestine in the Late Bronze Age (1550-1200 BCE) as Canaanite city dwellers left the economic and political turmoil in the lowlands and retreated to the highlands. Hence, patriarchal narratives hint at the social dynamics operative immediately before the emergence of Israel.

**Divine Names**: The narratives contained diverse names by which the patriarchs called upon God; the biblical authors implied that these were all names for Yahweh. We suspect these were names of different gods worshipped by people who eventually became Israelites, and their merger into the persona of Yahweh reflected the amalgamation of various peoples into Israel. If so, these would be authentic ancient names from the late Bronze Age and early Iron Age. However, a few scholars suspect that some of the names were artificial and others might be names that developed in the post-exilic period, so we should not claim these are historical memories from an early period.

We can make interesting observations about some of the names. Polytheists everywhere have assumed that all people have their own gods, and these gods were supreme in their own territories. Some gods, however, were viewed as "moveable," they could travel with their devotees. This was a common belief of pastoralists and later nomads. Such a deities were not tied to place but committed to a particular person, family, clan, or tribe. The patriarchal narratives seem to have deities who were both connected to a place and moveable. Some named deities appeared to certain patriarchs as patron deities, or what we call "gods of the fathers," a phenomenon often associated with semi-nomads, and such gods were "moveable." The patriarch received a blessing, divine protection, and a special name by which to call upon God. To Abraham, God was revealed as *magan-Abraham*, the "shield of Abraham" (Genesis 15:1); for Isaac, God was *pachad-Isaac*, the "fear (or "kinsman") of Isaac" (Genesis 31:42, 53); and for Jacob, God was *el-gibbor* or *gibbor-Jacob*, "mighty one of Jacob" (Genesis 49:24). For years scholars have suggested these were the names of deities worshipped in the highlands by pastoralist tribes who joined Israel, and the names continued as titles for Yahweh. Often familial religion can continue alongside of a high, national religion. Thus, the patriarchal narratives may not only testify to old religious piety from before 1200 BCE, they may recall the familial religiosity practiced throughout Israelite history. Patriarchs also called upon God with different names in various locales or places that became shrines (which makes you suspect that was the name of a deity once revered at that shrine). God was *El Bethel* ("God of the house of God") at Bethel, *El Elyon* ("God of the Heights") at Jerusalem, *El Olam* ("Eternal God") at Beersheba, *El Roi* (the "Seeing God") in the wilderness, *El Shaddai* ("God of the mountains") at various places, and *Ba'al Berith* ("God of the Covenant") at Shechem. (Some scholars suggest that some of the names, especially *El-Shaddai*, and perhaps all of them, come the post-exilic era and were artificially placed into these accounts.) These names were compounded with the names El and Baal, significant gods among the Syrians, Canaanites, and others who believed that their deities were manifest under different names at various locations. These would be fixed, territorial gods, and we call these Elim names. Patriarchs were portrayed as worshipping God under localized divine names.

If the patriarchs were polytheistic, the later biblical authors obviously wanted the names to appear as titles for one God, Yahweh. Maybe the accounts remembered ancient names and memories to merge them into one God, as the people merged to become Israel. Moses is told at the burning bush (Exodus 3) that some of these names were the names by which Yahweh was addressed in olden times, an obvious attempt to draw various gods together into one deity. Thus, the old gods could die as monotheism emerged.

**Family Customs**: The most important phenomena for us to observe are the social and familial customs in the narratives, which do not occur in the rest of the Hebrew Bible. However, we find texts testifying to these customs in Mesopotamia. Parallel customs were attested in legal documents from 14th century BCE Nuzi (in northern Mesopotamia), from 13th century BCE Emar, and especially from 6th century BCE Chaldean Babylon (where the Jews were exiled). In such parallel texts we discover that one may adopt a surrogate son for the sake of keeping inheritance in the family (Abraham and Ishmael and perhaps also Laban and Jacob), the adopted son may be disinherited by a natural born son (Isaac and Ishmael), a brother may function as spokesman for the bride (Laban and Rachel), creditors may adopt debtors to take care of them and debtors may adopt creditors to repay a debt by an inheritance (perhaps the allusion of Abraham to Eliazar of Damascus in Gen 15:2), deathbed blessings occur (Isaac and later Jacob), property exchange may occur (Abraham and the cave at Machpelah), teraphim or household gods may function as property deeds (Rachel's theft from Laban), adopted sons-in-law must continue the family cult of the father-in-law (perhaps implied by Rachel's theft of the teraphim), sale of birthright can occur (Esau to Jacob), slave girls are protected from jealous wives (Hagar and Sarah), barren wives provide concubines to birth sons for their husbands (Sarah and Hagar), and wives can be adopted as sisters (perhaps Abraham and Sarah). The biblical parallels appear to be most similar to the customs recorded in the 6th century BCE texts, which implies that the final crafting of the biblical narratives might have occurred during the Babylonian Exile. However, a few scholars have argued that we should not discount earlier texts from Nuzi and Emar as testimonies that the knowledge of these customs existed already in the second millennium BCE, thus permitting us to locate the plot line of the patriarchal narrative to an early period.

Years ago these parallels led some scholars to argue for the historicity of the accounts and their early composition, especially with possible connections to the 14th century BCE

Nuzi tablets. More recently we sense the greater connection with Babylonian laws of the 6th century BCE, so that apparently exilic biblical authors referred to the customs of their Babylonian neighbors to craft the plot line of their stories. That makes more sense than to suggest that an earlier biblical author drew upon distant Mesopotamian customs when telling the story in Israel. If so, the patriarchal stories were probably more fictionalized than historical.

If patriarchal narratives originated in exile, the patriarchs could be viewed by their audience as a landless people, as were the Jews in exile, who held the hope that the land of Palestine might be theirs once more. How interesting that returning exiles took the exact route that Abraham walked. According to the narrative Abraham left Ur of the Chaldees, and Ur was ruled by Chaldeans only in the 6th century BCE. Abraham went through Haran, which was an important city for moon worship under royal patronage, as was Ur, also in the 6th century BCE. Abraham's family was portrayed indirectly as moon worshippers, for their names indicate such. Little hints point to the exile as the time of final composition for the narratives. Though there are early memories about the ancestors' pastoralist origins and perhaps the memory of ancient divine names, it seems that much of the information points to the exile as the period when the narratives were crafted, using loose oral traditions from past years.

# Literary Aspects of the Narratives

The exilic author, presumably the Yahwist, may have drawn some of the patriarchal stories from oral tradition. Bards recited such stories at festivals and shrines, and they probably varied in different regions and changed over the years. Our written text still reflects characteristics of oral transmission. 1) The accounts have much humor in them, which reflects the desire of the village bards to make the stories entertaining. The plot line is quite simple, usually no more than two or three main characters appear in a story, and dialogue is often limited to two speakers. This may reflect the process of "smoothing" accomplished by the bards as they cast the story into a form easily recited or performed. 2) The narratives have popular memories of how certain customs and names of people and places came to be, what we might call "myths of origin." In biblical studies we call these aetiological narratives, or if they are part of a greater narrative, we call them aetiological motifs. 3) The narratives are loosely connected. With the omission of a few linking passages which describe ancestral relationships and maintain a narrative plot line, the bulk of the stories are independent and could stand alone. They may have been told in separate regions of the country, perhaps in shrines. 3) The tales are interested in the accomplishments of heroes who became the ancestors of later people, and the accomplishments of the hero, or eponym, are associated with the attributes or activities of later descendents. 4) Memories of old customs or foreign customs are found in the stories. 5) The heroes are sometimes portrayed as giants, a theme not to be found in later Israelite literature. And 7) the stories connect patriarchs to sites that later became shrines, which may imply that such stories were told orally at those shrines, and the original place names were displaced. These characteristics imply an oral origin to these tales before they were drawn together by historians.

The stories were gathered in the cycles of tales with the 7th or 6th century BCE Elohist, the 6th century BCE Yahwist, and later edited into their present written form by the 5th century BCE Priestly Editors.  These individuals might have been intellectually reflective, and their treatment of the stories indicates that these popular folk narratives were used for more serious purposes, including the attempt to recall the origin of the people and the attempt to provide religious messages to a later Jewish audience. The purpose of these narratives in their final written stage may have been to give hope to Jews exiled in Babylon and scattered all over the world.

**Aetiologies**: Narratives often explain the origins of place names, personal names, and customs.  We classify such accounts as aetiological legends (sometimes spelled etiological).  Scholars debate whether such legends or simple references arose in the oral tradition because people enjoyed such allusions, or whether the later writers included them because of their historical and theological significance. Later writers used aetiologies for serious reasons.  Even though a particular aetiology might be funny, it still had a serious message. Humor was sometimes the best way to communicate a serious message. Aetiologies include:  1) Genesis 28 recounted that the city of Bethel got its name when Jacob had a vision of God and declared, "This is Bethel, the house of God."  "Beth" in Hebrew meant house, and "El" was a name for God. 2) Genesis 32 remembered that the city of Penuel got its name when Jacob wrestled with a river sprite guarding a crossing of the Jabbok River, only to discover that it was his personal deity.  He encountered God "face to face, for "penu" meant "before the face," and "El" meant God.  In the same narrative we learn that since Jacob's hip or thigh was "touched" by the divine being, that nerve should not be eaten in any animal.  The name of the river, Jabbok (*Yabboq*) sounded like the Hebrew words for Jacob (*ya'aqob*) and "he wrestled" (*ye'abeq*).

**Eponymous Tales**: An eponym is a real or legendary hero whose name is connected to a group of people who believe they are descended from that hero.  This occurs in simple kinship societies, that is, societies wherein people view themselves as a large family, and social relationships are seen in familial terms of blood-kin or more commonly fictionalized blood-kin relationships.  Because so many people in Israel were adopted into various clan and tribal entities, very few people in a group actually were descended from one ancestor. People identified with the character traits of that ancestor or eponym.  Sometimes the eponym was a historic person, or a symbolic creation, or a composite of several people from the past.  The eponym could be from centuries in the past or simply a single generation. The patriarchs were eponymous ancestors of Israel, for the names of Jacob's twelve sons became the names of later tribes.

Memories of the ancestor and the activities of the tribal group that bore his name often blurred together, for the ancients viewed the achievements of a tribe as an extension of the ancestor's actions and personality.  (This does not imply, however, that they had a weak concept of the individual or the responsibility of the individual for particular actions.) As an eponymous ancestor, Esau was physically portrayed as red and hairy, and he acted like a wild ass (Genesis 25-27), which was the Israelite stereotype of Edomites, the supposed descendants of Esau. Edomites appeared red because they farmed in red clay and had red dust on themselves. "Edom" meant red dirt, and they acted like asses in the opinion of Israelites.

Jacob's sons symbolized later tribal politics: sons of Jacob's free wives (Rachel and Leah) were powerful tribes while those of the concubine wives (Zilpah and Bilhah) were smaller tribes. According to Genesis 34 Simeon and Levi destroyed the helpless men of Shechem, but other biblical texts hint that was the work of the later tribes of Simeon and Levi, which is why those two tribes disappeared as tribes. Rachel's sons were powerful tribes in the north (Ephraim, Manasseh, Benjamin), and Leah's sons were the strong tribes of the south (Judah, Reuben, and the tribes Simeon and Levi, both of which may have moved south after their attack upon Shechem to be merged into Judah). Patriarchal narratives sometimes contained symbolic allusions to later Israelite history.

**Origin of Stories at Shrines:** Patriarchal narratives may have been remembered orally at various shrines and their deeds may have been celebrated in cult. Each region of Israel may have recalled the memories of particular patriarchs. Abraham and Isaac stories may have been told in the south, in Judah, at shrines like Hebron and Beersheba, while Jacob stories may have been celebrated in the north, in Israel, at shrines like Bethel and Shechem. We suspect that because those particular sites were mentioned in the narratives about each of those patriarchs. Over the years memories recalled about particular patriarchs were intended to laud the shrine where they were told, and perhaps some cultic rites were connected with each of the patriarchs. When later writers collected these stories they connected the narratives and the shrines to speak symbolically of a unified Israelite people. However, some scholars suspect that the names of the shrines were put into the accounts late, and they may reflect the shrines that were important when the narratives were written down in the 6th and 5th centuries BCE, for these were the local shrines used after the destruction of the Temple or they were shrines established by exiles returning from Babylon.

Patriarchal stories were loosely connected, for with the removal of a few editorial passages that link the narratives, the stories could be easily re-arranged. This may imply their origin in oral form from different parts of the country. Each patriarch has a regional personality and was a hero for a select group of Israelites. Northern prophets used Jacob's name to symbolize the northern state of Israel, while Abraham was important for the Davidic dynasty in the south. Isaac seems to be a marginal figure who seldom appeared alone in an account. Maybe the little known Isaac traditions of the Negev (deep south) linked the memories of Abraham and Jacob, for obscurity made him a neutral figure to link the more dramatic personalities. Abraham was placed before Jacob to imply the more important status of Judah and Jerusalem. In the oral traditions Jacob may have been more known, for pre-exilic prophets refer to Jacob and not to Abraham. Maybe the Yahwist, with his southern bias, placed Abraham first in our present sequence.

Some accounts may have arisen among non-Israelite elements in the population. Motifs or even narrative sections, which were transformed by Israelite values, still appear to retain old elements of thought. Presumably Canaanite heroes were portrayed in old myths as semi-divine and giants. Jacob lifted up a stone pillar to God, and the object (*massebah*) elsewhere referred to a large sacrificial stone weighing several tons (Genesis 28:18). Jacob and Laban constructed a stone monument as a border between their lands (Genesis 31), and later Israelites viewed this account as the aetiology for the existence of a mountain in Gilead, thus implying both Laban and Jacob were giants. Finally, the Jacob's dream of God on the ladder in Genesis 28 reflected the Canaanite portrayal of the high god El being served by the lesser gods as he was seated upon his throne. Old mythic images were absorbed into patriarchal narratives, perhaps reflecting the gradual transformation of various peoples into the entity of Israel.

Overall, we are led to conclude that these narratives are best defined as epic literature: a mixture of historical memories cast into creative story form first by oral bards and later by theologically oriented scribal writers. The texts contain religious truths cast in dramatic form. The symbolism in these stories implies that the ancient Jews used them for teaching purposes.

# Theological Themes in the Accounts

The patriarchs were depicted as venerable epic heroes at times, and at other times their human finitude, so starkly portrayed, enables us to identify with them. They are both heroes and failures. Abraham almost sacrificed his son dutifully obedient to God, Jacob struggled with God and was transformed from scoundrel into noble patriarch, and courageous Rebekah determined the destiny of her sons, Jacob and Esau. Humorous tales show us the shortcomings and weaknesses of these epic figures. Humor may come from the entertaining bards who recounted the stories for years, but serious biblical authors used humorous tales to craft a serious message of human limitations and divine grace.

**Human Finitude:** In the ancient world, the ancestors (or eponyms) were semi-divine, born from the gods, superhuman in ability, worthy of the honor proffered by later generations. However, the way you laud your ancestors bespeaks how you view yourself and your culture's political and religious institutions. Perfect ancestors insure the perfect social institutions that need no reform. Praise your ancestors and you need not criticize and change your society. Divinize the ancestors and you legitimate the tyranny of kingship and powerful priesthoods. People speak this way even today and declare we have the perfect country that needs no change or reform. But Israel confessed the weaknesses of the ancestors in these narratives and thus acknowledged human weakness and sinfulness. They realized they existed because of divine grace and they needed to continue to grow and improve their society.

Our narratives often portrayed sinfulness and human finitude in the patriarchs. Abraham, fearful for his life, called his wife "sister," leaving her to the advances of pharaoh (Genesis 12) and Abimelech (Genesis 20). Old, blind Isaac was deceived by Jacob (Genesis 27), who then fearfully fled his brother Esau. Laban tricked Jacob into marrying Leah before Rachel and deprived him of a dowry by the supposedly generous act of adoption (Genesis 29). Jacob swindled Laban using cunning breeding practices with sheep (Genesis 31). Rachel stole her father's teraphim, or property deeds, and fooled the servants seeking them (Genesis 31). Simeon and Levi killed all the men in Shechem while they suffered in pain from the circumcisions demanded by Simeon and Levi in order to marry Israelite women (Genesis 34). The ancestors needed divine grace and forgiveness, as did the later Israelites. Dramatically, God was revealed to Jacob after Jacob cheated his brother and father and fled his home as a coward (Genesis 28), but before any moral transformation. God elected him as heir, when Jacob was totally undeserving and worthless, just as God chose Israel when they were slaves.

Humor can be used to communicate the finitude of human beings, for so often when we laugh at a character, it is because that character has made mistakes or is cleverly deceitful. Humorous stories about the ancestors reinforces their humanity. Biblical humor elevates the cleverness of the underdog, generates word plays and puns, which sadly are difficult to translate. Jacob and his mother, Rachel, deceived Isaac by pulling the wool over Isaac's eyes (so to speak) in masquerading Isaac in an animal skin to imitate Esau's hairy body. Laban tricked Jacob into marrying Leah before Rachel, and Jacob did not notice the switch until the next morning (strong punch at the wedding reception). Jacob used clever breeding practices that generated lambs with stripes, so that they became his property (a story meant to be funny rather than literal). Frequent puns fill the stories, but their meanings are often lost in translation. When Isaac said his wife was his sister, his ploy was unveiled when Abimelech saw Isaac fondling his wife in a closed courtyard (Genesis 26:6-11. A ribald pun in verse 8, used a word for caressing that came from the same verbal root as Isaac's name, so that Isaac was "living up to his name."

Sharp satire with serious meaning can also be found in the narratives. When Rachel sat upon the household gods and claimed that she could not move due to her menstrual period, the Israelite or Jewish audience recognized that the so-called "gods" of the nations became impure by proximity to Rachel, and they were powerless to protect themselves (Genesis 31:35). Menstruating women were not allowed near shrines or holy objects because their flow of blood made them impure. Ethnic jokes exhibit subtle political commentary. Esau, the red, hairy, wild ass of a man, ancestor of the Edomites, was the Israelite stereotype of an Edomite, and his failure to distinguish watery soup dyed red and meat soup reflected Israelite views about low Edomite intelligence. Moab and Ammon were conceived when drunken Lot impregnated his own daughters, and this story reflected Israel's disgust for these Transjordanian peoples. (Though, ironically, it is possible that Transjordanian people told a comparable tale about their national origins.)

**Human Nobility**: Sometimes patriarchs rose above their finitude, setting examples of obedience and courage. Abraham left his home for unknown lands in the west (Genesis 12), gave Lot the choice of the land (Genesis 13), rescued him (Genesis 14), and later pleaded with God to save the cities on the plain (Genesis 18). Jacob began as the thief who "supplanted" his brother, but after his experience at Penuel (Genesis 32), he became the noble patriarch who rejected and buried the idols (Genesis 35), which later Israelites should emulate. These patriarchal narratives were crafted to present inspirational models.

Though we use the term "patriarchal" to describe the narratives, "matriarchal" would be equally justifiable, for women often acted in more noble and courageous fashion than the men. In the ancient world, the status of women was low, yet these accounts portrayed women as strong and capable of shaping the destiny of Israel. Sarah was strong when Abraham nearly lost her through cowardice (Genesis 12, 20), and she determined the destinies of Isaac and Ishmael, not Abraham (Genesis 21). Rebekah decided to marry Isaac, when such decisions were usually made by men. Rachel was clever in the theft of her father's property and the ruse by which she avoided the search (Genesis 31). Later biblical authors kept some of these colorful accounts to affirm the status of women in an age when women were repressed.

**Religious Value of the Narratives:** In their present form, the accounts have been preserved for us by the Yahwist (who includes the Elohist) and the Priestly Editors, but as a final unity the narratives have significant religious messages. The ancestors were finite and sinful people, who were loved by God and chosen to inherit the land and give birth to a great nation. At times they could be noble, so that they were a complex mixture of "saint" and "sinner" in our modern language. The final biblical authors wished for the audience to identify with these people in their finitude and nobility. It was so often the custom in the ancient world to deify the ancestors, or to declare that the ancestors were half human and half divine. Describing your ancestors as sinful really is how you describe yourself and the social and political institutions you have inherited. Biblical authors undercut any pride that a later generation might seek to generate, as well as any attempt to justify political institutions as divinely and permanently instituted.

God's election of the ancestors entailed promises of land, numerous children, and a universal blessing through them to the world. Such promises meant something to landless sojourners of any age, but especially to exiled Jews in Babylon seeking to return to Palestine in the 6th and 5th centuries BCE. In their final written form, the patriarchal narratives addressed these landless Jews. Promises to the forefathers were a theologically unifying motif for the loosely arranged patriarchal narratives. These promises appear to have been developed in stages perhaps by both the Yahwist and the Priestly Editors. They indicated that God guided the patriarchs to a future destiny they did not understand. The promises in the narrative format foreshadowed the later narratives of Exodus, conquest, and the rise of David. This lent more concreteness to the theme of a God who controlled the destinies of a people and became an abiding divine presence throughout time.

The response of the patriarchs was obedience, which they sometimes demonstrated and sometimes failed to show. Patriarchs showed obedience to God by traveling to a strange land and following orders given by this God. The willingness of Abraham to sacrifice his only son demonstrated obedience, even though this act would have undercut the promises drastically. Jews in the Babylonian Exile hearing these narratives realized that they were called to the same radical obedience and to undertake the same journey, following the path that Abraham trod. Perhaps they understood the message that wherever they wandered in the diaspora, God would be with them to guide and protect them. The final editors, the Priestly Editors, knew that patriarchal promises were fulfilled once in the past with the entrance into the land under Joshua, but with the exile all of that had been destroyed. They believed the promise of divine presence would endure, so these blessings would come true again.

# Conclusion

Narratives of the ancestors have a universal and existential feel about them as they describe the experience of individuals in intense personal family relationships, the competition and anger between brothers, the conflict of women over the same man, the concern about progeny and inheritance, human greed, business cheating, and the drama of life and death. Perhaps that is why they made such good stories both in oral tradition as well as in written form. Biblical authors used these great stories as a medium to communicate religious truths. Probably many old oral traditions were not used by the biblical historians, so we can only guess at accounts which might be missing. In their final form these accounts honestly speak of humanity in its raw finitude, but it is a humanity loved and protected by God. Accounts mix historical memory and romantic fiction. The memories of pre-Israelite peoples in the highlands of Palestine were intertwined with memories and allusions from a later era when Jews were in exile. The mixture is so complex that scholars will argue endlessly about the nature of these stories and what precisely is historical and what is fictional. The romantic fiction created characters abounding with the universal traits of humanity, with both virtues and vices. The narratives entertain an audience with humor and drama and, at the same time, inspire listeners with examples of virtue and obedience.

# Bibliography:

Albrecht Alt. "The God of the Fathers." *Essays on Old Testament History and Religion.* Trans. R. A. Wilson. Garden City, NY: Doubleday, 1966.

Joseph Blenkinsopp. *The Pentateuch: An Introduction to the First Five Books of the Bible.* New York, NY: Doubleday, 1992.

Frank Cross. Canaanite Myth and Hebrew Epic: Essays in the History of the Religion of Israel. Cambridge, MA: Harvard University Press, 1973.

Ronald Hendel. *The Epic of the Patriarchs.* Harvard Semitic Monographs 42. Atlanta, GA: Scholars Press, 1987.

Gerhard von Rad. *Genesis.* Trans. John Marks. Old Testament Library. Philadelphia, PA: Westminster, 1973.

John Van Seters. *Abraham in History and Tradition.* New Haven, CT: Yale University, 1975.

John Van Seters. *Abraham, in Search of History.* New Haven, CT: Yale University, 1983.

Bruce Vawter. *On Genesis.* Garden City, NY: Doubleday, 1970.

Claus Westermann. *Genesis 1-11.* Trans. John Scullion. Minneapolis, MN: Augsburg, 1984.

Claus Westermann. *The Promises to the Fathers: Studies on the Patriarchal Narratives.* Trans. David Green. Philadelphia, PA: Fortress, 1980.

# Chapter 12

# Exodus and the Wilderness

Reading: Exodus 1-19, Numbers 10-14,16,20-25.

With the accounts of the Exodus and the Sinai experience, we enter into the narratives that testified to the beginning of Israel. We encounter memories of national origins and the revelation of laws that defined Israelites and Jews forever as the people of God. The foundational events were recalled in three cycles of tradition: Exodus, wandering in the wilderness, and revelation at Sinai.

## The Exodus

Exodus 1-15 recounted the memory of the Exodus and Moses. It told the story of Moses' birth, his encounter with Yahweh on a mountain, his call to lead the Israelites, confrontation with pharaoh, the plagues, flight of the slaves, and the destruction of the Egyptian chariot force. This was a dramatic narrative--powerless slaves of imperial Egypt liberated by God. A hero who fled the Egyptian court to become a shepherd returned to liberate a people. A rabble of slaves eluded pharaoh's army and sang victory songs over the once invincible enemy. A nation was born which has endured to this very day, giving rise along the way to Christianity.

Locating the Exodus in history has been difficult. Years ago historians believed that the pharaoh who knew Joseph was one of the Hyksos rulers, foreign Semites who ruled northern Egypt (1750-1550 BCE) until native Egyptians expelled them. The oppressing pharaohs were then native Egyptian pharaohs of the Eighteenth Dynasty (after 1550 BCE), and the Exodus was dated from 1480 to 1420 BCE. Current scholars observe that Israelites slaved at Pithom and Ramses, storage sites in north Egypt, both of which existed after 1300 BCE and were developed by Pharaoh Seti I (1302-1290 BCE). Ramses II (1290-1224

BCE) is often suggested as the pharaoh of the Exodus, even though we assume Moses did not have direct dealing with him. Violent movements of foreign Sea Peoples from the Aegean Sea caused destruction in Palestine from 1250 to 1100 BCE, making this a time when the Israelites could have invaded the country successfully. Landless outlaws called Habiru or Hapiru harassed cities in Palestine from 1400 to 1200 BCE. Most historians do not equate these people with the Ibri (the Hebrew word for "Hebrew"), but we suspect that Habiru people merged with others to become Israel. Sometimes in the Bible the word "Hebrew" refers to landless, poor members of society, like the word Habiru once meant. Archaeological artifacts (pots, houses, highland terracing, and later iron implements) connected to Israelite culture appear after 1200 BCE in central Palestine. Thus, biblical historians often date the exodus to 1250 BCE and entrance into the land around 1220-1200 BCE.

**Cultic Use of the Exodus Tradition:** Exodus 1-15 told a dramatic story, ready made for play or movie performance. Scholars suggest that maybe the text was acted out as a cultic play in ancient Israel to celebrate Passover. Cultic activity describes actions that people perform in connection with religious observances. Such actions recall great events of the past by involving worshippers in a symbolic re-enactment of those events. Worshippers believe that in some way they participate in those primordial events in mystical fashion. When the biblical text said that Israelites and Jews were to "remember" or "recall" the Exodus, it meant that the re-enactment brought those events alive again for worshippers. Christians today try to create that same feeling at Christmas and Easter, though we do not feel the experience as deeply as did the ancient people.

It has been suggested the Israelites celebrated the Passover in their villages and at local shrines, perhaps more in the northern tribal area of Israel than in the southern tribal area of Judah. At the annual performance people might have been adopted into the village community, and they symbolically affirmed that their ancestors participated in the Exodus under Moses. They identified with the experience of people under Moses and later Joshua, even though most Israelites did not have a direct ancestor involved in the historical Exodus. Passover was probably a family festival in those early years, though we cannot be sure how many Israelites observed it. Passover became a national festival and a pilgrimage festival under king Josiah of Judah after 622 BCE, at a time when it was feasible for people of the small province of Judah to pilgrimage to Jerusalem. Passover remained a significant pilgrimage festival for Jews until the destruction of Jerusalem in 70 CE. From that time onward Passover once more became a family festival for Jews, but the desire to celebrate it in Jerusalem remains a great hope for Jews even today.

**Sources of the Written Tradition:** Different layers of oral tradition have been woven into our present text. The signs of these layers may be observed, but use of this narrative in the celebration of Passover may have smoothed the narratives so much over the years that an easy separation of sources is extremely difficult, especially if biblical narratives were used in an annual performance. Doublets and parallel motifs testify to intertwined sources. Three versions of Moses' call are found in the text: Exodus 3:1-21, 4:1-17 combined a Yahwist and an Elohist version of the call, while Exodus 6:1-13 came from Priestly Editors. Plague narratives have different sources. In Exodus 8:1-4 the frogs came from the Nile (Yahwist), but in Exodus 8:5-6 they emerged because Aaron's rod waved over the canals (Priestly Editors). The Priestly account of the gnats or lice (Exodus 8:16-19) was a doublet of the Yahwist's plague of flies (Exodus 8:20-32). The Priestly version may have added the plague of boils (and perhaps darkness or death of the firstborn) as well as Moses' initial sign to pharaoh of turning the rod into a snake. It could be that the Yahwist had seven plagues and the Priestly tradition had ten plagues. Different perspectives have been merged into one fluid synthesis in our text.

**Theological Themes:** We may speak of this cultic drama as a "myth," which is not to say that it is a lie, but rather it is a symbolic story that speaks a greater truth than a mere historical rendition of brute facts. Myths point to deeper meanings than mere narratives can provide. "Myths" often have historical experiences behind them, but they are told so as emphasize religious or existential meaning rather than to recall mere events. In brief, a "myth" recounted in the Bible is sermonized history, or history interpreted from the "eye of faith" as events in which God interacted with the human realm. As a "myth" or symbolic story, the Exodus accounts spoke of a powerful God who reached into an alien realm to claim people. The Exodus narrative or "myth" proclaimed the liberation of people from slavery by the power and grace of God. In the Exodus narratives there were also additional sub-plots, each with its significant message.

Moses' birth-story in Exodus 2:1-10 paralleled other accounts of unusual births. Isaac was born to Abraham and barren Sarah late in life, Samson was born after a divine announcement to his parents, Samuel was born to barren Hannah, and Jesus was born to a virgin. These narratives testified that the person who was significant in later years was also special as a baby or small child, and he already reflected the divine charisma from birth. The name "Mose" in Egyptian meant "child" or "son of" of "born of," and it was found in the names of several New Kingdom pharaohs (1550-1200 BCE), including Ahmose, Thutmosis, and Ramses. The word sounded like the Hebrew word, mashah, "to draw out" or "one who draws," so the biblical author playfully connected Moses' name to the idea that he was "drawn" from the water.

The Moses account creatively used the political account told by the Mesopotamian ruler, Sargon of Akkad (2300 BCE). Sargon claimed that as a baby he was placed in a basket in the Tigris River, floated upstream, was drawn from the river, and raised in a foreign land by shepherds, but as an adult he returned with an army to southern Mesopotamia to liberate his people from the tyrant who had killed the royal family of the Sumerian city of Kish in whose palace he was born. Sargon used this as propaganda to justify his conquest and rule of both Sumerians and Akkadians in southern Mesopotamia. This narrative apparently was well known and influenced many other accounts in popular literature in the ancient world.

The Moses account reversed the plot, for whereas Sargon was born in the palace of Kish and raised by shepherds, Moses was born to slaves and raised in pharaoh's house. When he discovered his identity, he killed an Egyptian taskmaster and fled to the wilderness. Only in the wilderness did he find God, who commissioned him to return to the civilized river valley in Egypt. His goal was to take the slaves out into the wilderness to the sacred mountain. In the ancient world either the palace or the temple in the city was symbolically viewed as the "cosmic mountain" of the gods. The "cosmic mountain" was in the city, where the powerful kings and priests were the representatives of the gods.

But in the biblical account the true God lived on a mountain in the wilderness and awaited the arrival of slaves led by a shepherd, Moses. In the Sargon story, the goal was for the hero, Sargon, to return to the city and claim his throne, but in the Moses story, the goal was the wilderness where God would create a people out of a rabble of slaves. God was with the poor, the oppressed, the outcasts, and the slaves, who received a divine mandate to shape their egalitarian society.

If we diagram the movement of the two narratives, we discover the following. The heroic story pattern of Sargon has him move from palace to wilderness to palace, but the movement of Moses was from wilderness (slavery) to palace to wilderness (Midian) to palace to wilderness (Sinai). Sargon's narrative pattern paralleled traditional hero stories, where the hero was exiled as a youth but returned to claim his throne. The biblical narrative placed additional narrative material in this plot to make the wilderness the goal, rather than the palace. God was not with the king and the priests in the city, but with the slaves in the wilderness. Perhaps the addition of Sargon's birth narrative to the Moses account alerted the audience to notice the variation on the pattern of the heroic tale.

God appeared to Moses in Exodus 3-4 to send him forth and bring Israel out of Egypt. This narrative contained the call narrative format associated with later classical prophets. The Exodus text may have been influenced by those other prophetic calls, which made Moses appear to be a prophet but also gave greater authority to the prophets, who now were connected to Moses, the first of the great prophets. Later accounts in Exodus and Numbers ascribed to Moses the identities of judge, general, king, and priest.

God revealed himself to Moses under the name of Yahweh, and Exodus 3:6, 14 and Exodus 6:3-4 averred that Yahweh was the name of the deity known to the patriarchs under various names. The biblical historian connected the gods of the patriarchs clearly with the God of the Exodus. With this narrative Israelites could perceive that their ancestors with their different deities all worshipped the one true God under different names. The Yahwist projected the name of Yahweh back to the time of Cain, but most Israelites believed that the name came into Palestine from the wilderness with Moses and Joshua. (Biblical authors knew that other people used the name, including the Kenites and people in Edom, for it originated in the wilderness in or near Edom.)

The meaning of the sacred name Yahweh has puzzled folk for years. Popularly people understand the name to mean, "I am," or "I am who I am." The Septuagint translation rendered the name in Greek to mean "I am the One who is." This translation probably gave the greatest impetus to the understanding that the name should be translated in the first person singular present tense. The Hebrew text itself seemed to imply that the name meant, "I am," but the biblical text was simply playing a word game by pointing out that the name Yahweh sounded like "I am." Actually, in Hebrew the name cannot be in the first person with the prefix Ya-. Rather, the meaning somehow must be in the third person and in the future tense because of the prefix ya-. The consonants Y, H, W, H with different vowels would be the common verb, "he will be." The vowels would tell us what the mood of the verb is and how to accurately translate it. However, the true vowels to the sacred name were never written down in the text because of the sacredness of the name. In that way no one would be able to read the sacred name aloud in its correct form. Some vowels placed in our present Hebrew manuscripts were designed to let readers know that this was the sacred name and that they could read Adonai, "my Lord," rather than the sacred name, and other vowels were placed there simply to indicate that this was the divine name. Though we write it as Yahweh in our textbooks, that probably does not reflect how the name was originally pronounced. So over the years scholars have suggested several theories as to what the name might have originally meant: 1) It may have been some form of the simple verb "he will be," which implied that Yahweh will be with the Israelites on their journey. 2) It may have been a special causative verb form, an archaic verb system lost to us, which could best be translated as, "he will cause to be," or Yahweh will cause the Exodus and great acts of deliverance. 3) Or, it may be part of a longer title, "Yahweh of the Hosts, the creator of heaven and earth." This is suggested by the title, "Yahweh Sebaoth" ("Lord/Yahweh of the hosts") found in the prophetic oracles. Furthermore, spelling the word for "hosts" with an –oth ending rather than an –oh or –ah ending implies that another word at least was attached to this title. That invites speculation as to the longer name. If this latter theory is correct, then "Yahweh" was perhaps the verb form with a pronoun, "he who is of or with the hosts," and it became the shorthand version of the name, because it was the least sacred part of the name. How ironic, if that is correct, for Yahweh as a name ultimately became so sacred, it could not be uttered. As a footnote to the discussion, it should be pointed out that Jews used different vowels with the consonants Y, H, W, and H in their written manuscripts to avoid spelling the sacred name. One set were the vowels from the replacement word Adonai. These vowels with the YHWH consonants produced the word yehowah in manuscripts of the Middle Ages, which became Jehovah in the King James translation. Thus, Jehovah is not a real word, and that is why modern translations use Yahweh, or translate the divine name as Lord.

Exodus 4:24-26 related a bizarre story of how Yahweh tried to kill Moses, but Zipporah, Moses' wife, circumcised either Moses or Moses' son (the Hebrew is murky). Maybe the story originally spoke of an encounter with a desert demon or a tribal deity of Jethro's clan who opposed Moses' departure with his new wife without proper pre-marital circumcision or by his failure to circumcise his son. Circumcision may originally have been a rite associated with marriage (as Genesis 34 also seemed to imply). Perhaps Zipporah circumcised Moses or perhaps she circumcised the son and placed the bloody foreskin upon Moses' penis to make it appear as though Moses were circumcised. This appeased the deity and saved Moses' life. Overall, the story is archaic, difficult to translate and interpret. The Yahwist may have used the story to legitimate the custom of circumcision, which became an important sign of identity for Jews in the exile. Priestly Editors projected the custom back to Abraham to give it greater antiquity (Genesis 17).

**Passover:** The first Passover was recalled in Exodus 12:1-13:16, but the passage really recalled the later and more complete version of the Passover meal. Passover and Unleavened Bread were separate festivals that merged in Israelite culture. Exodus 12:34, 39 stated that originally the escaping slaves ate unleavened bread because they had no time for the bread to rise. Memory of this experience became a custom that expanded into Passover. A meal of sacrificial lamb (and perhaps unleavened bread) originated with pastoralists in highland Palestine, who engaged in such rites prior to seasonal movement of their flocks to protect themselves from danger (Passover of the angel of death). The wine and bitter herbs in the later Passover meal may reflect an agricultural festival of sedentary

Palestinians that may have included unleavened bread also (Festival of Unleavened Bread). With the gradual merger of these various peoples into early Israel, the elements of their sacred meals were brought together in a common sacred meal whose roots were connected to the simple fare eaten by those slaves fleeing Egypt, especially if unleavened bread was a common denominator in all three. Exodus 12-13 contained guidelines for the meal from a later age. Exodus 12:38 and Numbers 11:4 implied that the slaves were a "mixed rabble," not ethnically related as some later traditions would have it. Israel would always be a complex entity of people who were merging with each other. Calling these people a "rabble" appears to be an accurate memory of those fleeing slaves, who would bond in the wilderness and evolve into Israelites only in Palestine. Thus, our biblical author placed the guidelines for the later Passover meal here in the narrative that spoke of the first experiences of Israel, but the author also acknowledged that the first meal was a simple meal of unleavened bread, an accident of their circumstances. The evolution of the later meal reflected the merger of farmers and shepherds together in the worship of Yahweh.

**Power of Yahweh:** Two themes united Exodus 1-15; both expressed the total power of Yahweh to control the destinies of people and thus spoke especially to Jews in exile. The first theme was that the Israelites were liberated from slavery in Egypt by the power of a gracious deity. Yahweh, not Moses, saved the people. Yahweh led the Israelites in a pillar of fire by night and a cloud of smoke by day according to Elohist texts. Yahweh was manifest in the burning bush, the plagues, the crossing of the sea, and in the majestic theophany at Sinai or Horeb. This spoke to exiles in Babylon that that Yahweh could be present with believers scattered throughout the world.

The second theme was the struggle between Yahweh and the powerless or non-existent deities of Egypt. Everyone in that age, including most Israelites, was polytheistic and recognized the primacy of the various gods in every land. A defeated nation was encouraged by their conquerors to admit that their gods were defeated by the gods of the conquerors, but more often the conquered stated that their own gods had given them over in defeat because of their sin or impurity. Israelite slaves in Egypt certainly appeared to be the conquered. However, Yahweh invaded Egypt and defeated their deities by bringing plagues that Egyptian gods could not prevent. Particular plagues manifested Yahweh's power over the forces of nature that represented the different Egyptian gods. Turning the Nile to blood insulted Khnum, the guardian of the Nile; Hapi, the spirit of the Nile; and Osiris, for whom the Nile was his blood. The cattle plague offended Hathor, the cow goddess; Apis, the bull deity; and Mnevis, the sacred bull of Heliopolis. Hail from the skies usurped the authority of Nut, the sky goddess, and Seth, the protector of crops. The plague of darkness insulted Ra (or Re), Aten, Atum, and Atum-Ra, all deities associated with the sun, but especially Ra. Death of the first-born clearly assaulted the relationship between Osiris and his son, Horus, who was symbolized by the ruling pharaoh. In general, Isis, the goddess of life, was grieved by all the powers of death unleashed by the plagues. In a test of power against Egyptian magicians, Yahweh was victorious through the agency of Moses. Memory of the plagues was also found in Psalms 78:44-51 and 105:28-36. Interestingly, the plagues were not recalled in the same sequence, and Psalm 105:31 combined the plagues of flies and gnats into one plague. Perhaps this was poetic license in the Psalms or perhaps it testified to the diverse memories of the plagues in the oral tradition of ancient Israel.

The Hebrew word for magicians made the Jewish audience think of Mesopotamian astrologers and priests rather than Egyptian functionaries, which bespoke the power of Yahweh over Babylonian deities in 6th century BCE. When Moses threw down his staff and turned it into a snake that ate the snakes of the Egyptian magicians, the Jewish audience would think of the Mesopotamian goddess of chaotic waters, Tiamat, who was symbolized as a large snake or a seven-headed dragon, who had to be defeated by the creator god. The story of Moses was told to foreshadow the hope of a return from Babylon in the 6th century BCE.

The defeat of pharaoh and the Egyptian army was done without human help. In the ancient world kings claimed to be the agent of the gods in winning great battles, and they often praised their courage and prowess. This was not so for Moses. Yahweh commanded the sea to drown mighty pharaoh and his chariot force before the eyes of shivering, fearful slaves. Control of the sea belongs only to the most powerful of the gods, for the sea represented the ultimate force of evil and chaos. Yahweh was portrayed as the most powerful deity in the universe, destroying mighty pharaoh and using the sea to accomplish this. All this was done in order to liberate the slaves.

**Crossing the Sea of Reeds**: The crossing of the sea was the thunderous conclusion of the Exodus tradition. Scholars debate the location of the "Sea of Reeds" or the yam suph (in Hebrew). After 200 BCE the Greek translation of the Old Testament, the Septuagint, translated this phrase as Red Sea, which for them actually meant all of the water south of the Sinai Peninsula, including even the Indian Ocean. But originally the term had a narrower meaning. The term meant "papyrus sea" or "reed sea," and might have alluded to various marshy places in eastern Egypt. Possibilities include: 1) an inlet off the northern end of the Gulf of Suez where the winds can cause a tidal phenomenon capable of destroying a chariot brigade; 2) Lake Timsah or the Bitter Lakes, both inland lakes where the Suez Canal now exists, where prevailing winds can create tidal action; and 3) Lake Menzaleh or Lake Sirbonis, both major inlets on the Mediterranean Sea, where the tidal action of the Mediterranean Sea or more likely the possibility of a beach collapse under the weight of marching men or chariots could occur. A few scholars suggest that the biblical authors really meant the "Red Sea" (whose actual appearance in English translations results from a mistranslation of the original Hebrew). The term "Red Sea" meant the great sea of the south, including the Arabian Sea and Indian Ocean, as well as all the marshes. Symbolically, use of this term implied that Yahweh had great power to raise the monstrous sea of the south to combat mighty pharaoh, whose boasts of divinity were rendered absurd. The crossing of the Sea of Reeds expressed the heart of Israelite faith-- Yahweh saving a helpless humanity. Salvation in the Hebrew Bible was viewed in national, corporate, and this-worldly terms. Salvation at the sea was a political act by Yahweh, for the nation of Israel was born at that moment.

Israelites and Jews identified with that sea crossing as the moment of their creation as a people and the beginning of their freedom. Freedom brings responsibility. Freedom also brings loss of security. Freed slaves or free people of any age face the challenges of developing self-identity, personal responsibility, and self-direction. The open wilderness symbolized that new freedom, for it beckoned them to move forward, but with no clear roads. The people became afraid and cried out to Moses, "Have you brought us out into the wilderness to die?" (Exodus 14:11). They remembered the "security" of slavery in Egypt and the thin meatless broth they ate there was recalled as a "fleshpot," a hearty, meaty stew. They romanticized slavery, and those days became the "good old days." Such "good old days" always seem better to later generations, even in our society, especially when people wish to avoid present responsibilities. Later Israelite and Jewish thinkers in the Babylonian exile told the wilderness accounts to chide their audience for complaining, even though they had the presence of God. Imagine ancient Jews hearing the story of how their ancestors' complaints and laughing at how quickly their ancestors forgot the drama of the sea crossing. Then they would hear that they also romanticized their past and failed to face the challenges of the present.

In Exodus 14-15, we discern several traditions. The short "Song of Miriam" (Exodus 15:21), a poem in pre-Hebraic dialect, praised "Yah" for defeating pharaoh in battle by throwing him into the sea. It was attributed to a woman, Miriam, a leader in the wilderness experience. Perhaps, her women cohorts who sang would have been the natural singers of such hymns in early Israel. That Miriam's name was recalled betokens the importance of women in the early Israel's life; the settlement process saw the decline in the importance of women, for agricultural life diminished the status of women over against pastoralist life. Later reform laws and prophets spoke on behalf of women's rights to rectify this.

The "Song of Moses" (Exodus 15:1-18) expanded Miriam's song and may have originated in the 12th or 11th century BCE, early in the history of Israel, for its archaic poetry and language appear also to be pre-Hebraic. Again, Yahweh was the divine warrior who threw pharaoh into the sea in what appeared to be cosmic conflict. Neither poem mentioned Israel passing between the waters, so some scholars have suggested creatively that this old poem may recall that pharaoh and his troops historically crossed the water in ships or barges that capsized. The image of pharaoh and his troops being cast into the sea and sinking (Exodus 15:4-5, 10) fits with this theory. The reference to the Egyptian bodies on the beach (Exodus 14:30) also might reinforce this theory, or it might reinforce the image of a beach collapse or tidal action on the Mediterranean Sea.

The portrayal of Yahweh defeating pharaoh with the power of the sea was a mythic image. In the ancient world many people celebrated a New Year festival in which the creator god defeated a deity of chaos, who was often symbolized as water. In the Exodus account Yahweh used water, or the force of chaos, to defeat pharaoh. Yahweh was in total command of the mythic, cosmic force of water, so as to use it in the destruction of Israel's historic enemy, pharaoh. This was mythic imagery used to elaborate "historic" narrative. It has been suggested that perhaps Israelites celebrated a New Year festival in which Yahweh's defeat of watery chaos at creation was combined with talk about the defeat of the Egyptians in the sea.

In addition to the songs of Miriam and Moses, we have a narrative shaped by the Yahwist (Exodus 14: 5-7, 9a, 19-20b, 21b, 24, 27b, 30-31), which almost seems to be an actual account of what happened. This tradition said that an east wind blew the water back in the marsh, the Israelites crossed, Egyptian chariots charged into the muddy marsh, their chariots became trapped in the mud, and then the water returned in devastating fashion.

We might suspect that the historical Moses led the Egyptians into a trap because he knew the regularity of the tidal action in this area. But ancient Israelites and Jews would say, "It was a great act of Yahweh to work through such forces of nature to save our ancestors!" A miracle or sign does not have to overturn the laws of nature to be testimony to the divine. Perhaps, the Yahwist provided the memory of what happened, or perhaps not. The biblical authors were not interested in telling us what happened, but in proclaiming the religious significance of events.

Priestly Editors crafted symbolic imagery to describe a "creation" of the people Israel. Their account supplemented the Yahwist material in Exodus 14 by adding the image of two walls of water through which the Israelites passed. This alluded to the second day of creation in Genesis 1 (which came from the same era) wherein God separated waters above the firmament from the waters below the firmament (Genesis 1:17). Separation of water was a chief characteristic of world creation accounts in Israel and Mesopotamia. Thus, when Yahweh separated the waters into two piles during the Exodus, this became another great act of creation, the creation of Israel. Thus, the Exodus event was an act of both salvation and creation by Yahweh. These symbolic additions have been the inspiration for paintings and movies, rather than the narrative of the Yahwist. In three of the four traditions thus discussed, biblical authors praised Yahweh rather than actually recording what happened. We are obsessed so much with discovering what happened, that we fail to appreciate when the biblical authors tell us the meaning of what happened in literary and symbolic form.

# The Wilderness Traditions

Exodus 16-18 and Numbers 11-14, 16-17, 31-33 recalled the wilderness traditions. Israelites were slaves with no social institutions; they were de-socialized people. They lacked unifying identity; that would have to emerge with the giving of Law at Sinai. Presumably this "mixed multitude" or "mixed rabble" (Exodus 12:38) was composed of different races, speaking diverse languages, for among slave laborers many foreign elements would have been present, including prisoners of war taken captive by the Egyptians in Palestine. Many would have been dangerous, so their pursuit by the Egyptian military made sense (much more so than fleeing pastoralists). In the wilderness without a common identity, such a rabble would fall into anarchy and self-destruction.

**Route through the Wilderness:** Different routes are proposed for the fleeing Israelites: a long southern route to the southern tip of the Sinai Peninsula, a long journey across the Sinai into the land of Midian in north Arabia, a short journey into the central Sinai (where ancient shrines dating from 4000 to 2000 BCE have been found), or a short trip eastward of three days to Kadesh-Barnea and its oases. Maps frequently show the first choice, but it is the least popular choice among scholars. The southern route was popularized in the 4th century CE when the Roman emperor Constantine's mother identified Sinai with the tallest mountain in the Sinai Peninsula, which she felt befit the glory of God. Later Greek Orthodox monks built St. Catherine's monastery there. (You can depend on monks to choose and develop a truly austere site!) The central region of the Sinai contained old shrines at mountains like Har-Hakom, which were already in ruins when Moses arrived. They served wandering pastoralists for millennia, and one of these holy places could have been Sinai, for Moses encountered the burning bush while tending flocks at what seems to have been a holy site already. Some sites even have amphitheater conditions near a mountain or on a plateau where a speaker could address a multitude. The northern route attracts most scholars. It leads to Kadesh, a place often mentioned in the wilderness traditions, to which Moses told pharaoh that the Israelites would journey to worship. Modern archaeologists discovered ruins at this site, called Tell el-Qudeirat, indicating a significant settlement from the 10th to the 6th centuries BCE. (Perhaps, this settlement influenced the oral tradition and led the biblical authors to place Sinai there.) Oases near Kadesh could correspond to Marah, Massah, and Meribah, all sites mentioned in the wilderness journey. Modern Arabic names for these sites sound like the old Hebrew names, and modern Arabic names often are placed at the old biblical sites.

The location of Sinai (Yahwist name) or Horeb (Elohist name) is closely connected the debate over the route. The southern mountain, with St. Catherine's monastery, is the largest mountain in Sinai. References to fire, smoke, and thunder in the biblical text leads some scholars to suggest a volcano in Midian, in north Arabia. Midian was the land where Moses resided with Jethro and perhaps there he encountered the burning bush on the "mountain of God." This "mountain of God" may be the same as Sinai, or perhaps not. Several mountains in central Sinai, such as Har-Hakom, appeal to archaeologists also. Or, the imagery may be metaphorical, the mountain may be only a hill, in which case it could be a site in the north near Kadesh. Further arguments for Kadesh, in addition to the presence of oases, are references in old poetry (Song of Deborah in Judges 5:4-5) that refer to the holy mountain as Mt. Seir in the wilderness of Paran, which is only a little south of Palestine. However, the geographic reference could be vague enough to describe much of Sinai.

**The Murmuring Motif:** The biblical text recalled how Israelites "murmured," or complained about the leadership of Moses and God. They longed for the "fleshpots" of Egypt." The complaints of the Israelites were so obnoxious that Moses once asked God to kill him (Numbers 11:15) rather than to bear the burden of such people. Harsh honesty in recalling one's ancestors is rare in the ancient world and modern world, for what you claim about the ancestors is what you claim for yourself. Israel spoke honestly of the ancestors, confessing that people were sinful and human society was imperfect. Their view of humanity as finite and clearly separated from the divine realm (no half-human half-divine beings existed for them) was quite different than the political rhetoric we find among the inscriptions and epic literature of other cultures at this time.

**Manna:** Israelites complained about food, so Yahweh decided to "rain bread from heaven" (Exodus 16:4) in the morning and to provide flesh to eat in the evening (Exodus 16:8). Every day except the Sabbath, there was food. Manna was described as a white substance, "a fine, flake-like thing, fine as hoarfrost on the ground" (Exodus 16:14). In the evening exhausted quails flew into the camp and were captured for dinner. We think manna is a substance observed today clinging to tamarisk bushes in the Sinai. Produced either as an ooze on the bush when the plant is pierced by a certain insect or, as the excrement of the insect, it dries in the desert air to produce a substance that fits the biblical description, which said it was "like coriander seed, white, and the taste of it was like wafers made with honey" (Exodus 16:31). Quails migrating from southern Europe to Africa in the fall do fall exhausted upon the ground and could have been trapped by the Israelites. Israelite lack of experience with wilderness conditions made them vulnerable, so such natural phenomena were seen as gifts from Yahweh.

**Theology of later Biblical Authors:** Biblical authors added elements to the narratives to address later theological issues. For example, Aaron was persuaded by the Israelites to craft the golden calf. In Exodus 4:14-16 Yahweh made Aaron into Moses' chief spokesperson; then in Exodus 32-33 he betrayed this trust by creating the idol. This was an editorial comment by later theologians upon the character of priests, for whom Aaron was the symbolic ancestor, who worked with Jeroboam I of Israel and built golden calves at the shrines in Dan and Bethel. The king constructed these calves (1 Kings 12) to rival the Temple in Jerusalem, and this political-religious act was foreshadowed by Aaron's cowardly action. Exodus 32-33 (Aaron) closely paralleled the language of the earlier text in 1 Kings 12 (Jeroboam I). Perhaps prophets or the Elohist sought to condemn the priests at later shrines by the depiction of Aaron's treachery.

Korah's rebellion against Moses (Numbers 16) probably reflected later social or religious conflicts we no longer can identify. Korah's rebellion may have reflected post-exilic priestly conflict, for some Psalms were listed as coming from the guild of Korah, which implied Korah was a significant family or guild in that later era. The portrayal of Moses as a prophet reflects the beliefs of later prophets (maybe the Elohist again). Social and religious institutions were projected back into the wilderness to Moses to give them greater authority. Moses performed the functions of prophet, priest, lawgiver, judge, and military leader (king) to ground the authority of those roles in the hoary past.

# Conclusion

Israel was born in the Exodus from Egypt, liberated by God to become the chosen people. God was cast in the image of one who liberated slaves to become a special people. To make a great people greater would require no special power, but to elevate slaves testified to the power of a truly great God. Israelites were unique in the ancient Near East in claiming that their ancestors were so lowly. Later theologians of Israel, Judaism, and Christianity would recall the foundational events as ways in which God interacted with humanity, for in these events the Judeo-Christian tradition believes that the nature of God is revealed to be that of a loving and gracious God.

# Bibliography

Brevard Childs. *The Book of Exodus*. Old Testament Library. Philadelphia, PA: Westminster, 1974.

Mary Douglas. *In the Wilderness: The Doctrine of Defilement in the Book of Numbers*. Journal for the Study of the Testament Supplements 158. Sheffield, Eng.: JSOT, 1993.

Terence Fretheim. *Exodus*. Interpretation. Louisville, KY: John Knox, 1991.

Philip Hyatt. *Exodus*. New Century Bible. London: Oliphants, 1971.

George Knight. *Theology as Narration: A Commentary on the Book of Exodus*. Grand Rapids, MI: Eerdmans, 1976.

Brian Lewis. *The Sargon Legend*. Cambridge, MA: American Schools of Oriental Research, 1980.

Martin Noth. *Exodus*. Trans. John Bowden. Philadelphia, PA: Westminster, 1962.

William Propp. *Exodus 1-18*. Anchor Bible. Garden City, NY: Doubleday, 1998.

John Van Seters. *The Life of Moses: The Yahwist as Historian in Exodus-Numbers*. Louisville, KY: Westminster John Knox, 1994.

# Chapter 13

# Sinai and the Laws

Reading: Exodus 20-23,34,Deuteronomy 5,12-26

The crossing of the sea was the great act of deliverance for Israelites that created them as a people. But in the next stage of this drama Moses led the "rabble" of escaped slaves to a mountain where they received laws from God and their identity was defined forever. In modern language we might speak of them experiencing "socialization." The laws taught them how to live, how to rise above the level of barbarians, which is what slavery degraded them into being. They were "saved" by the Exodus, but "defined" and "civilized" at Sinai. Of all the laws, the Ten Commandments appear to perform the function of providing to directionless people the necessary guidelines for civilized life. Some scholars suggest these alone were the laws given to them by Moses, all other laws developed later. The Sinai experience prepared the people to enter the land of Palestine and to live as a unified folk. Later biblical authors declared that Israel's failure in the land was due to their inability to live by the "blueprint" given at Sinai. The later biblical tradition saw the experience at Sinai as one in which Israel "married" God (Hosea) or made a covenant with God (Deuteronomy). All the traditions saw Sinai as the time when God and Israel bonded forever, and the faithfulness of Jews even today is commended to them by the pact their ancestors made with God at Sinai.

## The Sinai Tradition

Israel's laws, found in Exodus 19-31, 33-40, Leviticus 1-27, Numbers 1-10, and Deuteronomy 12-26, arose over many years, but the biblical authors attributed them to the experience at Sinai. All of Israel's laws, even the obviously revised laws in Deuteronomy 12-26, were projected back to Moses, for symbolically with him the legal process began. In the ancient world law makers would insert later laws into an earlier law code and attribute their creation to the original legislator, for it was understood that those later laws were implicit in the earlier code. Revelation began with Moses, and later additions to his laws simply unfolded what was presumed to be present in that primal experience. Even the rabbis in the Jewish Talmud (100-600 CE) implied that teachings of the Talmud were given orally at Sinai, but not written down until later years.

Torah, or Law, means direction or a pattern for living. Yahweh provided for those escaped slaves at Sinai and for Israelites of all time a guide that enabled them to survive in social harmony with a just society. All aspects of life were addressed, for Yahweh was Lord over the entire domain of human existence. People obeyed the Law out of love because Yahweh saved them at the sea and made them a chosen people. Christians hear the word "Law" and attribute a negative connotation to it, but they should understand that for Jews the Law was the gift from a gracious deity to help humanity. Torah was given after the great act of deliverance, the Exodus. Jews were not the people of God by keeping the Law; rather, the Law was given after Yahweh saved and chose them in the Exodus. Obedience to Yahweh was not an onerous burden, but a loving response to God for deliverance from slavery and the subsequent gift of the land.

**Book of the Covenant: Exodus 21-23**: The laws in the Book of the Covenant or the Covenant Code reflected simple agrarian life in Palestine (Exodus 20:22-23:33) and addressed issues of everyday life. Disputes were adjudicated by local village elders, who sat at the gate of the village hearing arguments of villagers with legal complaints. They rendered decisions with a sense of what was just for each specific case. Thus, laws in the Covenant Code were advisory; they provided insight into how to make decisions rather than providing answers for every dispute. This is typical for corpora of oral law, which are shorter than written law codes. Scholars suggest that laws in the Covenant Code were in oral form for centuries before they were written down and revised. The written form of Exodus 21-23 may have come from the time of king Hezekiah in Judah who sought religious and legal reform (715-700 BCE). (Years ago scholars suggested that the code arose before the monarchy in the 11th century BCE.) The code reflected needs of a society experiencing economic development, as happened in Judah in the 8th century BCE. Some recent authors, however, attribute the code to the Babylonian Exile, a time when Jewish life again would have been rather rustic, but also in need of legal reform.

Individual laws were formulated mostly in casuistic fashion, as a legal example or case: "If such and such is the situation, then this shall be the penalty." This formulation was common in written law codes in the ancient Near East. Israelites may have known some ancient codes, especially the one by Hammurabi of Babylon (1750 BCE), as well as other Mesopotamia law-codes from the second millennium BCE. Hammurabi's laws were often copied in scribal schools as writing exercises, thus many people were familiar with them. Situations described in those codes were generic enough so that elders could fashion legal decisions to a variety of situations. Laws usually prescribed the maximum penalty to be imposed; mitigating circumstances could suggest a reduced punishment.

Generally, written law-codes in the ancient world (like Hammurabi's Code) were neither binding nor even used in law-courts. They were used to train writing skills to scribes, so that their influence was significant in terms of forming the worldview of scribal intelligentsia, some of whom might become judges. Royal Mesopotamian law-codes tried to affect existing legal practices, but probably did not have that much of an impact. Judges continued to use an existing corpus of laws that they knew by heart, oral laws. Likewise, biblical law-codes provided an advisory and inspirational function for elders in villages and jurists in law-courts. The codes were inspirational because they used a lively religious rhetoric to call upon people to be just. The biblical law-codes were more like sermons than actual tools for law-courts. We assume that the traditional oral laws that Israelite village elders used were quite similar to the Book of the Covenant, except that the Book of the Covenant was attempting to persuade elders to use some of the modified laws to bring about better justice, especially for the poor.

The principle of *lex talionis*, "eye for an eye, tooth for a tooth," was not the vengeful principle that so many people today assume. Elders could choose a lesser punishment, if conditions warranted it. The principle articulated that punishment should be equal to the crime, not greater. Often in Mesopotamian laws the punishment greatly exceeded the crime, especially for the lower classes and slaves. Laws in Mesopotamia were designed to keep such people in subjection and to protect property and privileges of the powerful classes. Israelites believed that the punishments had to be fair, so *lex talionis* protected the poor. It meant that poor people could not be brutalized with excessive punishment by the law, and rich people could not escape justice by simply paying a fine for a physical crime against someone. *Lex talionis* actually forbade cruel and unusual punishments and made rich and poor stand equally before the law.

**Ritual Decalogue (Exodus 34):** The ten or twelve cultic regulations listed in Exodus 34 supposedly was the second giving of the Ten Commandments in Exodus 20, after Moses broke the first tablets of the Law. What we really have is a clever narrative by which the biblical author presented both the civil (Exodus 20) and ritual (Exodus 34) decalogues. Some scholars suggest that Exodus 34 was really the older version of Exodus 20, and Exodus 20 did not arise until the Babylonian Exile. However, we shall assume in this textbook that Exodus 20, in some form, was really the oldest law-code. Since scholars usually count the imperatives in Exodus 34 to obtain twelve laws, they suggest that originally Exodus 20 had twelve commands to parallel Exodus 34. Exodus 34 contained directions for religious and cultic practices. Archaic language, including the old agrarian names for the three great festivals of Passover, Festival of Weeks, and Festival of Tabernacles, leads scholars to date this code variously from the late pre-monarchic era down to the time of Hezekiah (1050-700 BCE).

**Priestly Laws and Holiness Code (Leviticus 17-26):** Old cultic legislation in Leviticus 17-26 and other Priestly laws were not written down until the Babylonian Exile. Some believe these laws existed as early as 850-700 BCE. With the exile in 586 BCE, it became necessary to write down and expand laws that had been well known among the priests. These laws described sacrifice, ritual, cleanliness, kosher food, and many aspects of everyday life. Prior to 586 BCE these guidelines were only for priests; such ritual priestly guidelines are found worldwide (such as stipulations for Brahmin caste in India in the Code of Manu).

Priestly laws outlined various sacrifices: 1) The "holocaust" or "burnt offering" (Leviticus 1:1-17, 6:8-13) was an animal sacrifice in which the entire animal was burned on an altar, a dramatic offering made in extreme circumstances by the community or an individual. 2) The "grain offering" (Leviticus 2:1-16, 6:14-23) was a "gift" given to God made of flour and oil, part of which was burned on an altar and the rest given to the priests for their support. 3) The "peace offering" (Leviticus 3, 7:11-38) was for thanksgiving by the worshipper, or in response to the fulfillment of a vow, or simply a freely given sacrifice. 4) The "sin offering" (Leviticus 4:1-5:13, 6:24-30) and the 5) "guilt offering" (Leviticus 5:14-6:7, 7:1-10) provided for an animal to be sacrificed as a substitute for the human offender. The animal's blood was sprinkled on the altar, the fat burned and given to God (since fat was the "best" part of the animal for people who lived on the edge of starvation), and the rest of the animal was destroyed.

In the Babylonian Exile Jews risked losing their identity and merging into the Babylonian populace, as happened to the ten "lost tribes" of Israel in Assyria. But these priestly laws kept the Jews separate and holy, for guidelines that in pre-exilic era applied only to priests now were extended to all Jews. Jews became a "holy people of Yahweh" wherever they were scattered in the world. The entire world was the Temple of God, and Jews were Yahweh's priests in the world. In the New Testament Christians were described as a royal priesthood using this Jewish concept.

**Deuteronomic Legislation (Deuteronomy 12-26):** In the 7th century BCE, King Josiah of Judah undertook political and religious reform as Judah gradually felt Assyrian control weaken. A copy of the laws of Moses was discovered in the Temple during repair work, and Josiah immediately implemented these new laws. 2 Kings 23 gives us the impression that Deuteronomy 12-26 was that "discovered" code because of the similarity between Josiah's reform and the laws in Deuteronomy. (Later additions to the laws reflect and an awareness of exile, indicating revisions around 550 BCE.) The Deuteronomic Laws assumed a society with a well-developed economy, classes, judicial system, and kingship. The code revised laws from the older Covenant Code, and Deuteronomy was inspired by the rhetoric of 8th century BCE classical prophets. Specific laws in Deuteronomy revised and expanded similar laws in Exodus 21-23, and provided greater rights for marginal people. Widows, orphans, and resident aliens or sojourners were those people deeply in need of protection, and the lawgivers reminded their audience of how God saved them from slavery in Egypt, so they should take care of the poor in their own age.

**Decalogue (Exodus 20 and Deuteronomy 5):** The most highly revered law-code for Jews and Christians today is the Decalogue, or the Ten Commandments, referred to as the Debarim ("the words") in the Bible. The Decalogue arose in two versions with differences that hint at a long developmental process. Sabbath observance in Exodus 20 was grounded in the Priestly Editors' reference to the creation of the world (Genesis 1), while in Deuteronomy 5 the appeal was to the Exodus. In Exodus 20 Sabbath was a religious celebration; while in Deuteronomy 5 it was a day of rest for weary people, especially the poor. According to Exodus, Israel should "honor" or "keep holy" the Sabbath, and in Deuteronomy they "observe" the Sabbath. The Hebrew for "honor" had a religious meaning, the word for "observe" was a normal word used in other legal imperatives and meant "obey." In Exodus 20 the prohibition against coveting the neighbor's house occurred before wife, since the wife belonged to the "house" or "family" of the man, and "family" was the older meaning of the word. But in Deuteronomy 5 coveting of the wife came before house, because Deuteronomic laws attempted to elevate the rights and status of women. Deuteronomy reflected an age when "house" may have meant property because of economic development, and since the wife then was often viewed as property, the Deuteronomic reformers sought to avoid that interpretation. The word for "covet" Exodus 20 is hmd, which meant seizure and was a crime punishable by law. In Deuteronomy 5 the verb form came from awh and meant psychological desire. Exodus 20 contained the original form of the command, when it was civil law; Deuteronomy 5 presented the later meaning as the Decalogue evolved into a moral code.

Scholars sometimes hypothetically reconstruct the original oral form of the commands. If they were carved on two tablets of stone, they had to be much shorter than our present commands. They could have been two or three words in length, including the initial Hebrew particle lo, which meant, "do not" or "you shall not." They all might have been negative in form, whereas our present biblical text presents the Sabbath and parental commands in a positive form. The text and meaning would have been thus:

1. Do not worship other gods. (Pre-exilic Israelites did not deny the existence of other gods, this command told them to ignore those gods.)

2. Do not make images of Yahweh. (Images made people believe that they could manipulate the god(s), and it gave more power to priests who guarded the statues and to rich people who could afford to commission them, for statues often were made of gold and silver.)

3. Do not dishonor the name of Yahweh. (Do not use it to curse other people, or use it for witchcraft and divination, but rather use it for blessing! In later years, the command prohibited saying the divine name, Yahweh, aloud.)

4. Do not dishonor the Sabbath. (Freed slaves and marginal people needed a day of rest. Later in the Babylonian Exile, it also became a day for worship.)

5. Do not dishonor your parents. (Marginal societies often expose old people and weak members of society to die. Take care of old people and "your days will be prolonged" when you are old, too! Later the command legitimated the authority of elders in the kinship system.)

6. Do not kill. (It meant violent murder, for some forms of killing were sanctioned when done by the whole people in the name of Yahweh, such as Holy War and execution.)

7. Do not adulterate. (Do not steal or have sex with another man's wife, for that destroys the family, and in turn, the entire society suffers.)

8. Do not steal. (Since early Israelites had no property worth stealing, this might have meant kidnapping a person to sell him into slavery, or it might have referred to seizure of common property, like cattle, land, or water, by an individual to the detriment of the group. The command did not under-gird private property, but affirmed the right of access to necessary goods for all people.)

9. Do not perjure. (To lie under oath might lead to the death of another person in a trial situation, in addition to being another misuse of the divine name.)

10. Do not covet. (It might originally have meant actual theft, if stealing meant kidnapping. Eventually it meant trying to seize someone's property, as in Exodus 20, and later it meant internal greed, as in Deuteronomy 5.) (In Exodus coveting of the house was listed before coveting of the wife, and in Deuteronomy coveting of the wife was placed before coveting of the house. Thus, many argue over whether there is one coveting command or two.)

The commands were on two tablets of stone, and believers have disagreed for years on how to divide the commands between those two tablets. However, all of the commands might have been written on both tablets, since it was the custom in the ancient world to make two copies of important documents like treaties.

These commands were stated in "apodictic" form, as distinct from the "casuistic" laws in the Covenant Code. Apodictic laws were absolute, as though stated directly from God. Once we thought apodictic laws were unique only to Israel, but now we know that other contemporary societies used them. Israel, however, relied more on apodictic formulations, perhaps to stress the divine origin of such laws.

The Ten Commandments may have originated as civil law with death as the penalty for violation of most of the commands. This would make sense for Israelites in the wilderness, for it would have provided the most basic guidelines for order in society. When other laws evolved that covered civil crimes as well as religious violations, the Decalogue slowly transformed into a moral code to be placed at the beginning of other law-codes. The Covenant Code, for example, covered many of the same actions with more specific case examples. Both Exodus 20 and Deuteronomy 5 now preface larger legal corpora and function as introductions or generic summaries. They appear to us as great moral summaries of the law. One hint of this process might be the transformation of the word for "covet" from "seize" (a physical action) in Exodus 20 to "desire" (a mental attitude) in Deuteronomy 5.

The Commandments appear to have undergone change and reinterpretation before they assumed our present form. Further reinterpretation continued until the days of Jesus, and Jesus reinterpreted these commands by deepening and spiritualizing them. Christians have reinterpreted them, but use them to provide insight how the people should live and serve others. Christian theologians, teachers, and catechists recognize that the Ten Commandments are not literally binding upon Christians, for they are part of the law that became dead with the New Covenant, as Paul says. Yet they are used to educate the Christian community, for they describe universal moral actions.

It should be noted, as a final parting observation, that there are three different ways of numbering the commandments, because there appear to be eleven imperatives. 1) Roman Catholics, Greek Orthodox, Anglican-Episcopals, and Lutherans combine the command on graven images with the command to worship only one God and have two coveting commandments. 2) Other Protestants combine the two coveting commands and have a separate command on images, which is understood to call for simplicity in worship and liturgical art. 3) Orthodox Jews combine the image command with the command for exclusive worship and the two coveting commands; they then have the imperative, "I am the Lord" as the first command, which follows the pattern of imperative lists found in the book of Leviticus. If they are correct in assuming this phrase to be a commandment, and if there are two coveting commands, then there originally were 12 commandments, like the 12 tribes. Ultimately, alluding to the commandments by number can be confusing. The seventh commandment is adultery for some Christians and theft for others.

# Trajectories in the Legal Tradition

As we read the various law-codes we notice that certain legal issues were addressed repeatedly in the various codes, and these laws addressed problems in different ways. This, of course, is what led scholars to suggest a historical evolution of the law-codes from the Book of the Covenant to the Deuteronomic Laws and then to the Priestly Laws. Although we cannot be absolutely sure that laws and the law-codes built upon each other in this fashion; nonetheless, there are some specific laws that show an evolution through these three codes. This can be observed most directly with social-economic legislation. The evolution of those laws reflected the needs that lawgivers faced as Israelite society and economy became more complex. The laws evolved in a way that shows how lawgivers attempted to plug loopholes in the earlier laws. This is especially true with laws concerning interest and slavery.

Were the laws enshrined in the biblical text actually used by elders in the villages and in courtrooms of a later era, or were they created by religious intelligentsia and presented as literary-theological documents to envision an ideal society and inspire those who actually worked in courtroom contexts? Increasingly scholars suspect that the latter option is the case. But the post-exilic Jewish tradition treated them as binding guidelines for the creation of a religious lifestyle in service to God.

Interest was condemned because it often turned borrowers and their families into debt slaves, especially in a simple agrarian economy where most people were peasants. In complex societies, such as Egypt and Mesopotamia, high interest rates were placed on loans extended by temples (with their great sources of revenue) to merchants who could turn a significant profit in a trading venture. Interest rates of 20% to 33% could be repaid by merchants, but for a peasant these rates were a gamble. A very good crop yield could bring a 35 to 40-fold return, in which case the interest owed would be only 1% of the yield. But a poor crop year created by drought, insects, or foreign armies campaigning through the countryside, caused debt default on a wide-scale basis.

The Book of the Covenant contained perhaps the oldest condemnation of interest. If the code dated from the late 8th century BCE, it was an early attempt to mandate economic reform in response to the recent economic changes that put so many highland peasants in economic distress. Exodus 22:25 condemned the charging of interest on loans, especially loans extended to the poor. The Book of the Covenant also limited pledges taken from the poor in exchange for loans. Exodus 22:26 said that a cloak taken in pawn must be returned to a poor person at night, so he could sleep in it. Presumably, this law implied that other necessary possessions could not be taken for pledges on either a temporary or permanent basis.

Creditors circumvented these laws by redefining interest. A loan could be extended and a certain amount could be taken out of the loan, but the borrower was expected to pay the full amount back to the creditor. (So if you asked for $100 and received $90, you had to pay $100.) This was called a *neshek* or a "bite." Deuteronomic Reform addressed this new problem by condemning *neshek* on money and provisions (non-monetary items) in Deuteronomy 23:19-20. However, Israelite creditors were able to charge interest on loans to foreigners, since they probably were merchants from a distant land who operated routinely with the guidelines for loans and interest, and they probably made a good profit in Israel anyway. In reference to items of collateral, Deuteronomy 24:6, 10-13, 17 elaborated on the allusions in the Book of the Covenant. Not only was the cloak mentioned, but also a millstone for making bread was specifically listed. In addition, the creditor now was not permitted to enter the poor person's house to choose an item as pledge, but must wait for the poor person to bring out an acceptable pledge for the loan. Specific reference is made to the cloak of a widow, which should not be taken at all. Perhaps the widow might not have the courage to ask for her cloak back at night.

From this point onward creditors might demand an unspecified added amount, not called interest, on a loan. This would have been called a *tarbith* or *marbith*, an "add-on" or a "gift." (There is debate as to how this differs from *neshek*.) If *tarbith* was another way to sidestep laws against interest, then Leviticus 25:36-37 closed the loophole by condemning both *neshek* and *tarbith* on money and food. These interest laws show an evolutionary trajectory designed to provide protection for the poor against those who would sidestep such protection.

Debt slave release laws reflected a similar trajectory, but also demonstrated a greater urge for social reform. Some scholars suggest that even though these laws arose in different eras, they covered different situations. But most believe that these laws built upon previous laws to solve the economic woes. As legislation unfolded over the years to provide just treatment for debt slaves, we sense that the assumptions behind the laws led to a desire to humanize the institution of slavery, and eventually to abolish it.

People in the ancient world became slaves by being taken as prisoners of war or falling into debt. Needless to say, the latter case was more common in Israel. Children might be sold for debts (Exodus 21:7-11) or seized for debts (2 Kings 4:1, Nehemiah 5:5), and adults also could be seized involuntarily for debt (1 Samuel 22:2, Amos 2:6, Isaiah 50:1) or voluntarily submit for debt (Exodus 21:5-6, Deuteronomy 15:16-17). High interest rates could force people into debt slavery. The debtor would lose family members and ultimately himself as a debt slave to his creditor. This happened most frequently in Mesopotamia, where temples often gathered many debt slaves. Hammurabi's laws (1750 BCE) ideally decreed that no person could be enslaved for such debt more than three years, and periodic proclamations by other Amorite Babylonian kings in the early second millennium BCE, called *mishnarum* and *anduraru* decrees, proclaimed the release of debt and debt slaves. Israelites followed suit with their own legislation. Scholars see great similarity between these Mesopotamian decrees and the Sabbath Year in Deuteronomy and the Jubilee Year in Leviticus (the word for "release" in Deuteronomy is *deror*, which even sounds like *anduraru*).

Biblical authors mandated more situations under which debt slaves could be released. They were inspired by the rhetoric of the prophets and the memory of their ancestors' enslavement in Egypt. Beginning in the 8th century BCE economic changes in Israel caused a class of wealthy to emerge and a corresponding class of poor people and debt slaves. Amos 2:6 declared that a debt slave could be purchased for the price of a pair of sandals. Biblical authors produced the first laws in history to critique the institution of slavery. A respectful treatment of slaves demanded that they be permitted to share in the family religious life: Sabbath (Exodus 20:10, 23:12), sacrificial meals (Deuteronomy 12:12, 18), festivals (Deuteronomy 16:11, 14), and Passover (Exodus 12:44). Slaves were set free if the master beat a slave too severely (Exodus 21:20, 26-27), or if young slave girls were not allowed to become full wives at adulthood (Exodus 21:7-11). If a person kidnapped someone to sell him into slavery, the punishment was death (Exodus 21:6, Deuteronomy 24:7). A slave fleeing a foreign country was not to be returned to his foreign master, but could become an Israelite (Deuteronomy 23:15-16), which, of course, violated international law of slave return.

The evolving trajectory of Israelite law is demonstrated best with those laws directly concerned with debt slave release. The Book of the Covenant said that a debt slave should be released after six years of labor. If he entered debt slavery single, but married a woman provided by his master and had children by her, he had to leave his family behind. If he wished to stay with his family, he had to become a permanent slave after a special ceremony. The law released male slaves after six years, since no debt warranted service greater than six years. (Note how Jacob had to work six years each for Leah and Rachel.) No provision was made for females; perhaps they eventually were to marry their masters or be married off by their masters. Since the male slave could not leave with a family that was begun after he had entered debt slavery, crafty owners could be matchmakers and induce a debt slave to become a permanent slave. Furthermore, dishonest slave owners could fail to count the six years correctly and keep the debt slave for life. Any appeal to elders or a court could be futile, if the slave-owner bribed or intimidated the judges.

Because of such loopholes Deuteronomic legislators provided a broader set of guidelines for slave release in the Sabbath Year legislation of Deuteronomy 15:1-18, which covered both debt and debt-slave release. Debts were to be released every seventh year on a nation wide basis. Deuteronomy 15:12-14 attached debt slave release to this law to make slave release also appear to be universal every seven years, instead of being in the seventh year of an individual slave's service. (By itself the slave release law in Deuteronomy 15 does not appear to be a nation wide release.) This eliminated dishonest counting of years by individual slave owners. The slave release was extended to women. Such women might have been wives of debt slaves, some of whom might have been turned over to creditors before their husbands were seized, or perhaps they were in debt slavery and their husbands were too poor to pay off the debt. Finally, the law demanded that masters give provisions to newly freed slaves, so that they do not fall back into debt slavery. Together these laws constituted Deuteronomic Sabbath Year release.

Laws in Leviticus articulated a custom called Jubilee Year that combined debt release and slave release with land restoration, which provided even more drastic economic reform.

Leviticus 25:39-55 decreed that debt slaves were to be freed and land was to be restored to the original owners every 50 years (or 49 years as some interpret the text). Scholars have debated the mechanics of such land restoration, as well as verses that discuss pro-rating land, the right of kin to buy back a debtor's property, dwellings in cities, and the rights of Levities in this process (since they owned no land). Jubilee Year customs appear to us as an attempt to accomplish what previous legislation failed to do. Most have suggested Jubilee Year was created during the Babylonian Exile and was ideal legislation never put into practice, while the Sabbath Year practice in Deuteronomy 15 was observed regularly by post-exilic Jews. Jubilee Year was the most comprehensive attempt to restore economic equilibrium by canceling debts, freeing slaves, and even restoring land. The concept of Jubilee Year has continued to inspire Christians today who call for significant economic reform in third world countries.

In summation, the evolving legal tradition attempted to eliminate economic oppression of the poor. Through the years expanding legislation tried not only to assure that the debt slave would be free, but that he would have a solid economic footing to stay free from debt slavery. Such legislation was not found elsewhere in the ancient world, and is even radical reform by modern standards. But it was a bold attempt to create a society of free and self-sustaining peasant farmers.

One may observe an evolution in laws and customs in other areas not related to economic reform, where legislation sought to prevent people from circumventing earlier, simpler laws. Some legal evolution occurred as the religious understanding of Israel changed over the years. For example, one can observe that the understandings of festivals changed, and this may reflect evolving religious practices. In the Book of the Covenant the major Israelite festivals during the year were defined as the Festival of Unleavened Bread, the Festival of Harvest or First Fruits, and the Festival of Ingathering at the end of the year (Exodus 23:14-17). In the Ritual Decalogue they were called the Festival of Unleavened Bread, the Festival of Weeks or First Fruits, and the Festival of Ingathering (Exodus 34:18, 22-23). In both codes adult males were told to appear before the Lord at all three festivals, presumably at a local Israelite shrine. In the later Deuteronomic Laws these festivals were called Passover, the Festival of Weeks, and the Festival of Booths. Males were to appear at the place God will choose, most obviously Jerusalem (Deuteronomy 16:1-17). The gradual transition of names from Unleavened Bread to Passover, from First Fruits to Weeks, and Ingathering to Booths, suggests to scholars that over the years Israelites associated the great acts of God in Israel's history with simple agrarian festivals. This may betoken a corresponding emphasis on historical memory and ethical behavior rather than cultic fertility celebrations.

We can observe evolutionary trajectories in the laws, which implies the legal tradition was a living, dynamic heritage that changed over the years as economic, social, and religious conditions changed. This was not static timeless law, but rather an evolving theological legal tradition that tried to speak to Israelites and tell them how to relate to their God and how to deal justly with each other. If we appreciate that a process of legal development was preserved in the biblical text, not a systematic law-code, we are more likely to appreciate the spirit of the laws and what they sought to accomplish.

# Conclusion

At Sinai people received an identity from God and a mode of responding to God in gratitude for the salvation they had experienced at the sea crossing. They become Yahweh's pilgrim folk called to faithful obedience and a special identity as a chosen people. Jews of a later age, especially during the time of the Babylonian Exile, who also were a pilgrim people, could take hope in the same message. In the wilderness a de-socialized people bonded together to become a kindred people, a nation. They learned what freedom and responsibility both meant and entailed. The story of their wilderness wanderings spoke to later generations and demanded that they, too, accept their freedom and the responsibilities that came with it.

The later biblical theologians of Israel, Judaism, and Christianity looked to these foundational events for direction in addressing their own contemporary moral and social problems. Laws provided direction for people and a sense of identity in community. For the later Judeo-Christian tradition the spirit of justice found within the legal traditions is an inspiration for religious literature, preaching, and education. For Christians the specific laws of the Sinai tradition are not binding, but the spirit of justice found therein, which dovetails with the Christian message, is truly an inspiration and encouragement in the development of ethics and social teachings.

# Bibliography

Albrecht Alt. "The Origins of Israelite Law." *Essays on Old Testament History and Religion*. Trans. R. A. Wilson. Garden City, NY: Doubleday, 1966.

Hans Jochen Boecker. *Law and the Administration of Justice in the Old Testament and Ancient East*. Trans. Jeremy Moiser. Minneapolis, MN: Augsburg, 1980.

Calum Carmichael. *The Origins of Biblical Law: The Decalogues and the Book of the Covenant*. Ithaca, NY: Cornell University, 1992.

Frank Crüsemann. *The Torah: Theology and Social History of Old Testament Law*. Trans. Allan Mahnke. Minneapolis, MN: Fortress, 1996.

Anne Fitzpatrick-McKinley. *The Transformation of the Torah from Scribal Advice to Law*. Journal for the Study of the Old Testament Supplements 287. Sheffield, Eng.: Sheffield Academic Press, 1999.

Robert Gnuse. *You Shall Not Steal: Community and Property in the Biblical Tradition*. Maryknoll, NY: Orbis, 1984.

Walter Harrelson. *The Ten Commandments and Human Rights*. Philadelphia, PA: Fortress, 1980.

Dale Patrick. *Old Testament Law*. Atlanta, GA: John Knox Press, 1985.

Martha Roth. *Law Collections from Mesopotamia and Asia Minor*. Atlanta, GA: Society of Biblical Literature, 1997.

John Van Seters. *A Lawbook for the Diaspora: Revision in the Study of the Covenant Code*. New York, NY: Oxford University, 2003.

Christopher Wright. *God's People in God's Land*. Grand Rapids, MI: Eerdmans, 1990.

# Chapter 14

# Post-Exilic History and Priestly Theology

Reading: Ezra 10,Nehemiah 8,Genesis 1:1-2:4,9:1-17,17,Exodus 25-31,Psalms 1,8,22,46,73,93,121.

The post-exilic era was not an age of dead legalism or decaying Judaism, as too often scholars have assumed. Rather, it was an era of creative literary and theological productivity. The crises of the post-exilic era caused new values to arise, and the religious intelligentsia expressed the values of their traditional faith in new intellectual modes. Ultimately the literature, theology, and religious beliefs that developed in this era gave rise to both Christianity and Rabbinic Judaism. This era has various titles to describe it. It has been called the Intertestamental era, but increasingly scholars dislike that term, because it was not an age between the two testaments; much of the Old Testament was produced in this time. It has been called the post-exilic era, because it was the age that came after the Babylonian Exile. But that is to deny any real identity to the era. Jewish scholars prefer the term Second Temple Period or Second Temple Commonwealth, because in this era the most important symbol for worldwide Jewry was the Temple rebuilt by Zerubbabel (dedicated in 516 BCE) and refurbished by Herod the Great. Its destruction was the signal event that closed the era in 70 CE. Scholars now tend to use both terms, post-exilic and Second Temple eras, when speaking of this age.

Only the books of Ezra and Nehemiah provide a glimpse into the events of that age, and what they tell us is minimal. The Law and the Prophets became accepted written literature in that era, around 400 BCE for the Law and 200 BCE for the Prophets. Different genres of literature emerged: 1) post-exilic prophets, who slowly evolved from being radical proclaimers of hope into eschatological visionaries; 2) apocalyptic literature, which arose out of post-exilic prophecy, wisdom, and other intellectual sources; 3) the Psalms and other hymnic literature, which reflected priestly piety and a deep spirituality; 4) wisdom literature, a humanistic approach to reality that sought God in the created order and human reason; 5) novelistic literature, which was a didactic literary tradition somewhat related to the wisdom tradition; and 6) historiographical works, such as Chronicles, Ezra, and Nehemiah. Each type of literature contained a religious piety that sought the presence of God in some way: cult, internal piety, a new world order, reason, or creation. As Christianity emerged in the 1st century CE, it drew heavily from all these pieties to create its own synthesis.

# Second Temple Era

Our only historical memories from this era come from the literary tradition known as the "Chronicler," which includes 1 and 2 Chronicles, Ezra, and Nehemiah. (However, many recent scholars now view Chronicles as separate from Ezra and Nehemiah.) 1 and 2 Chronicles appeared around 400 BCE or thereafter (dates as late as 200 BCE are given) and retold the same stories as the Deuteronomistic History, especially in Samuel and Kings. The Chronicler produced an interpretation of history that came from a priestly perspective, and thus we include the discussion of the Chronicler's work with the consideration of the Priestly tradition. Some authors refer to the works of Chronicles as the "Chronistic History." The Chronicler claimed to have used sources, including the "Book of the Kings of Judah and Israel" (2 Chronicles 16:11, 25:26) or the "Book of the Kings of Israel and Judah" (2 Chronicles 27:7, 35:27), the "Book of the Kings of Israel" (1 Chronicles 9:1, 2 Chronicles 20:34), the "Chronicles of the Kings of Israel" (2 Chronicles 33:18), "Midrash on the Book of Kings" (2 Chronicles 24:27), and the "Chronicles of David" (1 Chronicles 27:24), but whether these were actual sources or whether the Chronicler creatively rewrote sections of Samuel and Kings is debated by scholars. The Chronicler gave us unique information that has been verified by outside sources. The period of prosperity assigned to the reign of king Jotham of Judah (2 Chronicles 27:3-6) corresponds with archaeological assessments of that era. Details concerning Hezekiah's tunnel, which archaeologists have discovered, are more complete (2 Chronicles 32:30) than those found in 2 Kings 20:20. The tradition that king Manasseh of Judah was a prisoner of the Assyrians (2 Chronicles 33:11) has been verified by Assyrian sources.

The Chronicler focused upon David and paid attention only to the kings of Judah. The history of kingship in the northern state of Israel was omitted, except where it intersected with history in Judah. David was viewed in a positive way: Nathan's Oracle in 2 Samuel 7 had negative elements removed and the affair with Bathsheba was omitted. Generally, post-exilic literature elevated David but perceived Solomon in a negative light, perhaps because he epitomized all the problems that kingship brought in terms of oppression and economic exploitation. However, Chronicles did not mention those particular negative things about Solomon. He did not tell us that Solomon gave 20 cities in Galilee to the king of Tyre (I Kings 9:11), and he legitimated Solomon's sacrifice at Gibeon in 1 Kings 3 by telling us that the Tent of Meeting was there (2 Chronicles 1:3). But we can intuit that in Chronicles Solomon paled next to David. Perhaps, the priestly authors envisioned David as a foreshadowing of a coming messiah, in particular, a priestly messiah. For the imagery of a priestly messiah surfaced in the much later literature of the Dead Sea Scrolls from Qumran, which was a community founded by alienated priests. If this was so, then priestly theologians had a view of a priestly messiah to parallel the developing prophetic view of a royal messiah. Since the perspective of Chronicles was a priestly one, the author stressed the importance of the Temple, the cult, and Levites for the overall history of Judah in the two books. The relationship of the kings to these religious institutions was stressed, so much so, that the kings, especially David, appeared to be priestly kings. The Deuteronomists were prophetic in orientation as they recalled the past, but the Chronicler provided a post-exilic priestly viewpoint of the past.

In the Chronicler's history there was no longer the need for the repentance that the Deuteronomists had demanded, for the punishment of the exile had come and gone. The Chronicler believed that what was needed after the exile was adherence to the Law of the priestly-led holy nation that had Yahweh as its king. David was the greatest king, but his real contribution lay in the establishment of a Temple-state system, even though he did not build the Temple. Chronicles gave David credit for building the Temple because David got the blueprints from God and gave them to Solomon. Judah was portrayed as a priestly people who rallied around the Temple prior to the exile. The Chronicler implied that post-exilic Jews needed to be a nation of priestly people serving God by obedience to the Torah and preserving the Temple worship as the capstone of their religious piety. Wars in Chronicles seemed like liturgical processions rather than real battles; people marched out in reverence and prevailed against their enemies. Priests were the true leaders of the people. Levites were important as Temple servants who assisted the priests not the prophets, as they did during Deuteronomic Reform. Chronicles wrote no history of the post-exilic era, but it gave a feeling for the piety of the age.

**Rebuilding Jerusalem**:  Cyrus the Persian seized Babylon in 539 BCE and permitted the Jews to return to their homeland in 538 BCE. As Jews returned home, events did not transpire as the prophet Second Isaiah had hoped. Rebuilding the city and the Temple took years, people were depressed, and they faced opposition from their neighbors. Samaritans north of Jerusalem were a people created out of old Israelite bloodlines mingled with people imported by the Assyrians after 721 BCE. They worshipped Yahweh, but their religiosity was different from the religion of the returning Jews, and tensions arose between the two groups. In some ways Samaritans preserved pre-exilic Israelite customs more authentically than did the Jews in Judah.

Cyrus appointed Sheshbazzar, son of king Jehoiachin, to be governor of the Persian province of Judah. Throughout the empire Cyrus appointed local leaders as governors to maintain continuity with the old social structures for stability. (Darius I ended that policy after regional revolts in the next generation.) Sheshbazzar was replaced by Zerubbabel (though some believe he was the same person). Zerubbabel completed the rebuilding of the Temple begun by Sheshbazzar, but disappeared after its completion in 516 BCE. Scholars suggest he became the focal point for a resurgence of Jewish nationalism, and he voluntarily left or was removed by the Persians. Haggai and Zechariah implied he was the "shoot of Jesse," the chosen king of independent Judah, and the messiah of the golden age. When he left, presumably the prophetic movement was discredited, and priests became extremely wary of the prophets. Never again would an individual prophet arise and publicly speak in his or her own name. With the removal of Zerubbabal, perhaps the high priest Joshua and his successors became the more important intermediaries with the Persians and later foreign rulers of Judah. Archaeological evidence, however, indicates that Judah would continue to have governors, and Nehemiah loosely referred to such governors, but we sometimes suspect that their role was not too important compared to the High Priest in Jerusalem. Perhaps, at least, in the eyes of the people their priests were the symbolic leaders. There were other leaders, perhaps a council of elders, so that the power of the priests was not authoritarian. The priests were the most visible leaders, and thus in 90 CE Josephus described Judea as a theocracy.

The significant political role of the priests continued until the days of Jesus. Foreign powers worked through Jerusalem's priests, especially the Romans, for the priests had no desire for national independence and were willing to collaborate with foreign powers to remove prophets or other spokespersons for national independence. Hence, the priests, the Sadducees, in Jesus' day would say, "It is good that one man die for the sake of the people," meaning that, in order to keep the peace, prophets had to be silenced.

**Ezra and Nehemiah:** From 515 BCE with the disappearance of Zerubbabal we know nothing until the arrival of Nehemiah as governor of the province in 445 BCE. He repaired the walls of Jerusalem and undertook social and political reforms in spite of resistance from the governors of Samaria and Ammon, who feared that he sought to create an independent state. Fortunately, the Persian government desired a strong province in south Palestine as a buffer against Greek military agitation in Egypt and coastal Palestine, so he had their support. Perhaps some of the disarray in Jerusalem he dealt with may have resulted from previous conflict of which we know nothing.

Ezra came to Jerusalem as a religious reformer with support from the Persian government. The traditional date of his arrival was 458 BCE in the seventh year of Artaxerses, king of Persia. But since there were two kings by this name, the date could be either 458 BCE or 398 BCE. Many scholars doubt that Ezra accomplished great reform in 458 BCE, thirteen years before Nehemiah found the city so chaotic; hence, they prefer a later date for Ezra. Also, the two passages in which Ezra and Nehemiah appear together seem like editorial glosses. Scholars conclude that Ezra built his religious reform upon the political reform of Nehemiah from the previous generation. Those who still argue for the 458 BCE, admit that Ezra was not as successful in his reform as the book of Ezra implies. (Everyone agrees that Ezra has been romanticized by the Jewish tradition much more than Nehemiah.) A third proposal suggests that Ezra 7:7 should read the 37th year of Artaxerses, thus placing Ezra's return in 428 BCE, which explains why the same people appear with both Nehemiah and Ezra.

Ezra was a scribe, and he brought the authoritative copy of the written Law to Jerusalem to use as the basis for reform. Later rabbinic tradition stated that Ezra wrote the entire Pentateuch by divine inspiration after copies of Moses' version had been lost. What may be remembered here is that Ezra probably promulgated the recent literary version of the old oral traditions, which had been created by the Priestly Editors in Babylon. Some scholars directly equate Ezra with the final Priestly author or editor. One could point out also that the Persian authorities probably sanctioned the creation and promulgation of such a text to bring identity and stability to the Jewish community.

Ezra sponsored a public covenant renewal ceremony in which the people swore that this Torah would be the basis of their social existence. The Torah may have been the five books of the Pentateuch or it might have been the Primary History, Genesis through

2 Kings. This ceremony committed them to the concept of a Jewish theocracy, rule by Yahweh. Jews who remained in the homeland during the exile did not share the exclusivism promulgated by Ezra and Nehemiah, who learned that such exclusivism worked in Babylon to keep Jewish identity intact. Ezra and Nehemiah succeeded in Jerusalem, especially on the issue of terminating mixed marriages. Jewish husbands sent their non-Jewish wives back to their homelands with children of those unions; according to Ezra 10, only a few refused. This was cruel, but it was seen as necessary for preservation of Jewish identity in the early years of reconstruction. Some literature in the Hebrew Bible (Ruth, Jonah) opposed the harshness of reforms.

**Greek Rule:** Alexander the Great conquered the Persian Empire in campaigns lasting from 333-323 BCE. With Alexander's entry into Jerusalem in 332 BCE, Judah was swept into a series of Greek empires. Alexander spread Greek culture everywhere; he and his successors engaged in a process of "hellenization." They were successful in Asia, creating Greek spheres of influence, Greek cities, and producing a hybrid culture in native societies. Jews fell under the influence of Greek culture, though they tried to resist it. Hellenization enabled Christianity to spread throughout West Asia and the Mediterranean world, for Greek culture united all people under Roman rule.

After Alexander's death in 323 BCE, a series of wars between Greek generals left General Pompey ruling Egypt and Palestine from the newly created city of Alexandria in the Nile delta by 301 BCE. General Seleucus held the eastern reaches of Syria, Mesopotamia, and much of Persia. Other Greek kingdoms arose in Greece, Asia Minor, Bactria (central Asia), and India, but for the Jews, the families of Ptolemy and Seleucus loomed significantly on their horizon. Judah was ruled by the Ptolemies from 301 to 199 BCE, and then by the Seleucids from 199 to 164 BCE. Under the Ptolemies, Jews were granted a degree of cultural freedom, for the Ptolemies isolated themselves in Alexandria and cared only to collect taxes and wage war. After wars lasting throughout much of the 3rd century BCE, the Syrian Greeks (Seleucids) wrested control of Palestine from the Egyptian Greeks (Ptolemies) and would have conquered Egypt itself had not the Romans persuaded Antiochus IV of Syria to retreat from Egypt. Seleucids aggressively hellenized their subjects to unify their geographically and culturally diverse empire. This caused Jewish resistance that led to persecution and finally a revolution (167-164 BCE).

Antiochus IV Epiphanes, who took the title "Epiphanes" to proclaim the "manifestation" of his divine status, was a great general and an aggressive hellenizer. He directed his efforts at the stubborn elements of Jewish society who resisted hellenization. Seleucid monarchs frequently claimed quasi-divine titles for themselves, such as *Soter* ("savior") and *Kurios* ("lord"). Both of these political titles were attributed to Jesus by Christians in a later age when to apply them to anyone other than Caesar (which was Latin for *Kurios*) in Rome was an act of civil disobedience and a capital crime. Antiochus IV took his titles more seriously than most hellenistic rulers, for he believed he was Zeus, the father of the gods. Ultimately, he erected a statue of Zeus in Jerusalem with his face and demanded Jews worship it. This was the golden statue of "Nebuchadnezzar" in Daniel 3, which Jews were forced to worship, and the story was veiled commentary on Antiochus. This statue gave rise to the reference of "the abomination of desolation" in Daniel and the New Testament, for the statue was erected in the Temple precincts. Later Jews and

Christians referred to the Roman erection of standards and altars in the Temple precincts after the 70 CE fall of Jerusalem with this same allusion.

Antiochus IV commanded Jews to sacrifice pigs to Zeus, both at his statue in the Temple and at local Jewish shrines. A priest named Mattathias left Jerusalem and settled in the small town of Modin. When Greek soldiers came to force Mattathias to sacrifice pig, the priest and his five sons killed the soldiers and started a revolt in 167 BCE. A son of the priest named Judas Maccabeus ("the Hammer") led the revolution, and by 164 BCE Jerusalem was liberated. Cleansing the Temple of Antiochus' cult and its re-dedication to pure Jewish worship are celebrated by Jews today in the "Festival of Lights" or Hanukkah.

The Hashmon family, from which Mattathias and his sons originated, formed a dynasty of rulers, the Hasmoneans or Maccabeans, ruling as kings and eventually as priest-kings over independent Judea. They controlled much of Palestine and even forcibly converted Samaritans to their brand of worship. Eventually, civil war in the family alienated them from the Jewish people, until the Roman general Pompey ended civil strife in 63 BCE. Though many Jews welcomed Roman rule at first, soon they realized that Roman rule was harsh due to the presence of a war zone near their land, the long-lasting conflict between Rome and Parthian Persian. In subsequent years Jews yearned for the days of Maccabean independence, and hope for a coming messiah and a renewed empire were fueled by that memory of independence (164-63 BCE). Into this atmosphere Jesus came, bringing the message of a "Kingdom of God." No wonder he caused such a stir.

**Roman Rule:** Rome had recently emerged as a great empire in the year Pompey marched into Jerusalem (63 BCE). Its quest for political and economic stability after the end of the Second Punic War in 201 BCE, combined with the adventurism of generals like Marius, Sulla, Pompey, Crassus, and Julius Caesar, created a monstrous empire encompassing the Mediterranean world. Rome frequently ruled through client states, or local leaders, in those early years of empire. Hence, Herod the Great, who had been loyal to the winning side in a Roman civil war, became "king of the Jews."

Herod the "Idumean" or "Edomite" was allied to Octavian or Caesar Augustus in the civil war between Marc Anthony (with Cleopatra of Egypt, last of the Ptolemies) and Octavian. Herod was rewarded by becoming the client king of the Jews 31-4 BCE. Since the Edomites were converted to Judaism forcibly by the Maccabeans, Herod had a claim to rule the Jews, for he was somewhat of a devotee to their God (they never accepted the idea, though). He endeavored to win the loyalty of his subjects by rebuilding the Temple as a magnificent edifice, rather than the shoddy creation Zerubbabel built in 516 BCE. Jews appreciated their new Temple, but not Herod. Herod died in 4 BCE, and his kingdom was divided among three sons. Archelaus ruled Judea (the newer name for Judah), Herod Antipas ruled Galilee to the north and Perea to the east, and Philip ruled Gentile regions northeast of Judea and north of Perea. Incompetent Archelaus was replaced in 6 CE by Roman procurators who ruled directly in the name of Rome. In 41 CE Roman procurators took charge of all the territories, and Herod Agrippa, son of Herod the Great, had the honorable title of king over all the Jews.

Abusive Roman rule caused Jews to rise in rebellion in 67 CE, which ultimately ended in a bloody disaster: Jerusalem and the Temple were destroyed. Jewish Christianity was forever weakened. Jews existed in the shadow of Roman rule in Palestine until another revolution against Rome (132-135 CE) under Bar-Kochba ("the son of the star"--a messianic title) led to another Jewish defeat. Jews were exiled from Palestine, and Judea became a Roman province. The Second Temple Era ended; the Rabbinic Era began.

# Priestly Editors

At the beginning of the Second Temple Period, Priestly Editors recalled their religious heritage to give exiles a firm identity in a new age. Scholars believe their literary and theological work was undertaken during the exilic and post-exilic years (550-400 BCE). These priests represented a minority among the pre-exilic priests, for the latter obviously included polytheists, whereas Priestly Editors were clearly monotheistic. These priests preserved their traditions during and after the exile by compiling the book of Leviticus, Exodus 25-31, 35-40, and Numbers 1-10, most of which existed in some oral form. The regulations for Israel's cultic life were preserved in this material. The codes extended beyond ritual decrees, for ethical principles were embedded in the legislation, and narratives were designed to define Yahweh religion apart from the religions of the nations. Jews could carry their sacred cult and sacrificial identity with them in symbolic form, the written scrolls (a fixed blueprint of the divine will), and be freed from a fixed Temple or shrine forever. Eventually, when the Temple was destroyed by Rome, Jews became the people of the Book because of these earlier efforts.

Priestly Editors worked with the entire Pentateuch, especially Genesis through Numbers, and some evidence of Priestly editing may be observed in Deuteronomy and Joshua. It is appropriate to think of Priestly Editors as scribes, for working with these texts was certainly a scribal task. The Priestly Editors prepared the first four books, or Tetrateuch, as a preface to the already written Deuteronomistic History that began with Deuteronomy. Priestly Editors reworked Yahwistic (and Elohistic) traditions and combined this material with the Deuteronomistic literature to produce the Primary History of Genesis through 2 Kings. Some scholars suggest that the books of Genesis, Exodus, and Numbers might have been reworked also by the Deuteronomistic Historians before the Priestly Editors received them. Priestly Editors were more than just editors, however; when they were finished with this literature, it was authentically their work. Their task might have been finished by 400 BCE, and perhaps this was the authoritative Torah brought by Ezra to Jerusalem in either 458 BCE or 398 BCE.

In priestly materials there were old traditions, especially in the book of Leviticus. Some suggest that the Holiness Code in Leviticus 17-26 came from the 8th century BCE and was preserved in oral tradition by priests in Jerusalem until it finally became part of the Priestly literature. Others suggest the reverse: that the Holiness Code was post-exilic but that other priestly materials in Leviticus 1-6 and elsewhere have origins in the 8th century BCE. In narratives associated with priestly traditions, however, there was continuity with other biblical traditions from the 6th century BCE exile in Babylon, including Second Isaiah in Isaiah 40-55. Both saw the creation of the world involving a symbolic division of waters. The verbs for "create" (bara') and "redeem" (ga'al) occurred predominantly in Second Isaiah and priestly texts. Ezekiel, Second Isaiah and Priestly traditions all referred to the "glory" (cabod) of Yahweh and to divine holiness. Second Isaiah and priestly texts also made references to narratives in Genesis that other texts appear to be unaware of: both referred to the promise given to Noah about no more great floods (Genesis 9:11, Isaiah 54:9) and the promise of great progeny given to Abraham (Genesis 22:17, 32:12, Isaiah 48:19). So we get the impression that the primary era of activity for generating priestly texts was in the Babylonian Exile and beyond.

**Priestly Theology**: Political institutions of Judah were gone with foreign rule, so Jews who returned to Palestine could no longer view themselves as a "nation." Most Jews remained in Babylon after 539 BCE, and for them the exile continued. If Jews were to retain any identity, it would be in non-political categories. Priestly theologians saw their people as a religio-social entity rather than a politico-social entity, more as a "people" than as a "nation." They were a theocracy, a "people" ruled directly by God without human overlords. Yahweh ruled over Jews throughout the world, and foreign rulers were unimportant. During the years in which Jews lived in Judah, they were subjects of Persians, Greek Egyptians, Greek Syrians, and Romans. Jews could ignore these rulers theoretically and turn their attention to God as their true overlord. Jews in diaspora felt united under the lordship of their God, who ruled the cosmos. This theocratic self-understanding required a strong monotheistic conviction. Hence, not only was the oneness of God emphasized, special attention was given to attacking the gods of the nations. Also, there had to be divine "sanctions" to encourage the worship of the one God, so priestly literature mandated laws concerning everyday life as well as the cult. Observance of these customs reminded believers of their Jewishness.

*Creation and Sabbath*: Monotheists proclaimed their deity to be not only a redeemer God but also a creator God. Priestly theologians responded to Babylonian claims about their god, Marduk. Marduk was said to have created the world after the defeat of Tiamat, whose dismembered body formed the waters above and below the earth. Marduk made humanity out of the blood of a defeated god (Kingu), and thus people were slaves of the gods, providing sacrifice to sustain the divine realm. The Enuma Elish, the Babylonian creation story, legitimated the Temple system of sacrifice and authority of the Babylonian priesthood. Re-enactment of the annual creation drama at the Babylonian New Year Akitu festival saw the Babylonian king play the role of Marduk in defeating the evil forces of chaos and re-establishing world order and fertility. Those who failed to participate in the rites endangered cosmic order. Needless to say, these rites also politically supported the authority of the Babylonian kings. This Babylonian religio-political ideology put pressure on Jews to conform and convert.

The entire Babylonian mythic worldview demanded a Jewish response. The sun and the moon, Shamash and Nergal, were powerful deities, and Chaldean Babylonian kings paid special attention to these two gods. The Babylonian king maintained cosmic order by participation in the New Year rites and sacrifice to the gods throughout the year. Mesopotamians saw themselves surrounded by threatening arid deserts outside the valley, and in the valley periodic flooding of the Tigris and Euphrates could destroy them quickly. Only the king and the priests maintained order by their intervention with the divine realm. Jewish priests had to respond to this worldview and the message of the Enuma Elish. Priestly theologians transformed this myth into the first of our two creation accounts (Genesis 1:1-2:4a). This chapter was a grand hymn, forming a prelude to the entire Pentateuch. It affirmed Yahweh as the only God, creator of the world, who accomplished this task in more noble fashion than Babylonians attributed to Marduk.

Genesis 1 was similar to the Babylonian version in many ways, but it also stridently critiqued the thought in the Enuma Elish. Yahweh created the heavens and the earth not by combat, as Marduk did, but by the spoken word. Opening verses contained subtle allusions to Tiamat: *tohu* or "void," *tehom* or "watery depths," and *tannin* or "whales, sea serpents," terms which were a translation, a transliteration, or a functional equivalent of Tiamat respectively. But these creatures posed no threat to the absolute power of God in Genesis 1. God commanded light to appear, independent of the sun and moon (three days prior). When the sun and moon were created, they were called the "greater light" and the "lesser light" in derogatory fashion to indicate that they were objects and not divine beings. The actual stages of creation were the same in Genesis 1 and Babylonian accounts, but the world lacked divine beings in the biblical version. The narrative was a polemic against polytheism and the worldview of the Babylonians.

God created humans on the sixth day. God created "man" to be male and female simultaneously, made them both in the divine image, and gave them both the authority to "rule" over the world. Babylonian kings were said to be in the "image" of Marduk, but the biblical author attributed this to all people. The word for "rule" was a term attributed only to kings, but in Genesis 1 all people "rule." People rule over nature, which for the Babylonians was the medium through which the gods confronted them. No longer was nature feared as the throbbing arena of the divine, but it was an arena of "things" over which people ruled wisely. Human beings were no longer slaves of the gods, as the Enuma Elish proclaimed, they were representatives of God, sharing the divine image, ruling over creation. (To many today this "rule" over nature may justify a wasteful abuse of natural resources by giving humanity an apparent absolute rule, but the biblical author understood "rule" as wise stewardship, and the account of the man and woman as gardeners of nature in Genesis 2-3 clarified that.)

In Genesis 1:27 "male" and "female" were created together, and both had the divine image and authority in equal measure. Priestly theologians may have corrected misinterpretations of Genesis 2 by readers who erroneously assumed the superiority of the man over the woman because he was created first. (If so, then all the animals would have been superior to the man, since they were created first in Genesis 1.) This is why the term "man" was used and subdivided into the categories of "male" and "female" in Genesis 1. The reader should sense that "male" and "female" were co-created together and thus equal before God.

On the seventh day God rested thereby instituting the Sabbath. There were actually eight creative acts of God; two acts occurred in day three and again in day six. The priestly writers compressed eight creative acts into six days, for they placed special emphasis upon the seventh day as a day when no divine work happened. An old Sumerian myth spoke of how the god Enki organized the world manor in eight days, so perhaps the Priestly theologians altered this format it to create their six plus one day pattern. This made Sabbath a religious observance for all people. Sabbath observance stood in opposition to the Babylonian emphasis upon the cosmic year, and Jews alone kept the Sabbath and thus kept the ordinance that all people should obey. This implied that by keeping the Sabbath Jews diverted divine wrath from others who foolishly thought that sacrifice to Marduk preserved world order. In Babylon the king played Marduk to impose order upon a chaotic reality and save people every year. But Jews maintained that world order was saved by the observance of divine Law by Jews.

In the flood story Priestly theologians added language that made the flood sound like the collapse of all cosmic order. In the Priestly additions to the flood narrative, the "firmament breaks" and the "fountains of the deep break"--these are the barriers created by God (and Marduk in the Enuma Elish) to separate the great bodies of water. Hence, unlike the Yahwist version of the flood with its rainfall, in the Priestly version the primordial waters came together again to cause total chaos. In the Yahwist version the flood lasted forty days, but in the Priestly version the flood lasted a full year, a cosmic year. Significantly, in the Priestly version of the flood, as opposed to the Babylonian creation accounts, God promised that such a flood would never occur again. Hence, the Babylonian fear of Tiamat bringing a worldwide watery destruction was unfounded. In Genesis 1 and other Priestly texts, we discover a polemic against polytheism, idolatry, and divination. In the Priestly theology, our worldview struggled to be born, and with its acceptance by the Jews, we find the beginning of western culture and values.

*Kosher Food and Circumcision*: Sabbath was one of the three customs put forth by Priestly theologians for people to observe that would preserve Jewish identity effectively; the other two were kosher food guidelines and infant circumcision. Sabbath and kosher food guidelines were observed by pre-exilic Israelites, but they did not receive the emphasis they would have in post-exilic times. Kosher food laws probably were kept by priests in Jerusalem. The laws appear old in the way they were recorded in Leviticus, but they were not written down until the exile, implying that they were recalled orally for years. Rules meant to sanctify priests were expanded to all Jews, so that all Jews would become a "holy people." Jews became symbolically God's priests in the world, for all people were subjects of Yahweh, and the world was the Temple of Yahweh.

Supposedly Moses received guidelines for kosher food (Leviticus 11), but the priestly story of Noah (Genesis 9) reported that Noah was to refrain from eating meat with blood. This was a central guideline in kosher food. By implication, Noah's descendants should eat kosher, but only the Jews did. Thus, Jews kept laws intended for all people, and their obedience prevented divine punishment from falling upon the world, even though foreigners might ridicule Jews for their strange lifestyle. Jews suffered "vicariously" for others, but preserved world order. This countered the Mesopotamian belief that sacrifice to Marduk at New Year's festivals preserved the world. We suspect that the idea of Jews suffering vicariously to preserve world order was a significant theme in priestly theology. This would resonate strongly with Second Isaiah's image of the suffering servant, in particular, with that interpretation which viewed Israel as the servant. Second Isaiah probably was a priest. Practically speaking, kosher food separated Jews from their neighbors. The foods that they could eat corresponded to the old diet of Palestine, which differed from the diet in Babylon. Jews could not eat in the homes of Babylonians; they had to live together in communities to provide each other with kosher food.

Finally, circumcision was a permanent sign, for once he was circumcised as an infant, the Jewish male bore this mark forever. Though he might be tempted to pass as Babylonian, his circumcision reminded him of his origin. Unlike the other customs, it was not a public sign, but it was permanent. Jews referred to it in later years as the sign of the covenant, which was also permanent according to the Priestly theologians.

*Priestly View of History:* Priestly Editors added narratives to Genesis describing the covenants made between God and humanity (Genesis 9, 17), and other revisions of the text gave the appearance that some form of covenant relationship was established, even though the word covenant did not appear in the text (Genesis 1, 35). The resulting narrative gave the impression that a succession of covenants existed between God and people. This subtly implied that even though the Mosaic/Sinaitic covenant, proclaimed by prophets and Deuteronomists, had been broken, God would make a new covenant. Ezra and Nehemiah both undertook public covenant "renewal" ceremonies in Jerusalem, perhaps reflecting priestly ideas.

The covenant format communicated numerous insights. In each covenant a different sign was given to people for them to observe. The most important of Jewish customs arose with each covenant and were placed into the primordial past, thus enhancing their importance and implying that all people should keep them. The divine name changed through the various covenants, implying that the self-manifestation of God unfolded progressively until the true self-disclosure at Sinai. The priestly view of history used such editorial additions to proclaim a process of divine revelation in history. The five covenants may be outlined as follows:

1. In Genesis 1 Elohim implicitly created a covenant with humanity and gave Sabbath as the sign.

2. In Genesis 9 Elohim established a covenant with Noah and his descendants, and ordained that meat should be eaten without blood (kosher food regulation).

3. In Genesis 17 El Shaddai created a covenant with Abraham and instituted the rite of circumcision. (Note that the Yahwist covenant was in Genesis 12 and the Elohist covenant with Abraham was in Genesis 15.)

4. Perhaps there was a covenant in Genesis 35 between El Shaddai and Jacob, in which idolatry was forbidden. Although this was not a custom, the prohibition of idolatry was one of the most important religious commands for post-exilic Jews.

5. Finally, the fullest disclosure came when Yahweh revealed the divine name and the Sinaitic legislation in the books of Exodus, Leviticus, and Numbers.

6. If Ezra and Nehemiah had covenant ceremonies, they implied that theirs was the sixth covenant. If so, the priests could have taught that there was a future seventh covenant that would come with a priestly messiah. This might have been one of the reasons why Christians spoke of Jesus as a priest and used covenant imagery.

The message to exiles was that God had not deserted them, but that God would renew the covenant relationship. The progressive revelation of the divine names would not introduce a name other than Yahweh in future covenants (though Christians assumed that with Jesus' name). This progressive revelation implied that the crisis of faith through which they passed might lead to a new and deeper relationship with God (as both Jeremiah and Ezekiel had implied when they spoke of the law being written on human hearts). Again, the universal mandate of these signs to all the descendants of Adam and Noah indicated that Jewish obedience was the fulfillment of a moral obligation owed by all people and that these signs were most important for Jewish identity.

Priestly Editors assured exiles that they could see themselves as the people of Yahweh wherever they lived, because the entire world was Yahweh's Temple, and they were the priests of God. They maintained this priesthood by keeping the law, especially the three signs which were the hallmark of their identity. Maybe some Jews realized that they were responsible for bringing the message of this one true God to the other peoples, and in future years Jews made converts. Ultimately, Christianity took this Jewish missionary impulse to the extreme by converting people to a Jewish religion free from its own law. In Priestly theology the world was stripped of deities and divine forces; the world was demythologized. In turn, the world was sacralized; it became the realm where Yahweh related to humanity, and people stewarded it wisely. One can see in Priestly theology many beliefs that would be inherited by Christians.

# The Psalms

A significant component of priestly piety was the Psalter, produced in the Second Temple Period as a hymnal for worship at the Temple. The word for psalms was *tehillim*, which meant "praises." The Psalms have a general piety of worship and devotion to God as creator of the world, sustainer of life, bringer of healing, and divine presence in life for the worshipping community and individuals. Yet one may sense the agenda of the Priestly tradition in the Psalter. The priests saw the presence of the divine in the cult or worship, and they avoided prophetic or historical language that lauded the action of God in the life of the nation or the social arena. The Psalms reflected this basic orientation; they were more personal and existential, speaking of God's abiding presence. We call the 150 songs that comprised the Psalter, "the hymnal of the Second Temple." The Psalms were created as a liturgical work for Temple worship. Even though some Psalms were pre-exilic, they were not written down and put in a collection until after the exile. In particular, Psalms 1, 2, 8, 18, 22, 30, 37, 41, 70, 77, 79, 91, 93, 95, 103, 119:1-8, 120-124, and 137 provide us with insight into cultic piety of the post-exilic period.

Psalms were only part of the literature produced by the Priestly tradition: other writings included the edited Pentateuch, 1-2 Chronicles, Ezra, Nehemiah, and other writings not included in our Bible. Piety in the Psalms sought the presence of the divine in the Temple cult, sacrifice, worship, and in a deep interior piety. Above all, this religious piety was a-political and non-historical; it departed from the theology of the Pentateuch and the Prophets that found Yahweh in human society and history. In the post-exilic era priestly piety provided a meaningful alternative for Jews who no longer saw God in political events; it enabled them to turn their faces from the pain of everyday political life and find God in a deeper religious dimension. This piety was carried by Jews into diaspora; the Psalter and its piety could sustain an individual or a small group in a distant land far from the Temple. Everyday actions were part of a liturgical drama, as the whole world was the great Temple of God. Believers were called to a mode of reverence and prayerful meditation in all aspects of life. The Psalms have provided Christians with the same piety for two thousand years.

Tradition ascribed the Psalms to David, but the Hebrew text implied that they were composed in his honor rather than by him." A "Psalm to David" is a better translation than a "Psalm of David." Priestly tradition saw David as the real creator of the Temple, not Solomon who was the example of a tyrant. Like Chronicles, the Psalter saw David as the founder of their Temple system. 1 Chronicles 28 credited David with receiving the design for the Temple for Yahweh, making him the founder of the Temple cult and the Psalter. Psalms that originated before the exile perhaps were used at local shrines, at Dan and Bethel in Israel, and in the pre-exilic Jerusalem Temple worship. Some, like Psalm 29, have a non-Israelite, probably second millennium BCE Canaanite origin. But most of the Psalter was post-exilic; Psalms 42-43, 137 refer specifically to the Babylonian Exile.

We have discovered continuities with the form and content found in the Psalms and comparable hymns crafted in Mesopotamia. Sumerian hymns (3000-2000 BCE) contained divine adoration of gods like Enlil, Anu, Utu, Enki, and Inanna, wherein devotees praised the gods for their power and glory, for their sense of justice and hatred of evil, for their creation of the world and humanity, for their presence in holy cities and temples, and their support of the king, all of which were also themes in the Psalms. In addition, we have classic lament hymns written both in Sumerian and the later Akkadian language (2000-1000 BCE), which bewailed the destruction of great cities in war (including Ur, Akkad, and Uruk), reminding us not only of the Lament Hymns in the Psalter but also the book of Lamentations. Thus, hymns of praise and lament existed in both Mesopotamia and Israel. Not only do we see strikingly similar themes, such as divine presence in the Temple in Jerusalem, the biblical Psalms sometimes reflect such a similarity of language with Mesopotamian counterparts, that we think the Israelites and Jews had Mesopotamian songs in their possession. This would have been true during the Babylonian Exile, but perhaps even earlier familiarity might have existed.

The Psalter has five divisions: Psalms 1-41 (Psalms 3-41 are called the "Davidic Psalter" by scholars), Psalms 42-72, Psalms 73-89 (Psalms 42-89 are called the "Elohistic Psalter" by scholars), Psalms 90-106, and Psalms 107-150. The divisions in the Hebrew text noted with Psalms 1, 42, 73, 90, and 107 might be indications of the stages of growth in successive editions of the written Psalter. Scholars believe the oldest psalms may be in the second and third part, called the Elohistic Psalter because of the use of the divine name Elohim. Some of these may have their origin in the northern state of Israel before the exile. (However, because two hymns in this section extol Jerusalem, the theory of northern origin remains tenuous.)

The Psalms performed various roles over the years. They may have been used at festivals in various shrines or local affairs such as weddings, and some commemorated great events in history. When they became the hymnal for the Second Temple, they were used by individuals and groups of people who came to worship at the Temple. With some of the hymns the sick or bereaved could lament; with others people could rejoice at their personal deliverance from illness or crisis, or just praise God in general. Some hymns look as though they were used for royal coronations in Judah before the exile, and later became hymns to Yahweh's universal kingship, perhaps celebrated on New Year's Day. Some may have been used in covenant ceremonies.

**Elements of Hebrew Poetry:** Hebrew poetry consists of rhythm in the poetic lines (lost in translation, of course) and "parallelism," the poet's use of alternating ways of expressing the same thought. There are three different ways of expressing this parallelism: 1) synonymous statements--the two halves of the couplet express the same concept using different words and images; 2) antithetic statements--the two halves express contrasting thoughts, perhaps comparing two actions or objects; and 3) synthetic statements--the second line or clause completes the thought expressed in the first line or clause. By our evaluation Psalms fall into certain types according to their message or content as well as form. Scholars disagree over the various categories and how Psalms are classified, but everyone agrees on the existence of Lament and Thanksgiving hymns.

Psalms of Lament provided language for addressing a range of human problems. Some psalms were in the singular (Psalms 22, 41, 70, 77, 109), others in the plural (Psalms 44, 74, 79, 80, 90, 137). There was a pattern in these lament hymns, though it was not followed in detail in every psalm. Rather, it was a pattern that a poet would follow unconsciously rather than deliberately crafting the poem around a rigorous outline. The parts were: 1) an invocation praising Yahweh's greatness, 2) the lament itself, which could occur in three different modes: first person lament–I/We have been cast down and suffer, second person lament–You, O God have forsaken me/us, third person lament–They, my/our enemies or former friends, laugh at or persecute me/us, 3) a petition which asked Yahweh to save the petitioner, defeat the foes, or rebuke the scoffers, 4) a confession of trust in divine mercy, expressed in a way which would motivate Yahweh to act, 5) a protestation of innocence from wrongdoing and of faithfulness to Yahweh, 6) a vow to sing the praise of Yahweh when delivered, and 7) a concluding formal doxology.

A special genre found in the ancient Near East was the lament over the destruction of a city. Tragically cities were frequently destroyed in war, and especially in Mesopotamia laments were generated to recall the horrid destruction of great cities such as Ur, Akkad, and others. Most of our representative examples are Sumerian and come from the late third millennium BCE. The destruction of a city was attributed to the patron deity of the city who became angry because his cult and worship were not properly observed. In the Bible the book of Lamentations conformed to this pattern, bewailing how the city of Jerusalem was destroyed in 586 BCE because of the sins of its people. It was a poignant lament reflecting the Deuteronomistic belief that the sin of the people brought punishment upon them. The book was crafted as an acrostic, that is, the first letter of each line in the poem began with the successive letters of the Hebrew alphabet. Each of the first four chapters was in acrostic form; chapter 3, in particular, had each stanza begin three successive lines with the same letter of the alphabet.

Psalms of Thanksgiving existentially followed the psalms of lament. They thanked Yahweh for deliverance from past crisis or illness. They also were used by individuals (Psalms 18, 27, 30, 40, 43, 73, 103) or communally (Psalms 66, 91). The pattern was similar to lament hymns: 1) proclamation of thankful praise in general terms; 2) an account of the adversity faced by the petitioner, reminiscent of lament hymn formulas, stated in the first person; 3) an account of the specific deliverance for which thanks were given, using the first, second, and third person language—I/We have been delivered, You (Yahweh) have done it, and they (the enemies) have been defeated or rebuked; 4) the vow to praise Yahweh was recalled from the lament hymn; and 5) a doxology.

Psalms of Praise were simple hymns of praise that did not necessarily refer to past tribulation or a lament. They praised Yahweh as creator of the universe, and their form was very simple: 1) a call to praise, 2) the reason for praise, and 3) doxology. Examples included Psalm 8, a product of priestly theology, and Psalm 93.

Pilgrimage Psalms, especially the "songs of ascent" (Psalms 120-124), were intended for use as songs for pilgrims on their way to Jerusalem. They were like hymns of praise, but they extolled the city of Jerusalem and the approach to the Temple. In post-exilic times, we suspect that pilgrimages to Jerusalem were quite common, as typified by the actions of Jesus and his disciples.

New Year Festival and Kingship of Yahweh Psalms have received much scholarly discussion. Many believe that, as part of the post-exilic New Year's festival, Yahweh was symbolically proclaimed king over the Jews and the entire universe. There were parallels to this in Mesopotamia rituals and hymnody. Psalms 8, 24, 33, 47, 93, 96-99, and 104 would have been good examples of such hymns. Other scholars suspect there was a pre-exilic ceremony wherein the Judean king was crowned anew on New Year's Day as the representative of Yahweh. In addition to the psalms mentioned above, Psalm 2:7 spoke of the divine adoption of the King as God's son, suggesting the image of divine adoption might have been part of the coronation ceremony. Perhaps both theories could be true, pre-exilic coronation psalms became post-exilic enthronement psalms, and the focus moved from king to Yahweh because Judean kings were gone.

Didactic Psalms is a category used by us for various psalms, some of which were Torah liturgies and others were related to wisdom thought and spoke of philosophical or existential issues. Torah liturgies praised or meditated upon the Law. Psalm 119, for example, was a long hymn devoted to the praise of the Torah, composed in an acrostic fashion with each eight verse section comprised of lines whose initial word began with the same letter of the Hebrew alphabet. Such acrostics were typical of didactic hymns. Wisdom Psalms treated issues of human reason, wisdom, folly, and reasons for suffering. Hymns typical of this genre included Psalms 1, 37, 49, and 73.

The various psalms testify to the rich diversity of hymnody in the Second Temple period. The Psalter may have grown gradually until its present form around 150 BCE. The later entries might be those psalms found after Psalm 106, which might have concluded the Psalter at the end of the Persian period. The five divisions of the Psalter listed in the biblical text might reflect those stages of growth. Thus, the Psalter contained a cross-section of piety from the pre-exilic era down through the entire post-exilic era to the Maccabean period. The Psalter remains one of the great contributions of the Priestly tradition to both Judaism and Christianity.

# Conclusion

Priestly Editors did their work both during and after the exilic period. The efforts resulted in the creation of the Primary History, the Pentateuch and the Historical Books. They created Judaism by the establishment of a Jewish identity that could survive exile and diaspora. Too often Christian scholars look upon Priestly literature as a form of dead legalism. Increasingly we recognize that they were creative theologians, masters of brilliant symbolism, and without their efforts Christianity could not have developed most of its concepts.

# Bibliography

Robert Alter. *The Art of Biblical Poetry*. New York, NY: Basic Books, 1985.

Joseph Blenkinsopp. *The Pentateuch*. New York, NY: Doubleday, 1992.

Richard Clifford. *Creation Accounts in the Ancient Near and the Bible*. Catholic Biblical Monograph Series 26. Washington, DC: Catholic Biblical Association, 1994.

Victor Hurowitz. *I Have Built You an Exalted House: Temple Building in the Bible in Light of Mesopotamian and Northwest Semitic Writings*. Journal for the Study of the Old Testament Supplement Series 115. Sheffield, Eng.: JSOT, 1992.

Clinton McCann. *A Theological Introduction to the Book of Psalms:* The Psalms as Torah. Nashville, TN: Abingdon, 1993.

Patrick Miller. *They Cried to the Lord: The Form and Theology of Biblical Prayer.* Minneapolis, MN: Fortress, 1993.

Sigmund Mowinckel. *The Psalms in Israel's Worship*. 2 vols. Trans. D. R. Ap-Thomas. Nashville, TN: Abingdon, 1962.

Joel Weinberg. *The Citizen-Temple Community*. Journal for the Study of the Old Testament Supplement Series 151. Sheffield, Eng.: JSOT, 1992.

H. G.M. Williamson. *Israel in the Books of Chronicles*. Cambridge, Eng.: Cambridge University Press, 1977.

Sara Japhet. The Ideology of the Book of Chronicles and Its Place in Biblical Thought. 2nd Ed. New York, NY: Peter Lang, 2001.

# Chapter 15

# Post-Exilic Prophecy and Apocalyptic

Reading: Isaiah 24-27,60-66,Zechariah 1-14,Daniel 2,7-11

Post-exilic prophecy continued the trajectories of pre-exilic prophecy for a century after the return. In later years Jews felt that prophecy had died by 400 BCE, directly after the time of Ezra. In reality, prophecy continued after 400 BCE (Jesus was certainly one, and Acts mentioned others), but prophets did not capture the attention of the crowds. A few Jewish intellectuals, like the historian Josephus (90 CE), tried to reconcile this disparity. He divided prophets into those who wrote (the biblical prophets), who were superior to all who followed them, and those who spoke (prophets after Ezra). He may have implied that he was one of those superior prophets because he reputedly foretold the future and wrote extensively.

Prophecy did not die, but transformed itself into apocalyptic literature. Post-exilic prophets became totally concerned with their vision of hope for the future, and their imagery became so increasingly bizarre and fantastic to proclaim such hope, that they evolved into apocalyptic seers. Apocalyptic literature emerged as a genre crafted by educated people who drew upon many intellectual sources, including mantic wisdom. Apocalyptic works were finely crafted pieces with symbols that communicated coded messages of hope to psychologically depressed or physically oppressed people. In reality, these works presented the prophetic message of hope cast in a new literary form.

## Post-Exilic Prophecy

We do not have as much material from post-exilic prophets as we do for pre-exilic prophets, for perhaps those who collected post-exilic oracles did not have as many to choose from. The poetic quality of post-exilic oracles is often characterized as poorer than pre-exilic oracles. However, the post-exilic prophetic message is more upbeat and exclusively hope oriented. Prophets saw the age of judgment as past with the end of the exile; what they envisioned was a future golden age for oppressed Jews. Post-exilic prophets were primarily eschatological, speaking of the future: a golden age, a messiah, an age of peace, the glorification of Jerusalem, and the recognition of Yahweh by all peoples.

Second Isaiah proclaimed a grand vision of hope for the return, but actual reality was dreary, and returning exiles soon became disillusioned. A new generation of prophets tried to give hope by reviving old images in a new, grand fashion. But when these visions were only partially fulfilled, another generation revived hope with an even grander message. Such was the pattern of post-exilic prophets, until the prophets exaggerated themselves out of existence, and Jews felt increasingly alienated by their radical message. Later Jews would say prophecy had ceased, but really prophets transformed themselves into apocalyptic visionaries. Several of these prophets deserve a closer evaluation.

**Third Isaiah:** Isaiah 56-66 contained classic post-exilic oracles from either one prophet, two prophets (Isaiah 56-59 and 60-66), three prophets (Isaiah 56-59, 60-62, and 63-66), or more, depending upon different scholarly reconstructions. The entire collection is called "Third Isaiah" and is dated anywhere from 530 to 330 BCE, either as a unit or as segments which emerged throughout that era. Most scholars believe a significant portion comes from 530 to 520 BCE because of references to the need for rebuilding the Temple. The style is reminiscent of Second Isaiah; thus, some suggest the prophet was Second Isaiah back in the homeland. Isaiah 56-59, in particular, addressed early postexilic concerns. The prophet uttered words of judgment that did not occur elsewhere in post-exilic prophets. The oracles had a sharper tone than Second Isaiah; the imperative was "to build" rather than "be comforted." There was critique of the people's attitudes when offering sacrifice and apathy in their observance of fasts. The issues addressed were contemporary with Haggai 1-2 and Zechariah 1-8. Jews were called upon to complete the Temple in order for Yahweh to be present among them.

Isaiah 60-66 sounds visionary to us, especially chapters 63-66, which are proto-apocalyptic in tone. Second Isaiah spoke of the coming events or "latter things" which would be comparable to creation and the Exodus, but Third Isaiah spoke of the "latter things" as being greater than anything in the past. Nations would come to worship Yahweh in Jerusalem after Yahweh conquered evil in a great war. Yahweh would rule by the "spirit" through an ideal king in an age with peace, prosperity, painless birth, and longevity. A "new heaven and a new earth" would come into existence. These themes became the hallmark of apocalyptic literature, so we date these oracles to 375-330 BCE.

**Haggai and Zechariah:** These were the last prophets whose actual names we know, for they spoke publicly. From 520 BCE to 518 BCE they called for Temple restoration with nationalistic fervor. (They provided us with dates for their oracles.) The Persian Empire was rent by civil war (522-520 BCE) before Darius I succeeded to the throne, but it was several years before people knew that the empire would endure. Haggai 1-2 and Zechariah 1-8 contained oracles which fanned the fires of revolutionary zeal. Zerubbabel, the governor of Judah appointed by Persia and heir to the Davidic dynasty, was hailed by both prophets as the coming king of the Jews (Zechariah 4:6-10; Haggai 6:20-23).

Zechariah cast his oracles in the form of dream visions (Zechariah 1:7-6:8), suggestive of the later apocalyptic format. The form of his dream reports reminds us of the symbolic visions of Amos rather than dream reports attributed to the patriarchs in Genesis. Zechariah saw four horns, four chariots, and four horses (foreshadowing the four horsemen of Revelation), symbolizing the universal extent of the Persian domain and its imminent collapse and replacement by Yahweh's kingdom. But such a vision was dangerous for Jews in the era of increased political stability after 520 BCE, and Zerubbabel, Haggai, and Zechariah disappeared silently. We cannot tell if they started a revolt that Persia crushed, or whether the Persians silently eliminated them, or whether Zerubbabel left or was removed by the Persians causing the prophets simply to go silent. Whatever happened, it may have been psychologically devastating for the Jews, and no account was left for us to know what happened. Prophets after this spoke anonymously, as though they did not appear in public. (Malachi and Obadiah were titles, not names.)

The oracles of Haggai and Zechariah would have been lost except that a prophet or prophets in a later generation salvaged them. Zechariah 9-14 was added to Zechariah 1-8 to project the coming Day of the Lord into the future and declare that Yahweh would bring it without any prior efforts of people. Oracles in Zechariah 9-14 were more poetic than Zechariah 1-8. In terms of content these new chapters had no visions, showed little interest in the Temple, had no reference to Zerubbabel, and listed no dates. References to contemporary events were vague, making this material hard to date. Zechariah 9-14 did not call for action; rather, it told people to wait for Yahweh's actions. The signs of the coming kingdom would be so spectacular that there would be no mistake about its arrival, thus people would not prematurely act and be crushed in a rebellion (as may have happened with Haggai and Zechariah). Deutero-Zechariah was either one prophet or two prophets (Zechariah 9-11 and Zechariah 12-14) who spoke sometime between 480 BCE and 330 BCE. Some scholars sense allusions to Alexander the Great in the last chapters, and are tempted to separate the last three chapters and date them late. The coming Day of the Lord was portrayed as a radical transformation, and chapter 14 especially appears to be a classic apocalyptic vision.

**Lesser Prophets:** Additional prophetic oracles were uttered after 500 BCE. Obadiah denounced Edomites for attacking Jerusalem during the Babylonian siege in 586 BCE, and he alluded to political events in the 5th century BCE. From 586 BCE onward Jews had a tremendous hatred of the Edomites, and this helps us to date other biblical literature with negative allusions to the Edomites. This is why Jews hated Herod the Great, he was an Idumean or Edomite!

Joel's style was both prophetic and apocalyptic or proto-apocalyptic. Hence, some commentators think that the oracles of two prophets are in this book. Some date the prophetic material back into the pre-exilic era. Joel described a plague of locusts to metaphor the Day of the Lord. In Joel 2:28-3:21 cosmic upheavals and an outpouring of the spirit were described, an allusion associated with the first Pentecost by Christians.

Malachi meant "my messenger," which was a title, not a name. It has been suggested that these three chapters once were the conclusion to the book of Zechariah, even though Malachi was a separate prophet. The chapters were separated by later scribes in the 2nd century BCE who wished to have twelve minor prophets, and Malachi made an additional prophet. Zechariah 9-11, Zechariah 12-14, and Malachi 1-3 appear to us as three specific units of oracles, each one beginning with the heading, a "massa" (which we translate as oracle). Hence, it appears as though these passages once were unified. Malachi damned Edom, but also reprimanded the Jews for their poor piety in sacrifice. Malachi offered hope for the coming of Yahweh, announcing that a "messenger" would come before the Messiah. When Yahweh arrives, it will be like a "refiner's fire" (Malachi 3:2). The messenger at the end of the book was Elijah (Malachi 4:5), for Elijah did not die, but was taken to Yahweh in a whirlwind (2 Kings 2:1-12). Popular Jewish piety suggested that Elijah was alive with God, and that Moses also was with him (popular piety ignored the story about Moses' death in Deuteronomy 34:5-6). Hence, in the New Testament accounts of Transfiguration, Jesus appeared between Moses and Elijah (Mark 9:2-13, Matthew 17:1-13, Luke 9:28-36). Also, the two witnesses in Revelation 11:1-13, who both ascended in a cloud after their mission was finished, may have been Moses and Elijah. Finally, this is why Jewish tradition believed that Elijah would come before the messiah, and why John the Baptist imitated the life style of Elijah.

**Decline of Prophecy:** There are a number of reasons why prophecy declined and lost the attention of Jews after 400 BCE. Contrary to popular opinion, it did not cease; prophecy still continued, but prophets received little attention. Six reasons may be given for prophecy's gradual decline.

*Loss of the Monarchy*: Kings were the usual targets of prophetic criticism. Kings sponsored religious activity and cults, such as those at Dan and Bethel, which were condemned by the prophets. Royal families and their powerful friends were responsible for oppressing the poor in the pre-exilic era. Pre-exilic judgment prophets attacked these abuses, but after the exile, kings were gone along with polytheism and social injustice. The first real prophet, Samuel, coincided with the first king, Saul, and the last two named prophets, Haggai and Zechariah, were contemporaries of the last possible candidate for kingship, Zerubbabel. Since some prophets functioned as court prophets in the court of the king, the institution of prophecy also was supported, in part, by kings. Often the prophets in our canon appear to have criticized these court prophets, and so the royal support of some prophets indirectly fostered some of the oracles that appear in our Bible. Kings not only received criticism, but they could become role models for prophetic visions of an ideal future. Prophets spoke of an ideal messianic figure who would come someday and epitomize the best virtues of kings.

*Written Scriptures*: Written scriptures were created in the post-exilic era, especially after Ezra returned from Babylon. The Pentateuch was fixed by 400 BCE and the emerging Prophetic corpus took shape by 200 BCE. With authoritative writings from the past, Jews felt they should not listen to "unproven" spokespersons of the present. They would rather heed the words of past prophets, whose oracles were written down and accepted, and reinterpret those old words for a new situation than heed the oral message of a contemporary prophet. If a person wished to proclaim a prophetic message, he or she had to become a scribe and write a commentary or "midrash" on the old prophets. Such commentaries are found among the Dead Sea Scrolls from the settlement at Qumran. This tendency to comment upon past texts and not speak a new authoritative word was why people were amazed when Jesus spoke with his own authority (Mark 1:22).

*Priestly Domestication*: Priests in the post-exilic era tried to subordinate prophets under their authority. They portrayed prophets as serving in the Jerusalem Temple and speaking oracles under the authority of the priests. Prophets also were portrayed by the two books of Chronicles as Temple servants who assisted in worship. For example, 1 Chronicles 25:1-31 spoke of the priestly sons of Asaph, Heman, and Jeduthun who prophesied for David with musical instruments. 2 Chronicles 20:14-17 spoke of a Levite named Jahaziel, who uttered a prophetic oracle. Thus, the priestly intellectuals sought to "domesticate" prophecy by making it appear as one of the many functions of the Jerusalem priesthood. It was an effective way to subordinate and trivialize prophets.

*Priestly Suppression*: Some prophets were nationalistic, and threatened the peace, especially the delicate relationship Sadducean priests in Jerusalem had with the foreign powers. Priests wished to preserve the Temple and sacrificial cult; political independence could lead to war and the possible destruction of city and Temple. Priests, especially after Haggai and Zechariah, may have removed prophetic figures to keep the peace. We are reminded of the priests in Jerusalem who became convinced it was necessary to remove Jesus "for the sake of the people," lest he incite a rebellion among the large Passover crowds against Romans. Priests were respected by Jews for being intermediaries with Yahweh, but hated for being political traitors. Upper and middle class Jews generally supported this priestly compromise, because they would profit socially and economically from political stability, while the poor were prone to oppose the priests and heed the words of revolutionary prophets. Furthermore, political leaders in any age are prone to condemn public voices that could pose a potential threat, even if the prophetic voice seems to be an ally of the political leaders. Political leaders, religious or secular, tolerate no competition. Thus, prophets were driven underground, spoke anonymously after 500 BCE, and took to writing oracles, especially apocalyptic visions.

*Popular Disillusionment*: How could people identify a true contemporary prophet, especially when two prophets disagreed with each other, like Jeremiah and Hananiah in the 590's BCE? People remembered how conflict between prophets often occurred. Early prophetic conflict flared between prophets of Yahweh and prophets of Baal in the days of Elijah. The true prophets of that age spoke in the name of Yahweh, but by the post-exilic era no one spoke in the name of Baal anymore. In the pre-exilic era prophets authenticated themselves by appealing to a call experience, but eventually every prophet appealed to a call experience and used the correct formula. Every prophet was rooted in the old prophetic tradition; even the so-called false prophet Hananiah used imagery of Isaiah. Moral rectitude was no guideline for telling a true from a false prophet, because a prophet was touched by Yahweh and often acted strangely. Isaiah and Jeremiah both walked around naked, Jeremiah criticized the Temple abrasively, and Ezekiel acted bizarrely in a number of oracles. The only substantial guideline was if the prophet's words came true, and even that was not a perfect guideline, because Yahweh could change the divine decision contingent upon human response. Ultimately fulfillment of the oracles was the only criterion a listener had. The problem was how long did the audience have to wait until real fulfillment occurred? If the audience waited too long, would it then be too late to heed the prophet's warning and act appropriately? Certainly that was the experience of Jeremiah's audience. They knew Jeremiah was a true prophet once Jerusalem fell, but then it was too late. In the face of prophetic conflict and uncertainty as to the identity of a true prophet, normal human response in any age is to simply stop listening to prophets. People simply tired of the prophetic message coming from the living prophets, especially when they had the writings of the prophets from the past.

Prophetic Exaggeration: The message of hope begun with Second Isaiah was repeated by successive generations of prophets, but each generation had to exaggerate the imagery of the previous generation to capture audience attention and engender hope. For example, Second Isaiah implied that the return from Babylon would be as great as the "former things" (creation of the world and the Exodus), but Third Isaiah said that the future would bring events greater than those "former things." The portrayal of the messiah became grander with successive prophets, so that the messiah hardly seemed human, as in Zechariah 12-14. Eventually, prophetic imagery became so grandiose that prophets were no longer prophets, but apocalyptic seers. Prophecy exaggerated itself into apocalyptic. This level of intense imagery in envisioning the future was so evident in the latest oracles of this period, Zechariah 12-14, Isaiah 24-27, 60-66, that we sometimes call this material "proto-Apocalyptic" or "early Apocalyptic."

# Apocalyptic Theology

Apocalyptic evolved out of prophecy between 400 and 250 BCE. Good examples of this new literary and theological genre in the Bible include Daniel 2, 7-12, 2 Esdras or 4 Ezra (in the Apocrypha), and Revelation (in the New Testament). Other works not in the Bible include Enoch, 2 Baruch, Testament of the Twelve Patriarchs (partially), Book of Jubilees (partially), Assumption of Moses, Apocalypse of Adam, and Sibylline Oracles. The list can be lengthened with other smaller writings: Treatise of Shem, Apocryphon of Ezekiel, Apocryphon of Zephaniah, Vision of Ezra, Apocalypse of Sedrach, Apocalypse of Adam, Apocalypse of Elijah, Apocalypse of Daniel, and Assumption of Moses. The names of these writings reveal a significant characteristic: they claim authorship by a famous person from the distant past. Since people believed that Yahweh no longer spoke through prophets or inspired authors after 400 BCE, they would not heed a contemporary prophet. Thus, apocalyptic authors had to use a pseudonym, a "false name," to gain an audience. Perhaps they did not deceive everyone in their audience, for it may have been known that this was a common literary convention, among Jews as well as others in the Mediterranean world and the Near East.

The word "apocalypse" meant "that which is revealed." An ancient seer supposedly had visions of the future (which really was the reader's recent past and present), wrote these visions, and hid the book. Then the book was discovered in the age of which the ancient seer spoke. Since the ancient seer had correctly predicted future events that had come to pass, the message that accompanied the visions was valid. It was the message, not the predictive timetable of history, which was truly important for the readers. The "accuracy" of the so-called predictions was excellent for events close to the time of the actual creation of the literary work, and this helps us date many of the apocalypses. Hence, the final edition of Daniel can be dated to 164 BCE before the Maccabeans retook Jerusalem, and the book of Daniel "foresaw" many events in that age except for knowledge about the actual beginning of Maccabean rule in Jerusalem.

The message of these texts was that God would deliver faithful believers, that the oppression and evil they experienced did not deny the power of God, but was part of a divine plan that would ultimately work out for good for all who faithfully endured. The audience was not obsessed with the symbols or portents that "predicted" events, as is the case with modern sectarian interpretations of Revelation; rather, they saw the message of the whole text, God was in charge of history and would save faithful believers. The language and bizarre imagery was understood symbolically, not literally.

Some Jews, however, did take the visions and imagery seriously, and it caused them to rise up in revolution and get killed. We suspect that the apocalyptic authors may have been educated authors weaving creative and inspirational works, but they did not view their imagery as literally as some of those who became familiar with the works and became active in radical apocalyptic movements. So apocalyptic authors were a different class of people than the revolutionaries, and some of them could have been priests or sages. Works that inspired apocalyptic authors included Ezekiel and Second Isaiah, who were priests, and Zechariah, who had affinity with priestly thought. Thus, scholars use distinctive definitions. "Apocalypticism" refers to a general worldview that most people in that age shared, as well as the common language they shared. Jesus used this language and imagery because people understood it. "Apocalyptic movements" refer to groups of people who engaged in revolution or withdrew from society because they took the imagery seriously. Often these people were marginal and oppressed people, whereas the authors of apocalyptic literature might have been middle or upper class. "Apocalyptic literature" refers to the literary and theological writings written by highly educated authors to inspire others. These people were not marginal, and sometimes their literature addressed people other than the poor in proclaiming a radical transformation of the world that even the leaders of society might desire. However, some scholars believe that apocalyptic authors actually did, at times, take their imagery very seriously and enter into the very worldview they created. Such does appear to be the case with some modern individuals who lead and inspire millennial or apocalyptic movements.

**Literary Characteristics:** Certain literary and ideational motifs identify apocalyptic works. A venerable seer observes the course of human events either in visions or in a journey to the heavenly realms, and the seer writes down the vision in highly symbolic form. In a later time the scroll is discovered, read, and readers sense that most of the predicted events have transpired. History is often divided into distinct ages, usually four in number; the early ages are good (symbolized by gold or silver) and the later ones are evil (symbolized by bronze and iron). As evil increases, believers suffer persecution until only a "righteous remnant" remains. Social upheavals and natural catastrophes occur toward the end of time. Evil rulers and cosmic powers arise to oppose God, but finally are defeated. A new heaven and earth are created out of the destruction of the final war and the judgment. Everything in history unfolds according to divine will. As the apocalyptic work was read, the reader or listener sensed that most of the signs had been fulfilled except for the intervention of God. Readers were reassured in their tribulation that God would deliver them soon.

Certain symbols recurred frequently in apocalyptic literature. Because the works were hostile toward priests and foreign rulers, symbols were bizarre and obscure so that only insiders or faithful believers could understand the code. The same phenomenon occurs today among oppressed people who create "coded" language to use so that authorities do not understand their discourse. Thus, animals (real and imaginary), astral bodies in the heavens, astrological symbols, numbers and their multiples, and other strange images were used to refer to actual political events and people. The authors were fascinated with numbers, in particular, as were many people of that age. Sometimes the numbers they used were actually coded for the historical events, so numbers might refer to an actual number of kings. At other times simply the symbolic meanings of numbers were evoked. Evil numbers were 6, 11, 13, or permutations thereof, 17, 19, 36, 66, 216 (6 x 6 x 6), 666 (obviously), obtained by addition or multiplication of the base evil numbers. Prime numbers were considered evil, too. Good numbers were 3, 7, 10, 12, or permutations thereof, 21, 30, 36, 70, 120, 144, etc. If we know the historical period that an apocalyptic work addressed, often we can determine references for the symbols.

Apocalyptic authors were well educated. They used symbols from mythologies of old religions (like the old Canaanite religion, Persian Zoroastrianism, or pre-exilic polytheistic Yahwism), from narratives in the Old Testament, and from the contemporary milieu of syncretistic and Hellenistic thought in the Near East and classical world. For example, they spoke of El and the great dragon from old Canaanite mythology, images like the kingdom of light and kingdom of darkness, angels and archangels, demons and archdemons, fire at the judgment, four ages, all taken from Zoroastrianism, and to this they added traditional Old Testament ideas like Messiah, Son of Man, divine warrior, Day of the Lord, and others. The scenes in their writings were fantastic and dramatic.

In the future new age, oppressed believers will be vindicated. The Messiah will come and defeat Yahweh's enemies, the Son of Man will judge the enemies, and a golden age will commence as Yahweh rules the world from Jerusalem. The Messiah and the Son of Man were separate figures. Perhaps Christians combined the figures and attributed both images to Jesus, and then added the imagery of the Suffering Servant to the portrait. In some texts there were two messiahs, one priestly and one royal.

**Daniel**: The book of Daniel provided the best example of apocalyptic literature in the Old Testament. Chapter 1-12 in Hebrew and Aramaic arose in 164 BCE, and later chapters may have been added in Greek in Egypt. Apart from the short novelistic accounts in Daniel 1, 3-6, the rest of the book provided visions of the future by a seer named Daniel during the Babylonian Exile. His name reminds us of the Canaanite sage Daniel of the second millennium BCE tale of Aqhat. Daniel (or the king) had dream visions of future world history pertaining to the Jews, visions of Chaldean Babylon, Media, Persia, Alexander the Great, and the Hellenistic kingdoms of the Ptolemies and the Seleucids. In the end, these kingdoms would be replaced by divine rule.

In Daniel 2 Nebuchadnezzar had a dream of a statue made out of various metals which was destroyed by a stone from the sky. Daniel reminded the king what the dream was about (for he had forgotten the dream) and then interpreted the parts of the dream. Daniel described the statue with gold head (Babylon of Nebuchadnezzar's day), silver chest (Media), bronze belly (Persia), iron legs (Alexander the Great), and iron and clay feet (Greek Ptolemies in Egypt and Greek Seleucids in Syria). The stone that destroyed the statue became a great future kingdom, which for the author of Daniel stood for a truly future kingdom, and not the Maccabees.

In Daniel 7 Daniel himself had a vision of a lion with eagle's wings (Babylon), a bear with three ribs or tusks in its mouth (Media with its three kings), a leopard with four wings and four heads (Persia, which ruled the four corners of the earth), a horrid beast with iron teeth and ten horns (Alexander and kings in the successor states of the Ptolemies and Seleucids), and a little horn which displaced three of the other horns and attacked the people of God (Antiochus IV who killed competitors to become king and persecuted Jews).

In Daniel 8 Daniel had the vision of a ram with two horns (the dual empire of Media and Persia) destroyed by a he-goat (Greeks) with a large horn (Alexander), which was replaced by four horns (four Greek kingdoms which arose by 301 BCE after the collapse of Alexander's empire and civil war), followed by a little horn that persecuted the saints (Antiochus IV again). This vision regarded Media and Persia as a dual monarchy and not as separate empires as they were in Daniel 2 and 7, which implies that these visions might come from separate sources, or that the author had poetic license.

Daniel 9 contained a vision of 70 weeks, which was a chronology from the time of the Babylonian Exile to the Maccabean revolt. However, our author may have used a different chronology than what we know today to fit 490 years into the time from 586 BCE to 164 BCE (70 years too many). But the vision set up for the longer vision in Daniel 10-11. In Daniel 10-11 an extremely complex vision unfolded about kings of the north (Seleucids) and kings of the south (Ptolemies), who warred with each other over God's holy land (Palestine), and these visions reduplicated the complex politics of 301 to 164 BCE. There were allusions to the wars of Ptolemy I of Egypt and Seleucus I of Syria in the early 3rd century BCE, to Bernice of Egypt and her marriage to Antiochus II of Syria which led to the deaths of both of them at mid-century, and to the wars of Seleucus II, Seleucus III, Antiochus III, and Antiochus IV of Syria against Ptolemy IV, Ptolemy V, and Ptolemy VI of Egypt in the late 3rd and early 2nd centuries BCE. The complexity of detail in these visions indicates to us that the events occurred rather recently in relation to the composition of the book, since apocalyptic works obviously spent the greatest detail on the recent events most well known to the audience.

The book was circulated to encourage Jews to be faithful to God during the persecution under Antiochus IV and the Maccabean revolution. The final Jewish capture of Jerusalem after 3 and 1/2 years of war fulfilled the anticipation (probably inserted after the event) that the tribulation would last for that length of time. So the book was vindicated by the victory of the Maccabeans. Even though the world did not end and the golden age begin, Jews realized that God acted for them in dramatic fashion, as the book promised. Daniel was cherished and ultimately became part of the sacred canon. We fail to appreciate this saga of the faith when we naively use the book to interpret politics in our world today, such as predicting a Russian or Chinese invasion of the Near East, as some popular writings suggested in the 1970's and 1980's.

# Evaluation of Apocalyptic Literature

There are theological problems with apocalyptic literature. First, it creates a mechanistic view of divine inspiration by portraying Yahweh's dictation of the words to an ancient seer. Elsewhere in the Old and New Testament, inspiration is perceived as a dynamic relationship between God and human individuals, wherein God speaks through the knowledge and language of that person. Second, it fosters the notion of determinism, a worldview opposed by the classical prophets. The literary technique of a seer predicting the future gives the impression of an unalterable timetable of history that denies human freedom. Granted, this made sense to people like the Jews who felt trapped by forces of history beyond their control, but for believers, then and now, this is not a good worldview to have. It makes people unresponsive toward remedying the social evils in our world. Third, it flirts with dualism by granting too much importance to the devil, archdemons, or evil in general. By speaking of the great battle between evil and good, it almost makes evil or the devil into a divine being equal to God. Many Christians in their rhetoric today give too much attention to the devil and detract from the responsibilities of human beings for their own actions. Ultimately, this is why most apocalyptic works written by Christians and Jews were not put into the Bible.

Not everything in apocalyptic literature is bad. It speaks of God's ultimate rule over all things; it says that no matter how bad our world may become, God is able to deliver humanity. It offers people encouragement to hold onto faith and endure hard times, and to all humanity it promises that God has a vision for the future. For persecuted people, it is the rhetoric of hope for tomorrow and divine justice in the world. It speaks to the downtrodden in our world. The greatest abuse occurs when people with means, such as Americans, take the images literally, then sit back and wait for God to come, comfortably assured that they are the "righteous remnant," and that God will deliver them from their persecution (which they suppose they experience). Such people pay no heed to social injustice, world hunger, the environmental crisis, and so forth, because the world is going to end shortly, and they alone will be saved.

We need to hear the prophetic word instead. The prophetic word gave birth to apocalyptic literature, and both are valid messages when they are heard by the appropriate audiences. A contrast of these two genres yields the following observations: The prophet proclaimed a public oral message with clear symbols everyone could understand; the apocalypticist delivered a message anonymously or pseudonymously in a secret written document with esoteric symbols to be interpreted only by the community of faith. The prophet declared that Yahweh acted through the historical process; the apocalypticist spoke of Yahweh ending the world order because the world was totally evil. The prophet spoke a word of judgment or hope to the audience, and judgment and hope was upon both the people of God and foreigners, depending upon the social circumstances; the apocalypticist spoke of judgment upon "them" (the priests and foreigners) and salvation for "us" (the righteous), so that there obviously was little mission outreach in apocalyptic communities. The prophet called upon hearers to respond in freedom to shape society, for Yahweh worked through the present world order to make things better; the apocalypticist counseled patience and endurance to suffer through the pessimistic experience of the present evil world until Yahweh destroyed it. Prophets face the world; apocalypticists flee it. Early Christians used apocalyptic symbols, as Jesus did, but they were a prophetic not an apocalyptic movement.

# Conclusion

Prophetic traditions continued after the exile to meet the religious needs of Jews. Post-exilic prophets were messengers of hope in a dreary age, who generated images that became significant to the heritage of both Judaism and Christianity. As they evolved into apocalypticists, they created literature that would not be placed in the Bible, but they spoke a meaningful message of hope to Jews during severe persecutions and hard times. Their imagery inspired Jesus and became part of the Christian heritage, albeit in modified form. Prophetic and apocalyptic are different sides of the same phenomenon. One speaks an imperative to people with the ability to change society; the other speaks a radical word of hope to helpless people. Theological discourse is not an absolute set of unchanging teachings; it is an ever-evolving message that addresses the human situation.

## Bibliography

Robert Carroll. *When Prophecy Failed: Cognitive Dissonance in the Prophetic Traditions of the Old Testament.* New York, NY: Seabury, 1979.

James Charlesworth, ed. *Old Testament Pseudepigrapha*, vol. 1: Apocalyptic Literature and Testaments. Garden City, NY: Doubleday, 1983.

John Collins. *The Apocalyptic Imagination: An Introduction to Jewish Apocalyptic Literature.* 2nd Ed. Grand Rapids, MI: Eerdmans, 1998.

Paul Hanson. *The Dawn of Apocalyptic.* Rev. Ed. Philadelphia, PA: Fortress, 1979.

Sigmund Mowinckel. *He That Cometh.* Trans. G. W. Anderson. Nashville, TN: Abingdon, 1954.

Otto Plöger. *Theocracy and Eschatology.* Trans. S. Rudman. Richmond, VA: John Knox Press, 1968.

Norman Porteous. *Daniel.* Old Testament Library. Philadelphia, PA: Westminster, 1965.

Mitchell Reddish. *Apocalyptic Literature: A Reader.* Nashville, TN: Abingdon, 1990.

D. S. Russell. *Divine Disclosure: An Introduction to Jewish Apocalyptic.* Minneapolis, MN: Fortress, 1992.

D. S. Russell. *The Method and Message of Jewish Apocalyptic.* Old Testament Library. Philadelphia: Westminster, 1964.

# Chapter 16

# Didactic Literature

Reading:  Proverbs 1-9,Job 1-2,38,42,Koheleth 11,Genesis 38,39-41,Daniel 1,3-6,Jonah

he books of Proverbs, Job, Koheleth, Sirach, Wisdom of Solomon, and several novels in the Old Testament offer us examples of didactic piety.  Didactic piety was a new way for Jews in the post-exilic era to perceive God's presence in their midst.  Priestly piety and the piety of late prophetic and apocalyptic literature provided alternative visions to people quite opposite in nature.  Priestly piety was a-political and accepted the status quo of foreign rule, while prophetic-apocalyptic piety yearned for a golden age and Jewish independence.  Didactic piety spoke more to a middle-of-the-road piety, perhaps for middle class people, which encouraged Jews to find God in everyday life, the created order, and human reason.  This piety may have appealed to people alienated from the priests with their ritual and sacrifice (and their power in society), as well as the wild visionary hopes (and revolutionary zeal) of the later prophets and apocalyptic seers.  This literature offered practical guidelines for successful living and encouraged moral behavior in everyday life.

## Wisdom Literature

Wisdom literature in its narrow sense refers to the five Old Testament books listed above.  These books contained intellectual and literary teachings we call "Wisdom."  Wisdom sayings and literature sprang from an intellectual and literary tradition that extended across many cultures and ages.  From sages of Egypt in 2500 BCE to the sayings collected by Ben Franklin in *Poor Richard's Almanac* to our modern era, people distilled the reasoned insights of their age and expressed it in sophisticated, polished form, especially in pithy sayings or comic jokes.  The wisdom tradition of Israel and the Jews fit readily into this international genre.  These biblical books included the five books, as well as other segments of the Old Testament that have been called wisdom literature by various scholars over the years. More recently, however, scholars have limited their discussions of the wisdom tradition to these five core books.

**Characteristics of Wisdom**: Wisdom sought to understand the order of the universe so as to enable people to cope with everyday life. Wisdom was both speculative and practical. Sages were like the philosophers of ancient Greece in their attempt to apply reason to questions of existence. (In fact, philosophy means the "love of wisdom"). Sages communicated insights by formulating clever sayings that could be understood and remembered. Sages observed reality in nature or society, perceived patterns, and summarized their insights in short maxims. The maxim or proverb impressed the listener with ironic humor and the ability to communicate great insight in a pithy, clever fashion, so that the listener internalized the message. The focus was on the order of creation, rather than redemption by Yahweh. Wisdom sought to discover cause and effect relationships in the world with human reason rather than relying on divine revelation for the answers to the great problems of life. Wisdom, therefore, was "secular" or everyday advice. One can appreciate the message of a proverb without adhering to a religious creed. The expression, "A penny saved is a penny earned" from Ben Franklin is the same as, "A slack hand causes poverty, but the hand of the diligent makes rich" in Proverbs 10:4.

Wisdom sayings took several forms. The most common was the *mashal*, "proverb" or "rule," a word that meant both a measurement and a mandate for living. Every proverb was an observation of reality and an encouragement to be diligent and prudent. A riddle also expressed wisdom insight; it was a proverb turned into a question. Though our present collection of the sayings in the book of Proverbs contains virtually no riddles, scholars suspect that in oral form some of our present proverbs may have been riddles. Proverbs were often two-line statements; they came in the "parallel" form that we notice in the Psalms. In addition to these short forms, wisdom literature had longer literary forms, including parables, allegories, fables, prayers, debate speeches (such as those in the book of Job), psalms, and perhaps even short stories. Jesus's "Sermon on the Mount" was in the form of wisdom language, short, pithy, evocative sayings. The parable, used by Jesus to speak of the Kingdom of God, was a classic wisdom genre. Jesus' discourse was the language of a sage, for this mode of teaching had become popular by Jesus' day.

**Development of Wisdom**: Wisdom literature was not connected to historical texts or the language of "salvation history," thus it is difficult to date the literature. But scholars suggest four phases in the development of Israelite wisdom literature on the basis of evolution in Egyptian wisdom literature and a critical study of the biblical texts. These stages are: 1) early optimistic wisdom, 2) later reflective wisdom, 3) critical wisdom, and 4) reconstructed positive wisdom or realistic wisdom. This paradigm is over-generalized, but it provides a useful paradigm to study wisdom.

*Early Optimistic Wisdom*: Oral proverbs in the pre-exilic period were optimistic, affirming the individual's ability to perceive the nature of reality and respond with a lifestyle that would bring success. Wisdom was concerned with secular, everyday matters; it lauded temperance, moderation, caution, diligence, and hard work. It assumed a fair universe in which such positive virtues brought success, and it probably assumed a simple, agrarian society in which that was possible. Though we label these proverbs "secular," we must be cautious with that stereotype. The proverbs were religious in assuming God's existence, and certainly more religious than modern secular literature. These proverbs did not frequently refer to religious values, though they assumed God and a divinely ordered creation. Nor did they refer to specifically Israelite and Jewish religious beliefs. The collectors of the proverbs sought something more universal rather than something specifically Israelite or Jewish.

This stage of wisdom was represented well by Proverbs 10-31, a collection containing many pre-exilic sayings written down in their present form around 400 BCE. These proverbs were optimistic, simple in form, and they discussed everyday matters. Maxims contrasted the wise person and the fool to encourage the student to work hard and strive for success. The proverbs would remind us of the early 18th century proverbs in America, which Ben Franklin collected. Proverbs such as, "Early to bed, early to rise, makes a man healthy, wealthy, and wise," betoken an ethos that believed hard, honest work brought you success. Proverbs 10-31 reflected this same attitude. The proverbs suggest to us an origin in rural village life and appear to be "clan wisdom." In those rural villages the old men observed that honest, hard work, combined with common sense brought success. Perhaps, the sayings were first articulated by these villagers, then some of the proverbs were collected in the royal court, as implied by the traditional ascriptions to Solomon and more seriously to the scribes of Hezekiah (Proverbs 25:1). Hezekiah may have been the first king to collect proverbs, and to give authority to his collection he attributed Solomonic authorship to it. These proverbs may have been used in the court not only for instruction of young men, but also as writing exercises to help teach young men aspiring to be scribes.

*Reflective Wisdom:* Jewish wisdom became more reflective in the post-exilic period and addressed religious issues. The wise person was equated with the believer and the fool with the unbeliever. Wisdom was personified as a divine force that aided Yahweh in the creation and preservation of the world. Intellectual issues were discussed in more systematic fashion, and literary forms became more complex. Whereas Proverbs 10-31 was a loose collection of sayings, Proverbs 1-9 was a unified composition reflecting this later theological discourse. The message of Proverbs 1-9 indirectly said that the quest for knowledge by the sage brought deeper insight into the nature of God. God may be encountered in an intellectual quest by a sensitive and reflective individual. This provided an alternative mode of divine revelation for people in contrast to the cultic experience provided by the priests or the hope of a glorious future envisioned by prophets and apocalyptic seers. Those attracted to the worldview of the wisdom tradition perhaps felt that their experience of God was more foundational and relevant.

Theological wisdom in Proverbs 1-9 was optimistic; knowledge can bring deep wisdom, and that was more important than physical success, even though success was still a reward of seeking wisdom. Wisdom formerly meant skill or technical knowledge, after the exile it began to mean "philosophy," a systematic way of thought and life. Somewhat later wisdom became personified as a semi-divine force, usually feminine in nature. Literature spoke of wisdom poetically as a woman, or even a divine being, and "She" was viewed as an emanation from God. Proverbs 8, Job 28, Sirach 24, and Wisdom of Solomon 7 were hymns that praised and personified wisdom as feminine, and each one portrayed her as increasingly important in the cosmos. For later Jews wisdom was the "Torah," and for Christians wisdom became the *Logos* ("Word") or Jesus (John 1). Jewish authors may have drawn imagery from the Isis cult in Egypt in portraying wisdom as well as old imagery connected to the worship of Asherah in Palestine. In the case of Asherah imagery, it could be that biblical authors undercut some form of old, popular devotion to Asherah by attributing her characteristics to a philosophical principle.

Once wisdom sayings and thought moved into the religious sphere, faith was foundational to wisdom ("the fear of the Lord is the beginning of wisdom" was a common expression). However, when they associated the wise person with a believer and a fool with an unbeliever, certain problems arose. The equation reads as follows: a wise person is a believer and one who is successful in life, while the fool is an unbeliever and one who fails or suffers in this life. Obviously wisdom did not intend to say that suffering signified unbelief or divine punishment for folly, but that was a common misunderstanding. Critical wisdom emerged to criticize that.

*Critical Wisdom*: Difficult times for Jews in the post-exilic era impressed upon people the unfairness of the world; after all, God's special people were an insignificant and oppressed group. This led wisdom thinkers to challenge some of the simplistic conclusions into which their methods led them, especially the equation of folly, evil, punishment, and suffering. Eventually, wisdom as a movement became more self-critical and challenged the human ability to know reality. Intellectual uncertainty, even agnosticism, was admitted within the boundaries of the wisdom movement.

The book of Job attacked the ability of wisdom to know the answers to great existential and theological questions. Job was the ultimate innocent sufferer; he represented Jews in the post-exilic era or any individual who suffered unjustly. He questioned the reason for his suffering, assuming that it must be punishment, and his three friends tried to assure him by providing explanations for his suffering, all of which assumed that it must have something to do with sin. By challenging the friends' arguments, Job criticized the principle of individual retribution as taught and implied by wisdom thinkers, especially in the more comprehensive system of thought in Proverbs 1-9. He ultimately critiqued the ability of wisdom thinkers to answer great questions, such as the reason for human suffering. When God finally appeared to Job after a long debate between Job and the friends, no answer was given for his suffering, for there was no answer that could be given. More importantly, God was present for Job in his suffering.

Job bore a striking resemblance to Mesopotamian works, which may have been known by the author of the book. Three, in particular, have drawn the attention of scholars: 1) "A Man and His God" or "The Sumerian Job," dated to the early second millennium BCE, contained the laments of an individual to his god because he suffered from physical and mental degradation. He asked for forgiveness and at the end of the work he was restored to health. 2) *Ludlul bel nemeqi* or "I Will Praise the Lord of Wisdom" was an Akkadian poem from the late second millennium BCE in which a sufferer offered thanks to Marduk who delivered him from distress, but only after the petitioner struggled for a long time in prayer with the deity. And 3) "Babylonian Theodicy" from around 1000 BCE contained a dialogue between a sufferer and his friend about the unfairness of the gods and the universe, in which the friend spoke of the inscrutable will of the gods. The poem ended with a prayer for help from the gods. It seems that our biblical author may have combined elements from all three of these works.

The book was organized into several parts. In the prose framework of Job 1-2, 42, Job was a pious man who accepted the suffering and the loss he experienced, and remained faithful to God when three friends came to visit him. In the last chapter Job was rewarded by God, and the three friends were told to sacrifice for their sin of speaking. Perhaps, in an old original prose story the three friends told Job to curse God and die, as did Job's wife. That portion of the old tale was removed by the author, if our theory is correct. In the poetic dialogues of Job 3-31, Job challenged God, and the three friends defended God's justice in the world as well as the principle of individual retribution. It appears that our author took the old prose tale and inserted these poetic dialogues (which were made to appear archaic). In the new literary creation, the personalities of Job and the friends have been switched. Job became angry with God, and in arguing with the three friends, he refuted their arguments to make sense out of his suffering and their attempts to defend the idea of moral order in the universe. They suggested that Job somehow suffered for sins he committed, or thought, or the good he has failed to do. They even suggested he suffered for sins of his children, or because of universal human finitude, or because of his defiance, or for the sake of a test. But the reader knows from chapter 1 that Job was "perfect" in his life and that all of these arguments were untrue or inappropriate. Job's refutations thus ring true for both ancient and modern readers.

The author used Job to indicate that no truly good reason can be given for human suffering. Ultimately the author implied that the principle of individual retribution, that is, suffering as a punishment for sin, does not exist in the universe (although corporate retribution may not be rejected). Furthermore, the author implied that the person who suffers has a right to complain to God and should not be silenced by "friends." This was why God, in our author's final form of the tale, spoke to Job but demanded that the friends, who defended God, seek forgiveness for the sinfulness of their words. After the debate between Job and his friends in Job 3-31, there came the speech of Elihu, self-proclaimed prophet, whose words are diversely interpreted by modern commentators as either a serious attempt to summarize and move beyond the words of the friends, or the attempt of a blathering fool who merely repeated what had been said and functioned as comic relief before the appearance of God. Those who suggest the latter opinion also believe the Elihu speeches were added in a second edition of the book of Job to provide distance between the debate of Job and his friends and the appearance of God. The two divine speeches appear in Job 38-41, and God spoke in dramatic and bombastic fashion about the natural order in the world. This puzzles commentators, for God did not address the issues of human suffering and individual retribution. Does this imply that as nature is beyond human understanding, so also the mystery of suffering is beyond human grasp? Or does it imply that there exists in the universe only a throbbing, powerful natural order, directed by God, and in the human social realm there is no order, only human freedom, which results in the suffering of the innocent? If there is no moral order, Job suffered for no reason. His consolation was that his angry quest for the answer to his suffering obtained for him a revelation, and God came to be present for Job, but not to answer a question for which there was no answer. Ironically, God came to the person who screamed angrily at the divine. But then in his defiant screams Job engaged in what we would call prayer. The three friends never cried defiantly at God, or to God, they merely talked about God smugly. God appeared to the person who prayed, the person who cried out with lament (and Job's language was very similar to the language of the Psalms of Lament.)

The book may be written in a masterful fashion that enables readers to identify with Job at different stages in their own personal struggle with grief. Commentators have disagreed for years whether Job submitted in the end to the majesty of God and admitted that he spoke too boldly about mysteries he could understand, or whether at the end of the book Job was still the defiant rebel speaking strong angry words to God, whose divine graciousness permitted Job this continued catharsis of anger as response for his suffering. The crux of the problem is the interpretation of ambiguous statements by Job to God. In Job 40:4-5, Job stated that he was too small to respond to God and that he would cover his mouth and not speak again. Was he portrayed as speaking with the piety of reverential awe or the petulance of an angry child who will not respond to the parent (or the frustration of a human being cowed by the tyrannical power of a god)? In the second response of Job in Job 42:2-6, Job said that God could do all things, that he had seen wonderful things, that now he had seen God, and that he despised himself in dust and ashes. At first, this sounds like Job stood in awe before God and repented. Or was Job saying that God was a tyrant who could do what he pleased, that Job had seen overwhelming evidence of this unbridled divine power, and that he "felt sorry" (not repented) for "dust and ashes" (that is, all humanity who must serve this powerful deity). The first interpretation attributes piety of repentance to Job, the second interpretation sees Job maintaining the angry defiance he exhibited in his speeches during the debate with the three friends (Job 3-31). I believe the author has crafted for us a grand double entendre in Job's response. Those people who are going through a time of crisis or grief in their lives may read the book and identify with the imagery of an angry Job confronting God; at some later time when the crisis has passed and they have attained some resolution in their lives, they may read the book and identify with the Job who is more at peace with God and accepts the inscrutable divine will. If so, the book of Job should remind us of the tension between the Lament Hymns and the Hymns of Thanksgiving in the Psalter which are meant to be read at different points in the life of a community or a person who has gone through a grief process and struggled with God. Job is a masterpiece of religious and psychological literature.

Ecclesiastes or Koheleth appears less pious and even more critical of wisdom's ability to understand ultimate questions, such as the existence of justice and the nature of God. All life is "vanity," that is, a wisp of smoke. God exists, but is very distant, and what happens in this world does not appear to happen according to a divine plan that is to our benefit. There are great patterns in the universe, especially in nature, but life in the social realm transpires without an apparent order that we can discern. Nothing pursued for its own value, brings ultimate reward. All things in life perish and come to the same end, there is no hope for an afterlife. A person can become wise, but wisdom comes late in life, too late to help you be successful. The book taught intellectual skepticism; nothing was sure, and so the book reacted negatively to the message of Proverbs 1-9. All we can do in this world is to live boldly, enjoy life, and still respect God. God is sovereign, there is an order to things, though it is beyond our understanding, so we can only accept the sovereignty of God and the fact that life still goes on. It may seem strange to many readers that such a pessimistic book is in our Bible. But its inclusion was a testimony to the painful nature of reality, and it was to stand in tension with Proverbs, Sirach, and Wisdom of Solomon. It is so often in the tension of intellectual positions, both in philosophy and theology, that we find the best explanation of reality.

We date the book to the 3rd century BCE in a Jewish Palestine ruled by the Greek Ptolemies of Egypt. Commentators guess that the author might have been an old man (maybe a misogynistic bachelor), a retired wisdom teacher, who provided insights to life. Commentators suggest the author's familiarity with Greek philosophy (Stoic or Epicurean thought) and even Buddhist beliefs. Pious tradition attributed the book to Solomon in his old age, after he had repented of his many mistakes in life. That other intellectuals had problems with his negative attitudes is demonstrated by the two postscripts at the end of the book. Koheleth 12:9-11 praised the author for critical insight, and Koheleth 12:12-14 warned the reader not to contemplate such issues too long.

*Positive Reconstructed Wisdom:* Critical literary works in the wisdom tradition probably brought forth a response from the authors of Sirach (also known as Jesus ben Sira or Ecclesiasticus) and the Wisdom of Solomon. These works tried to reconstruct a positive, but realistic wisdom perspective. They would be included in the Christian version of the Old Testament but would not be found in the Hebrew Bible or Tanak.

Sirach originated with a teacher in Jerusalem (Jesus ben Sira) who lived around 200 BCE. Our present book was translated by his grandson from Hebrew into Greek: he claimed he began the translation during the reign of king Ptolemy VIII Euergetes (132-117 BCE) and finished it after his death. These dates are important because in the Prologue to the book the grandson referred to the Jewish "Law" and the "Prophets," which tells us of their recognition by Jews as authoritative sacred texts by the late 2nd century BCE. He did not refer to the "Writings," which implies that our present Hebrew Bible or Old Testament had not yet come into existence. Although Sirach was not included in the Hebrew canon (for it circulated in Greek and not Hebrew); nonetheless, its thought influenced later Pharisees and Rabbis.

The grandfather discussed Wisdom from a traditional Jewish perspective, but unlike earlier wisdom sages, his religious faith and commitment to belief in the redemptive acts of Yahweh, formed the basis of his wisdom thought. Wisdom, personified in Proverbs 8 and Sirach 24, was equated with Torah and the fear of the Lord in a grand synthesis (Sirach 19:20). In this regard, Sirach foreshadowed the later Pharisees and Rabbis. Sirach attempted to call Jews back to their traditional faith, but he cast this faith in contemporary values of that age. He merged traditional wisdom thought with the traditional theology of the Hebrew Bible, demonstrating sensitivity for the themes of the prophetic corpus and the view of a God who acted in the lives of the people and society. He accepted the traditional notions of obedience to God, divine justice and retribution in the world, and the call for social justice. In Deuteronomic fashion the book stressed the importance of the divine-human relationship in this world. Sirach sought to strengthen wisdom thought by merging it with traditional concepts of salvation history, and this was most apparent in the section that extolled great heroes of the faith (Sirach 44-50), which followed his discourse on the created order (Sirach 42-43). The author wished to show the superiority of traditional Hebrew thought over contemporary Greek thought.

All attempts to reconstruct the wisdom tradition faced the issue of "theodicy," the justification of God in the face of evil and suffering, which Job and Koheleth focused upon in their critique. Most wisdom thinkers were unwilling to use the notion of an afterlife as a way of explaining evil, though Sirach supposed that evildoers received punishment in the form of nightmares. Sirach sensed on this issue a response had to be made to the authors of Job and Koheleth. He tried to offer a nuanced view of reality by affirming that although people were free, God still destined things for good, so that even evil decisions would be used ultimately by God to bring about fulfillment of the divine will. The universe was harmonious; there was ultimately equilibrium.

The Wisdom of Solomon introduced Greek categories into the wisdom synthesis rather than conservatively relying on the old Jewish traditions, as Sirach had done. We suspect that the book originated around 50 BCE. Years ago scholars dated the book a century later and attributed it to Judaeus Philo, the great Jewish philosopher-theologian of Egypt. Like Sirach, this work was produced in Hellenistic Egypt, but it partook deeply of that intellectual milieu to a far greater degree, especially the philosophical tradition of Greece. The author sought to give a new and meaningful articulation of Jewish faith to appeal to Jews who were tempted to disappear into the Greek culture of their age. Perhaps the author also wrote the book as an "apology," or a defense of the faith, in order to appeal to or even convert pagans to a liberal form of Hellenistic Judaism.

The heart of the book was the first nine chapters, where the crucial concepts were expressed. Here we find classic Greek writing style, concepts, and terminology, which indicate the author's familiarity with Greek philosophy, especially Middle Platonism with its talk of divine emanations. Chapters 10-19 retold the traditional stories about the Exodus and the wilderness journey. Though commentators characterize these chapters as poorly written; nonetheless, they tell us much about the piety and interpretative technique of that age.

For the first time in Jewish literature, we encounter the notion of an immortal soul, the classic Greek concept that regards the good soul as trapped in a mortal, evil body. However, the soul was portrayed not as inherently immortal, but immortal only by divine grace, and evil souls could die, contrary to Greek thought. Appeal to an afterlife was his answer to the problem of retribution in this life; God would reward the righteous in the next life. On this point the author of Wisdom of Solomon parted ways drastically with Sirach. Also, in Wisdom of Solomon, we discover reference to virtues as emanations of God and the rule of God portrayed in Greek terms like the ideal state or Greek polis (city-state). One senses continuity with the tradition of the Greek philosopher, Plato. This differed significantly from Sirach's traditional view of the people of God. The author of Wisdom of Solomon identified "wisdom" with morality or a righteous life, and sometimes wisdom appeared to be divine providence. Wisdom was personified, said to have divine origin, and given attributes that remind us of images attributed to Isis in the Egyptian mystery cults of that age.

Wisdom of Solomon was too liberal for the later Jewish tradition, so it was not included in the Hebrew canon, even though it bore Solomon's name. It was written in Greek initially, which also made Jews wary of it. (Sirach, which may have originated in Hebrew before circulating in Greek, was excluded from the Hebrew Bible because it identified the author as living after the age of inspiration.) Wisdom's emphasis upon the immortal soul ran counter to the Jewish and New Testament stress upon the resurrection of the body, an image that proclaimed that the physical world was inherently good and redeemed from human sin by divine grace. The concept of an immortal soul concept by itself gave the impression that the physical world was inherently evil and unredeemable.

These same stages of evolution in the wisdom movement from early optimism to later pessimism and realism also characterized the development of wisdom elsewhere. In ancient Egypt, early optimism (3000-2400 BCE) gave way to more critical wisdom (2400-1000 BCE) that overlapped a more pious stage (1200-1000 BCE). What is interesting is that Israelites from the very beginning had access to all the wisdom literature of the ancient Near East, both the positive and the negative. Why did Israel not immediately borrow critical and pious modes of wisdom discourse early in the development of their own wisdom tradition? Why did literature, such as Proverbs, resonate an optimistic view of reality, when the authors had negative wisdom literature at their disposal from other countries? For example, Proverbs 22-24 drew heavily upon an Egyptian work called the *Wisdom of Amenemope*. This Egyptian work reflected the religious piety and intellectual pessimism of the wisdom tradition in the New Kingdom era. Ironically, the section in Proverbs that paraphrased the Egyptian material does not give us that same feeling. Proverbs was more optimistic through the selection of particular sayings and their translation into Hebrew. How was this possible? It was because Israelites were not ready to resonate negative Egyptian thought until their society had experienced its own disillusionment in the post-exilic era. A society may read the texts of another culture, but not resonate intellectually with such texts until they are ready. Soren Kierkegaard was a famous brooding existentialist author in early 19th century Denmark, whose writings were ignored in America, until we were really ready to hear these intellectual reflections in the post-World War II age. The same was true for the Jews, who also went through a comparable evolution of thought. Subsequently, only after the deep pessimistic reflection of Job and Koheleth were they ready to move forward and create the synthesis of thought found in Sirach and Wisdom of Solomon.

# Novels

The didactic tradition also included a number of post-exilic novels. Technically, they were not part of the wisdom tradition, because they ranged into broad theological issues. Yet there were great similarities with wisdom and the novel genre, so we discuss them in the broader category of didactic literature. Some scholars have evaluated certain novels as wisdom literature in the past, but now scholars are more inclined to keep them in a separate category. Novels flourished as a genre in the post-exilic period, for they communicated significant values to people in popular form. Examples included Ruth, Jonah, Esther, Tobit, Judith, Daniel, Susanna, Bel and the Dragon, and the expansions in Genesis 37, 39-50, the Joseph novel. What characterized these stories was a unified plot, a coherent set of related themes, and character portrayal of the main personages.

**Joseph**: The Joseph narrative in Genesis 37, 39-50 may have been the earliest novel, if we exclude the Succession Narrative in 2 Samuel 9-20, 1 Kings 1-2 (850 BCE or later). The Joseph saga may have existed in the early Yahwist and Elohist narratives, but in much briefer form than our present text. The present Joseph narrative was a unified story reflecting quite accurately the living conditions in Egypt from 650 to 400 BCE. (Reference to coins in Genesis 42:35, 43:21-23 betrays a date after 550 BCE.) This present story has expanded the old epic memory of Joseph and created a meaningful paradigm for Jews living in diaspora, perhaps in Egypt.

The story was humanistic, the plot moved as people made decisions, but Yahweh controlled the course of events from a distance. This led scholars in past generations to call this a wisdom novel, but few today would agree. Joseph was portrayed as moral, wise, and noble (except when he "toyed" with his brothers), who could be a model to Jewish youth. He exemplified a Jewish boy who worked with foreign authorities without compromising his religious or moral beliefs, and that was an important message for diaspora Jews. Furthermore, his cooperation with the authorities brought blessings to other Jews. The story has other messages to share. Even though wicked people persecute Yahweh's chosen ones, Yahweh will turn evil into good. Joseph said to the brothers, "You meant evil against me, but God meant it for good, to bring it about that many people should be kept alive, as they are today" (Genesis 50:20).

**Ruth and Jonah:** These two novels advocated universalism and tolerance in response to the exclusivism of Ezra and Nehemiah. Ruth was a Moabite woman, married to an Israelite man, who came to live in Israel with her mother-in-law, Naomi, after the death of her husband. Naomi prompted her to entice Boaz, a kinsman, to marry her and fulfill the Levirate custom wherein a kinsman had to enable a woman to give birth to an heir after her husband died. The child she bore would be the great-grandfather of David. Post-exilic priestly custom forbade anyone who was a third-generation descendant of a Moabite from entering the Temple, and that would have included David, according to the book of Ruth. Yet in the book of 1 Chronicles David was given credit for Temple construction rather than Solomon, and David was glorified even more than in pre-exilic texts as the proto-type of the ideal king. The point was that if David could not enter the Temple in the days of Ezra and Nehemiah, something was wrong with their narrow legislation.

Jonah, the reluctant prophet, was dragged to Nineveh by God to proclaim a message of repentance to the hated Assyrians, who brutally oppressed Israelites for years. Jonah did not want the Assyrians to repent and be saved. When Jonah attempted to escape by sea, Yahweh brought him back in a big fish. Even with Jonah's very crass and short proclamation of a message of doom, the Assyrians repented. Jonah hoped that they would not repent and deserve the punishment they would get, and it would be worse for the Assyrians, if they killed him. Jonah sulked outside the city because the Assyrians repented. When Jonah complained about the death of a gourd that gave him shade, Yahweh reprimanded him for having more concern over a plant than for people in the city. The book taught that Jews were not the only people of God. Jonah resonated the same themes found in Second Isaiah about Yahweh's message for all people (Isaiah 45:12-14, 51:4-5). Ruth and Jonah both have the universalistic message that Christianity inherited. For Jesus the sign of Jonah was the imperative to preach to the Gentiles.

**Esther and Daniel:** These two stories celebrated the survival of Jews among people hostile to their beliefs. Both stories came from the eastern diaspora, Babylon and Persia, though we know little about the experience of Jews in those lands. Jews still celebrate the festival of Purim in the spring by merry-making and gift giving; the only serious part of the celebration is the reading of Esther. This celebration began sometime after the Maccabean Revolt (164 BCE), and the book supposedly explained the origin of the festival, but we are not sure whether the festival or the book came first.

Esther was a Jewish girl married to the fictional king Ahasuerus of Persia (who may have been a parody on Xerses I, 486-465 BCE, who failed to conquer Greece). Ahasuerus put aside his first queen, Vashti, and married Esther, not knowing she was Jewish. Esther's cousin, Mordecai, angered the prime minister of the king, Haman, who sought to have all Jews killed. Esther had to decide whether she had the courage to expose her identity and risk her life to save her people. She invited the king and Haman to a private dinner where she interceded successfully for her people. When Haman discredited himself foolishly, he was hanged on the gallows he prepared for Mordecai. Mordecai became prime minister, and Jews were permitted to attack their enemies. In its present form, the novel is fictional; the final revenge may reflect the Maccabean revolution. But it cast the challenge to every Jew in diaspora by saying, "Do you have the courage to stand up and admit your Jewish identity for the good of your people?"

Daniel also addressed Jews in diaspora tempted to surrender their faith, and in its final form the book addressed Palestinian Jews who were severely persecuted for adhering to their Jewish beliefs. One senses that the intensity of persecution is greater in Daniel than in Esther, for it reflects the Palestinian setting where the persecution and revolt occurred. The book was composed of two different types of material, short stories about Daniel and his friends in the Babylonian Exile (Daniel 1, 3-6) and apocalyptic visions. Both parts addressed the question of suffering for the faith and the reward for enduring until the end. Scholars suspect that some of the stories may have arisen in the 4th and 3rd centuries BCE, but the final form of the stories and the apocalyptic visions emerged in the 2nd century BCE, during the persecution of Antiochus IV Epiphanes of Syria and the Maccabean Revolution (167-164 BCE). The book may have gone through several editions during the revolution itself and thereafter, which would explain why the Greek Septuagint has additional chapters (after Daniel 12:13) that the Hebrew Massoretic Text and traditional Protestant translations lack.

Daniel and his friends represented Jews in a foreign land or in persecution. Though pressured to forsake kosher food observance, they remained faithful and actually began to be more successful under the foreign king. The message to all Jews everywhere was that they should remain faithful and thereby bring prosperity to foreigners as well as to fellow Jews. Some of the stories reflected brutal persecution--the fiery furnace in Daniel 3 and the lion's den in Daniel 6. These narratives emerged with Antiochus' brutal program of forced hellenization, including the erection of a statue of Zeus in the Temple with his own face upon it. Nebuchadnezzar's statue (Daniel 3) was a veiled commentary on this event in 167 BCE. These stories circulated among Jews in Palestine together with the apocalyptic visions to encourage resistance to forced hellenization. With the Maccabean victory over the Seleucids, the book was vindicated and assured of being accepted as canonical.

Two entertaining accounts were placed at the end of the book. *Susannah and the Elders* related how a young woman resisted the sexual advances of two elders but was accused by them of adultery. Daniel cross-examined both elders separately and vindicated the young girl's story, and the elders were executed. In *Bel and the Dragon*, Jews were forced to worship an idol that supposedly ate food left before it overnight. Daniel revealed this to be a hoax, for powder left on the floor of the sanctuary showed that the priests came up through a trap door to eat the food during the night. The idol and priests were destroyed, and Jews were permitted to keep their religious observances. Both stories may have been added by Jews in Egypt; hence, they appear in the Greek translation of the Hebrew Bible, but not in the Hebrew Bible itself.

Daniel as a book emerged from many sources, old novelistic tales of Jews in a foreign land, newer tales of faithfulness during persecution, and apocalyptic visions. The dream reports with subsequent interpretation (Daniel 2, 7) were inspired by the Joseph dream reports in Genesis 40-41. In its final form, it was an emotional testimony of faithfulness and divine vindication.

**Tobit and Judith**: These two novels do not appear in the Massoretic Text of the Hebrew Bible. They are found in the Septuagint alone, and both novels were written in the Greek language originally, which would explain their exclusion from the Hebrew Text.

Tobit was a fanciful tale of a pious but grievously afflicted Israelite at the time of the Assyrians. Tobit had a son named Tobias, who journeyed to a far land with the angel Raphael in human disguise. Tobias married a woman whose previous husbands were killed on their wedding night, but Tobias survived due to his piety (great scripture reading at weddings!) Eventually Tobias became wealthy, and Tobit was healed of his blindness. Everyone was blessed because of faithfulness to Jewish belief.

Judith recounted how a young girl killed evil Nebuchadnezzar of the Assyrians (obviously a historical distortion, one of many in the book) and thus saved her people. (Deliberate historical distortions in this novel, in particular, as well as other novels, signaled to the audience that the narratives were parables, not historiography.) Like Esther, Judith used her beauty to save her fellow Jews. While dining with the king in his tent and pretending to seduce him, she beheaded Nebuchadnezzar and slipped away with the head in her basket. (Never go on a picnic with Judith!) When the Assyrians attacked her village, she displayed the head and demoralized them. She was a great example of a heroic woman, surrounded by incompetent and cowardly men, who stood firm in the faith and saved Judaism.

Both tales were generated late in the post-exilic period. Tobit is dated in the 3rd or 2nd century BCE with uncertainty, while Judith appears to be from the late 2nd century BCE due to its indirect awareness of the Maccabean Revolution. Like most of the other novels, it was a story of religious faithfulness rewarded.

All of the novels conveyed powerful messages to their readers, but the primary focus was faith in Yahweh in the midst of adversity. Early novels proclaimed the universal nature of the Jewish faith in the face of exclusivistic tendencies in Judaism (Ruth, Jonah);

others encouraged Jews to preserve their religious values in diaspora (Genesis 37, 39-50, Tobit), and most encouraged Jews to hold firm to their faith despite persecution (Esther, Daniel 1-6, Judith, Bel and the Dragon). For Jews living in Palestine and the diaspora, the post-exilic era was depressing and oppressive; literature such as this strengthened their faith. The literature proclaimed that Jews should remain faithful to God and their Jewish traditions. If they remained faithful and served those with whom they lived (including Gentile rulers), God would be faithful and they would be blessed.

# Conclusion

Wisdom literature and the novels strike us as being more humanistic than religious; this literature spoke of emotions and insight, it testified to human actions guiding events and wisdom or folly determining the outcome. Though commentators speak of this literature as secular, God was present in the background, guiding affairs from a distance. Wisdom sayings implied God was in the created order that the wise person studied. The novels implied that God worked through decisions made by the chief characters. God was present, but in a subtle way. This literature created a new piety predicated upon the assumption of divine distance in an age when people felt God was distant. Wisdom literature and the novels declared that God was present, but manifest in the wisdom and decisions of human beings. It is as though the literature said look no more to the heavens, but look within for the presence of the divine. As the Pentateuch and the Prophets became sacred scriptures, these new texts testified to the presence of God in the lives of people. Jews in the post-exilic period felt that God was no longer vividly in their midst as in the lives of their ancestors. Wisdom spoke to that need by saying look elsewhere for God, not to the cult or history of the nation, but to the human mind, created order, and the lives of individual people. Didactic literature spoke not of a God in the past, but of the God in the present.

# Bibliography

Richard Clifford. *The Wisdom Literature*. Interpreting Biblical Texts. Nashville TN: Abingdon, 1988.

James Crenshaw. *Old Testament Wisdom: An Introduction*. Rev. Ed. Louisville, KY: Westminster John Knox, 1998.

Norman Habel. *Job*. Old Testament Library. Philadelphia, PA: Westminster, 1985.

James Limburg. *Jonah*. Old Testament Library. Louisville, KY: Westminster John Knox, 1993.

Roland Murphy. *The Tree of Life: An Exploration of Biblical Wisdom Literature*. 3rd Ed. Grand Rapids, MI: Eerdmans, 2002.

David Penchansky. *The Betrayal of God: Ideological Conflict in Job*. Literary Currents in Biblical Interpretation. Louisville, KY: Westminster John Knox, 1990.

Leo Perdue. *The Sword and the Stylus: An Introduction to Wisdom in the Age of Empires*. Grand Rapids, MI: Eerdmans, 2008.

Gerhard von Rad. *Wisdom in Israel*. Trans. James Martin. Nashville, TN: Abingdon, 1972.

Robert Scott. *The Way of Wisdom in the Old Testament*. New York, NY: Macmillan, 1971

Lawrence Wills. *The Jewish Novels in the Ancient World*. Ithaca, NY: Cornell University Press, 1995.

# Epilogue: Toward the New Testament

hristianity was born at the end of the Second Temple period, not too long before the destruction of the Temple (70 CE) brought the period to an end. Christianity emerged out of the diverse theological and literary currents that made up Second Temple or post-exilic Judaism. We have stressed the pieties of the priests, the late prophets and apocalyptic authors, and the sages or wisdom thinkers who produced didactic literature. All of these currents flowed into the river of Christianity. Jesus spoke with the sayings and parables of a sage, he proclaimed his message with the zeal of a prophet, and he created a sacred meal before his death to replace the sacrifice of the priests. Christianity drew heavily upon the language of literature of those three traditions.

## Socio-Theological Parties

These theological trajectories may be discussed from the perspective of social-theological parties. The diverse types of piety gave rise to theological and political views that were held by various people. Over the years scholars have proposed a typology that reflects the various categories of literature: 1) Priestly literature, including the redacted Pentateuch, the Psalter, and historical literature, like 1 and 2 Chronicles, Ezra, and Nehemiah, were the ideological literary works of Sadducees or hierocrats ("priestly rulers") in Jerusalem. They were the *de facto* upper-class leaders of the Jews by virtue of their cooperation with foreign powers, and priestly literature, with its non-political perspective, reflected their agenda. Sadducees maintained only the Pentateuch was authoritative scripture, for it alone contained the laws. For them God was experienced in the cult and worship. 2) Those excluded from power often turned to prophetic and apocalyptic modes of discourse. The revolutionary nature of this literature fueled the fears and hopes of dispossessed and lower class people. They envisioned a golden age, when Jews would be free, a great David would rule, and Jews would experience an age of glory. 3) The people in the middle of these two extremes were probably folk we would call middle-class, perhaps they were somewhat literate and had professional craft skills. Their leaders may have been intellectuals, perhaps teachers, people who turned to wisdom or didactic traditions to address life's problems. They saw God active in the everyday events of life, the created order, and felt that God was accessible through human reflection.

The famous Jewish historian Josephus testified to four Jewish parties that existed around 50 CE, including the Sadducees, Pharisees, Essenes, and Zealots. These groups arose only late in the post-exilic period, but their religious and political convictions were held by Jews throughout the era. Critical scholars recognize that his categories are extremely over-generalized and that he described groups around 50 to 70 CE, which makes it tenuous for us to project them back in time. But we have no other paradigms with which to work, and there is truth in Josephus' descriptions. In reality, there was a spectrum of groups all merging into each other, but those complex relationships cannot be reconstructed by us.

A good example of complexity may be found in some of the late post-exilic prophets. Ezekiel, Second Isaiah, Zechariah 1-8, and perhaps even Zechariah 9-14 were rooted in the theology of the priests, for the first two individuals were probably exiled priests, and the literature in Zechariah was supportive of Temple reconstruction and contained hierocratic language. The distinction between priestly and prophetic theology can be blurred. Furthermore, since late prophetic traditions evolved into apocalyptic, it is worth noting connections between apocalyptic literature and the priestly traditions. Since Ezekiel, Second Isaiah, Zechariah 1-8, and Zechariah 9-14 were proto-apocalyptic, then apocalyptic literature need not always originate in the hands of the oppressed, it can come from priestly circles. Jewish *de facto* leaders may have envisioned a grand transformation of society that promoted them to a higher position of religious authority. The apocalyptic literature of the Dead Sea Scrolls, emanating from Qumran, came from alienated priests who withdrew from Jerusalem to Qumran. Hence, our categories, and those of Josephus, may be convenient pedagogical tools, but history was more complex.

**Sadducees**: The term Sadducee came from the name of the high priest in Jerusalem appointed by David, Zadok, who replaced Abiathar. It was a term for the priests and their families, a significant class of people in post-exilic society. Priests maintained the Temple cult; they continued to offer sacrifice in the Temple up to the very moment in 70 CE when Roman soldiers burst in and killed them. They sought to shape the Jewish people into a liturgical community whose purpose was to praise Yahweh, and the greatest sign of their success was the actual survival of Jews as a people. Political concerns were subordinate to cultic priorities; political independence was a bane rather than a blessing. Political independence could bring the diplomatic maneuvers that led to war and the destruction of both city and Temple. Political power fell into their hands by default, for they were the only public officials through whom foreign powers worked. Foreign rulers sensed the priestly apolitical stance made them good intermediaries.

The Pentateuch alone was their religious authority, for it contained the laws that formed the basis for cult and Jewish identity. Sadducees were noted for their rejection of notions, such as resurrection, not found within the Pentateuch. Sadducees rejected prophetic books because of the prophetic critique of priests found therein and because prophets hearkened to the hope of a golden age and a national state. The Former Prophets or historical works of Joshua, Judges, 1-2 Samuel, 1-2 Kings were unacceptable, because they spoke of independence, wars, and a national state, which could cause resurgent nationalism. Priests were nervous about public prophets who might disturb the political order, bring about war, and cause the destruction of the Temple once more. (Apocalyptic thought usually was their nemesis, except for the Qumran sectarians, who were alienated priests that became apocalyptic in their worldview.) Sadducees held to a style of traditional Jewish cultic piety and had no need for the concept of afterlife, for the divine presence was experienced in religious or meditative activity. Textbooks thus speak of their theology as being "conservative." Their accomplishments were significant. They promulgated written scriptures; Ezra brought Jews to recognize the official Torah in a public covenant ceremony, and this led to the emergence of the other portions of sacred canon. They created an identity for Jews that was theocratic, enabling Jews to survive both in diaspora and as a province in larger empires. Finally, they gave us the meditative piety represented by the Psalms. Judaism and Christianity owe much to the Sadducees.

**Essenes and Zealots:** Post-exilic prophets were visionaries dissatisfied with the social structures in their society. Beginning with Haggai and Zechariah, dissent was sounded through later anonymous prophets who envisioned the end of Judah's status of subjection and the dawn of a golden age. This vision gradually exaggerated until it evolved into apocalyptic visions by 200 BCE. They believed that Yahweh would act in history in a dramatic way to create the final golden age, and they never relinquished the cherished hope for national independence.

Due to their suppression prophets became anonymous or pseudonymous and produced written apocalyptic visions. In this literature the priests deserved judgment as did foreign nations. There were passive visionaries who withdrew from society to anticipate a coming golden age in which they would be given authority to rule (such as the Essenes at Qumran, perhaps), and active visionaries who believed that if they began a revolt, Yahweh would bring the golden age when they were in the grand, final battle (Zealots). These latter folk tended to go into battle expecting Yahweh to intervene, and they usually lost. Such were the dynamics behind the Jewish Revolt against Rome in 67 to 70 CE. Revolutionaries holding the city of Jerusalem against the Romans were not only inadequately supplied, they even fought each other in the city as the Romans attacked. We know little about these prophetic, apocalyptic, visionary groups. We suspect there were many types; some appear to be very prophetic, while others had a priestly agenda. The fact that the name Zealot appeared very late, after the time of Jesus, should caution us about using these categories too facilely.

Essenes emerged around 150 BCE as they withdrew from Jerusalem to found desert communities around the Dead Sea. Priestly in origin, they were extremely concerned with matters of cultic purity. The famous community at Qumran, which produced the Dead Sea Scrolls, perhaps was one of those communities. Dismayed by corrupt Maccabean rulers, especially when a Maccabean king also became the high priest, they withdrew to the wilderness to await the coming of Yahweh. Some of their literature reads like classic apocalyptic. Their views were best expounded in works like the *Manual of Discipline*, a rule for community life, and *The War of the Children of Light against the Children of Darkness*. Romans destroyed their communities around 70 CE, assuming them to be revolutionaries. They may have influenced Jesus and John the Baptist with imagery, such as the "war between light and darkness" and ideas associated with the Kingdom of God. John the Baptist may have been connected to the Essenes because of his presence in the Jordan valley, close to where Essenic communities were located. Language of the Essenes was well known in Jesus' day, so both Jesus and John may have used it to communicate effectively. We cannot determine the extent of contact between Essenes and the first Christians.

Though Zealots did not emerge as an actual party until 50 CE, just before the Roman wars, there were always revolutionary groups in post-exilic Palestine. The Maccabees in the 2nd century BCE were such a group, and they won independence for the Jews. Memory of their success fired the minds of Jews. Zealots were strong in the rural areas, especially Galilee. Revolutionary thought appealed to the poor and dispossessed. Zealots thought in political terms, religion was often subordinate to their political values, and they despised the Sadducees with their a-political views. Zealots were rooted in apocalyptic, especially imagery associated with the Day of the Lord and the Kingdom of God. They believed they should take the first step toward revolution once they had discerned the "signs of the times," and then Yahweh would bring the golden age. (Certain post-exilic prophets, like Third Isaiah, Zechariah, and Haggai, maintained humans must act first before Yahweh brings the blessing of the new age.) Their leadership in the Jewish wars of 67-70 CE and 132-135 CE (revolt of Bar-Cochba) led to their rejection by the later Rabbis and the exclusion of apocalyptic literature from the Hebrew Bible (except for Daniel 7-12 which was carried in on the strength of the novelistic material in Daniel 1-6).

**Pharisees or Sages**: Among educated people, merchants, craftsmen, artisans, and others a new perspective emerged. The wisdom tradition may have appealed to these people, for it said that Yahweh could be found in the totality of life. Though they respected cult and accepted both the Torah and the Prophets (including the Former Prophets or Historical Books), they looked for a new form of piety. Hence, the later wisdom tradition became more religious, perhaps under their direction, and addressed life's questions from both religious and philosophical perspectives.

This piety was concerned not only with reasoned observation; it also generated interpretations of the biblical text germane to everyday existence--the emergence of the first commentaries. Much of this lore was written in the Mishnah of the later Jewish Talmud. This piety accepted both the Law and the Prophets and sought further interpretations for life. Spokespersons were sages, sometimes called the "pious ones" or the "people of the land" (Hasideans). Eventually, the people we call Pharisees emerged out of this movement. The name Pharisee was associated first with a political party that supported the Maccabees, probably coming out of a broader category of rural, faithful Yahwists called the Hasideans or Hasidim. Hasideans may have included visionary and revolutionary groups, too. They were also called the "people of the land," a term used for the groups who supported Josiah's reforms in 622 BCE, so Pharisees perceived themselves as having a long ancestry. Pharisees were a powerful political party until many were executed in the Maccabean civil strife around 100 to 90 BCE. They disappeared and resurfaced only in 30 BCE. At that time they were no longer political, but were interested in teaching morality and interpreting the Law and the Prophets.

These lay teachers, whose strength lay in rural areas and in local synagogues, applied Torah to everyday life. Ironically, the word Pharisee was used by lay teachers to insult other teachers of different ideological persuasions. We find not only in the Gospels, but also in the Talmud, that lay teachers or sages insulted their opponents with this label. Thus, the sages did not call themselves Pharisees; Josephus used that term, lacking a better one. We should call these people sages or teachers, even though those two words are very generic. There were many schools of sages with different modes of interpretation. Some were pacifists, others were revolutionaries, and some were priestly oriented, but most were critical of cult and emphasized teaching. We must avoid simple stereotypes given by Josephus, for there were tremendous variations in this movement.

A succession of famous teachers was recalled by the later Rabbis, many of whom were fictional. Two truly historical leaders in 30 BCE created parties that became extremely significant over the years. Shammai, a conservative, promoted a strict interpretation of Torah that created a "hedge" around Torah to insure that Jews would faithfully keep the Law. In addition to the more than 600 laws in the Pentateuch, the Shammai school created an additional 10,000 guidelines for Jews to observe, especially to clarify Sabbath observance. Hillel, a liberal, maintained that the laws in the Torah were sufficient and additional rules were not needed. Rather than keeping the "letter of the Law," as Shammai did, we should keep the "spirit of the Law" according to Hillel. For Hillel the Torah could be summarized as, "Love the Lord your God with all your heart, soul, and mind; and that which is hurtful to your neighbor, do not do!" Jesus was a Hillel Pharisee, and the Golden Rule was a positive paraphrase of Hillel's statement. His stress upon the spirit rather than the letter of the Law brought Jesus into conflict with the Shammai "Pharisees" constantly, as observed in the Gospels. Christianity began as an offshoot of the Hillel tradition, a fact forgotten by later Christians.

Sages accepted the Law and the Prophets, and in addition they used materials from the wisdom tradition. Their use of apocalyptic was restrained, and after the Jewish wars they eliminated it. Sages frequently used sayings, parables, allegories, and other didactic teaching devices, as did Jesus. They alone survived the Jewish wars. Zealots and Essenes were wiped out and their thought was condemned for leading the Jews to destruction. Loss of the Temple removed the reason for Sadducean existence. Only the sages survived. They formulated the Hebrew Bible at a training school in Jabneh or Jamnia from 90 to 132 CE. (Jamnia was not a council as so often textbooks state.) Law and Prophets were supplemented with "Kethubim" or "Writings" containing much wisdom literature and novels, with the inclusion of the most significant priestly works (Psalms and some historiography). Sages evolved into Rabbis, who praised as their great co-founders, Hillel and Shammai. Actually they favored Hillel in this tension, for the Shammai school had been condemned around 40 CE for being too legalistic. (Jesus obviously was not alone in his observations.) Later Rabbis rehabilitated Shammai to strike a balanced interpretation of the Law that sought to keep the "letter of the law" after interpreting according to the "spirit of the law."

# Conclusion

In conclusion, we have observed the trajectory of theological themes in the post-exilic period and their corresponding social-political movements. The thought of these movements created the setting that gave rise to the Christian movement and fed directly into Christian beliefs. As the Old Testament era came to a close, the twin religions of Christianity and Judaism arose out of Second Temple period Judaism, especially after the destruction of Jerusalem in 70 CE, which brought this era to an end. The destruction of Jerusalem brought the entire Old Testament era to an end, but in another sense, it was the beginning of a great new era for Jews and Christians.